AMERICAN PHOTOJOURNALISM

Medill School of Journalism
VISIONS *of the* AMERICAN PRESS

GENERAL EDITOR
David Abrahamson

Selected titles in this series

MAURINE H. BEASLEY
First Ladies and the Press: The Unfinished Partnership of the Media Age

PATRICIA BRADLEY
Women and the Press: The Struggle for Equality

DAVID A. COPELAND
The Idea of a Free Press: The Enlightenment and Its Unruly Legacy

MICHAEL SWEENEY
The Military and the Press: An Uneasy Truce

PATRICK S. WASHBURN
The African American Newspaper: Voice of Freedom

DAVID R. SPENCER
The Yellow Journalism: The Press and America's Emergence as World Power

KARLA GOWER
Public Relations and the Press: The Troubled Embrace

TOM GOLDSTEIN
Journalism and Truth: Strange Bedfellows

NORMAN SIMS
True Stories: A Century of Literary Journalism

AMERICAN PHOTOJOURNALISM
MOTIVATIONS AND MEANINGS

Claude Cookman

Foreword by Richard B. Stolley

MEDILL SCHOOL OF JOURNALISM

Northwestern University Press

Evanston, Illinois

Northwestern University Press
www.nupress.northwestern.edu

Printed in the United States of America

10 9 8 7 6 5 4 3 2 1

Library of Congress Cataloging-in-Publication Data

Cookman, Claude Hubert, 1943–

American photojournalism : motivations and meanings / Claude Cookman ; foreword by Richard B. Stolley.

p. cm. — (Medill School of Journalism Visions of the American Press)

Includes bibliographical references and index.

ISBN 978-0-8101-2358-8 (pbk. : alk. paper)

1. Photojournalism—United States—History. 2. Documentary photography—United States—History. I. Medill School of Journalism. II. Title. III. Series: Visions of the American press.

TR820.C6595 2009

070.4'90973—dc22

2009007881

♾ The paper used in this publication meets the minimum requirements of the American National Standard for Information Sciences—Permanence of Paper for Printed Library Materials, ANSI Z39.48-1992.

For Joyce, Colin, and Alex

CONTENTS

Photographs follow page 98.

FOREWORD

Richard B. Stolley

"F8 and be there" is the ancient formula for successful photojournalism. Like most clichés, it still applies. "F8" is the all-purpose lens opening that rarely fails. "Be there" is obvious, the proximity of shooter to subject. Being there is clearly essential for the long-form photojournalism that is celebrated in this fine book by Claude Cookman, not just for the shutter-click moment that news coverage requires, but for the days, even weeks, that are needed to tell complicated stories in pictures and words. I speak from experience. I worked in close collaboration with photographers as a correspondent for the weekly magazine *Life* for seventeen years and later published many of those photographers' efforts as editor of both *People Weekly* and the monthly *Life*. I chased countless news stories as bureau chief in Atlanta, Los Angeles, Washington, and Paris, and because *Life* was a thriving magazine then with scores of pages to fill, I also helped contribute longer photographic essays that were always timely and occasionally memorable.

Their broad variety was an indication of how a weekly publication could use photo-essays to background news events and trends. As examples, here are four I worked on:

- Synanon (1962), a controversial private drug-rehabilitation center in Los Angeles that achieved amazing results at a time when national despair over narcotics was growing;
- the New York State Thruway (1955), the first of the Eisenhower interstates, that monumental engineering feat that

connected America with multilane highways from coast to coast;

- paleontologist Richard Leakey (1969), who was searching for more evidence of early man in northern Kenya (during which assignment I actually discovered a Stone Age scraping tool myself); and
- teenage marriages in North Carolina (1959), a phenomenon that was worrisome to parents and school officials but was clearly preferable to the rise in unwed teenage pregnancies.

All of these essays carried the photographer's byline, as they should have. We correspondents labored in virtual anonymity, but we were essential to the editorial process, as I believe most photographers would testify. We researched the story beforehand, provided a rough shooting script, negotiated photographic access to places and people, took careful notes, and afterward submitted both captions and text for polishing by an editor at *Life*'s headquarters in New York. These published words, as limited as they usually were, constituted a necessary ingredient, in my view. Pictures without words is mere photography; pictures with words is photojournalism.

I say most photographers were grateful for our help, because a few were dismissive of us and reluctant to share any credit. Theirs was the finger on the shutter, and that's all that mattered. But on most photo-essays, the collaboration was genuine and amiable. Yet, it was important for us reporters to understand that good photographers are a roiling mix of supreme self-confidence and overwhelming paranoia. And I say that with great respect and affection for those well-known *Life* photographers I worked alongside: Alfred Eisenstaedt, Eliot Elisofon, Grey Villet, Ralph Crane, Bill Ray, Gordon Parks, to name a few.

Their self-confidence was never expressed more succinctly

than by famed sports photographer Neil Leifer, who once told the *Los Angeles Times,* "What separates a really good photographer from the ordinary is, when things happen, when you are lucky, you don't miss. I didn't miss."

The paranoia came from the forces that photographers always felt were arrayed against them: recalcitrant subjects, lousy weather, insufficient time. They also were never sure what they were getting. Today, in the digital age, a photographer knows in the blink of an eye exactly what he or she has shot. Back then, their work was hidden inside rolls of 35 mm film that had to be shipped off to the magazine's photo lab. On assignment, some of them nervously called the lab every day, from anywhere in the world, to make sure their exposures were correct.

Even the most celebrated had moments of doubt. I vividly remember the photographer on the New York State Thruway essay, the world-famous Margaret Bourke-White, telephoning a top editor in Manhattan and confessing, "I think I'm getting some beautiful pictures, but I'm not sure how they fit into the story." The editor had been through this before. "Maggie," he soothed, "great pictures never hurt a story yet." It was what she needed to hear.

Most photographers had two other virtues. One was a keen sense of psychology, of when to charm, when to push. Bourke-White needed to infiltrate off-limits highway construction sites, and with a dazzling smile and a hard hat perched jauntily on her snow-white hair, she succeeded. When Michael Rockefeller disappeared in the ocean off New Guinea, Eliot Elisofon put aside his occasional imperiousness and persuaded the Australian air force to fly the two of us on a restricted search mission. In northern California, when a schoolteacher was being harassed for her liberal views, Bill Ray and I played good cop–bad cop to convince a hostile conservative to cooperate with us. In this case, the photographer blustered, I calmed, and the man finally relented.

A photographer's second virtue, as Professor Cookman so ably demonstrates, is the desire to improve "the human condition." I was witness to two examples. The first was *Life*'s coverage of school desegregation in the South. All members of the press were frequently in danger then, but photographers, not just ours, were especially targeted. In 1956, *Life* photographer Bob Kelley escaped uninjured from a stone-throwing mob in Tennessee only to break a leg that night running from another crowd of angry rednecks. A couple of years later, freelancer Don Cravens had three shotguns pointed at his chest when he (and I) approached the farmhouse of a man suspected of involvement in a Mississippi lynching.

Photographers were in the crosshairs because they were showing America and the world what racism and its evil proponents looked like. Their pictures of courageous black children entering all-white schools, police dogs attacking black protestors, tobacco-chewing rural sheriffs smirking during their trials for murdering civil rights workers—these all shamed the South and the nation. This powerful coverage, from dozens of brave photographers, was critically important in encouraging the decent citizens of the South ultimately to accept the rule of law. It was the most inspiring triumph of photography that I have ever known.

A second example of how photography has changed the world is a curious one. It was not news pictures or even a photo-essay; it was film, the 8 mm home movie taken by businessman Abraham Zapruder of the assassination of John F. Kennedy in Dallas. I was the first reporter to contact Zapruder late that same night and the next day bought editorial rights for *Life*. The film's grisly frames show first the wounding of the president and Texas governor John Connally and then, seconds later, the fatal head shot. Still pictures from the film were printed in *Life* a few days later, demonstrating to the world in unprecedented detail how Kennedy died. His murder created a political deity, helped pass his civil rights legislation, and transformed the way presidents are guarded in this country.

This was photojournalism at its tragic best, and yet most ambiguous, too, because of the way the film has been used since. For the Warren Commission that investigated the assassination, Zapruder's film was key evidence in deciding that a single gunman, Lee Harvey Oswald, was responsible. And yet since 1963, conspiracy theorists insist that Oswald had help and cite the same film as their proof. The quarrel rages on.

It is a frustrating dispute that ironically could not happen if those ghastly events were ever to be repeated. Nearly all spectators today would record the crime on a cell phone, which dramatizes how photojournalism is adapting to our technological society. Where that photojournalism is being seen has changed too. It's on the Web, to be sure, both in still pictures and video, much of it (but not all) overwhelmingly personal and meant to enlighten us about the photographer, not the world. Television qualifies as photojournalism, too, of course, even when it is concentrating on the grotesque behavior of drunk or drugged-out celebrities. In my view, photojournalism's house has many mansions.

Its future in print is less clear. Despite their current economic woes, newspapers and magazines publish more pictures than ever before, but the photo-essay is, unhappily, in short supply. Perhaps we are in the mood, culturally at least, for the rebirth of a picture magazine, in print or even online, like the ones that gave birth to the photo-essay. I would hope so. As is so aptly quoted in the pages that follow, a *Time* editor, Daniel Longwell, long ago observed that "the quick nervousness of pictures is a new language." No longer new, but more indispensable than ever, it is a language that we need to preserve and encourage.

PREFACE

Like most histories, this one contains its share of dates and facts, events and people, causes and effects, evolutions and ruptures. For me, though, its most interesting contents are ideas, specifically the discussion of the four major forces that shape contemporary photojournalism. These ideas have percolated in my thinking during the dozen years I worked as a picture editor and nineteen years as a teacher. I thank Bill Luster for giving me the first occasion to articulate them when he asked me to write copy promoting the 1985 National Press Photographers Association's Flying Short Course that he was chairing. I thank Northwestern University Press for giving me the opportunity to bring them into deeper focus in this book. While my understanding of the forces that motivate photojournalists was already established in the mid-1980s, my graduate studies at Princeton University and my research as a historian of photography at Indiana University have enriched it immensely. Photojournalism is a fascinating subject. When its images combine with ideas, it becomes irresistible.

All authors owe more debts than they could possibly repay. Each new book arrives as the latest comment in a conversation that stretches far into the past and will continue across future horizons. If we are lucky, we may add a fresh insight to the conversation, perhaps one that will outlast us. But we are always aware of how the authors who preceded us have made our contribution possible. In the case of this book, those authors are found in the bibliography, but one bears special mention: Michael Carlebach, author of a two-volume history of photojournalism from its origins through the 1930s—*The Origins of Photojournalism in America* and *American Photojournalism Comes of Age*—stands at the head of the line of those to whom I owe so much.

Special appreciation to my wife, Joyce McMahan Cookman, and our sons, Colin and Alex, for their love and support. Gratitude to my editor, David Abrahamson, for his patience and guidance, and to the anonymous reviewer of this book's proposal for many welcome suggestions. I have been fortunate to study with great teachers who taught me photography and its history, including Peter C. Bunnell, Arthur Rothstein, Don Anderson, and Susan Moeller. My grateful acknowledgments to all who made suggestions, provided corrections, helped establish facts, served as sounding boards, and offered encouragement, including Bonnie Brennan, Rich Clarkson, C. Thomas Hardin, Dave Hamer, Jim Kelly, Steven Raymer, Bryan Moss, Radhika Parameswaran, Pam Spaulding, Zoe Smith, and Donald R. Winslow. My apologies to any whom I have inadvertently omitted.

Thanks to my students, who energize me and sharpen my mind with their questions. Finally, admiration to the photojournalists—prominent and nameless alike—who form the subject of this history, especially to those who enriched my life and taught me our profession as colleagues at the Associated Press in New York City, the *Louisville Times,* and the *Miami Herald.* Without them, there would be no book.

AMERICAN PHOTOJOURNALISM

ONE

———————◇———————

FOUR STREAMS NOURISH
PHOTOJOURNALISM

Four broad streams flow through the history of American photo-journalism. Three are traditions of practice: bearing witness to history, promoting social reform, and embracing human-ism. The fourth is the evolution of photographic technology. In the early twenty-first century, these streams converge to frame photojournalism's practices, shape its images, and motivate its adherents.

Most photojournalists accept and embrace these streams. Out-side the profession, in the 1970s, academic theorists began exam-ining photojournalism from critical perspectives. Positioning it in a broader cultural context, they applied such methodologies as feminism, Marxism, semiotics, structuralism, and poststructuralism to critique its images and methods. This book tells the story of the four streams, while acknowledging the critical perspectives.

The first tradition—the desire to witness and record important events and people—is closest to journalism's primary mission of reporting the news. Eight years after the announcement of pho-tography's invention in 1839, an anonymous daguerreotypist took the first war photographs during the Mexican-American War, launching this tradition. When Mathew Brady and his contemporaries photographed President Abraham Lincoln and other politicians, they expanded it from events to people.

Since then, photojournalists have recorded events, big and small, and portrayed people, important and ordinary. While their immediate objective may be the next morning's front page, many hope their images transcend the ephemeral nature of a newspaper or magazine to form a visual record of their era. Like Robert Capa's images of D-day or Margaret Bourke-White's portrait of Gandhi at his spinning wheel, they aspire to preserve the visual history of their era. W. Eugene Smith, a legend in twentieth-century photojournalism, expressed this idea: "The final desire of nearly every photographer-artist who works in journalism is to have his photographs live on past their important but short life span in a publication."[1]

Historical consciousness animates this statement by Carl Mydans, who photographed the Great Depression and World War II:

> My major motivation is to record what is happening in my time. I began with a view as a historian when I made pictures for the Farm Security Administration. This is America. This is what is happening to my land. . . . And that was true in covering the war, the dead and injured, the terrible lives of refugees. That is what is happening. That is history. That is my job. No matter what, to cover it.[2]

It is a commonplace that "journalism is the first draft of history," but there are important distinctions between news stories and photographs. The verbal first draft is rarely more than one source among many for historians. Its key facts are extracted, evaluated, supplemented, paraphrased, combined with other data, and—always—rewritten. It is difficult to rewrite photographs. While they may be cropped, retouched, recaptioned, and altered in other ways, they retain their integrity in a way that sets them apart from the written word.

The role of photographs as visual history recalls the phrase "mirror with a memory," applied to photography in the first years of its existence. *Mirror* referred to the shiny, reflective surface of the daguerreotype plate. *Memory* expressed the realization that photographs could preserve a trace of departed loved ones for future generations. The value attached to this preservation derived from the fact that, from its beginnings, photography enjoyed unprecedented authority as a witness of unimpeachable veracity. As the nineteenth-century public saw the perfect perspective and tonal gradations of the first camera images, it recognized the fidelity of the photograph over paintings and drawings.

This acceptance caused photography to excel as a medium of visual communication from its announcement to the present. The two original processes were introduced with claims that they would be useful for documenting and communicating. When François Arago presented Louis Daguerre's invention to the French Senate in 1839, he emphasized its utility in making visual records for science, industry, geography, and ethnography. The British inventor William Henry Fox Talbot, in promoting his negative-positive process in *The Pencil of Nature,* cited such practical uses as making a photographic inventory of one's possessions. Central to both statements was an absolute faith in the unprecedented veracity of this new process for making pictures.

Unlike drawing, painting, woodcut engraving, or lithography, all of which relied on an artist's hand, photography used a machine, lens, light-sensitive plates, and chemistry to let light draw the picture. It eliminated the deliberate alterations artists made to bend reality to their aesthetic vision and their unwitting mistakes resulting from poor drawing skills. The philosopher Ralph Waldo Emerson captured the idea when he said there "is no interference" between the subject and picture, and any imperfections in the latter "are not the blunders of an artist."[3]

It took another forty years to develop photomechanical reproduction, which allowed photographs to be published in newspapers. In the interim, visual communicators practiced proto-photojournalism, pasting photographs into books and selling them as album prints, stereograph views, and postcards. At newspapers and magazines, photographs functioned as sketches for craftsmen who based woodcuts and steel engravings on them.

The mechanization of picture making coincided with the height of the Industrial Revolution. Although they may not have known the name *positivism,* most Europeans and Americans subscribed to this philosophy's faith in science as the basis for certainty and progress. Photography's mechanical-optical-chemical process impressed the nineteenth-century public as the epitome of objectivity. Indeed, the French word for a camera lens was *objectif.*

Faith in the truth-value of photography persists to the present, despite numerous cases of photographic manipulation and despite the attempts of critical theorists to dislodge it. A wide range of critical perspectives originated with such European thinkers as Roland Barthes, Jean Baudrillard, Walter Benjamin, Simone de Beauvoir, Jacques Derrida, Michel Foucault, and Jean-François Lyotard. They were adopted by American critics and scholars who explored and expanded the implications of the Europeans' ideas. These perspectives—feminism, Marxism, structuralism, and poststructuralism—were often grouped under the heading of postmodernism. Today, many theorists working in these methodologies call themselves cultural historians.

They begin by pointing out that no photograph is unmediated. The relationship between a photograph and what was in front of the camera when the exposure was made is tenuous at best, they argue. A photograph is a representation and must never be confused with reality itself. Every photograph is the product of such a large number of decisions by the photographer that any claim of objectivity is deceptive. The photograph freezes an instant from the flow of time, extracts a small rectangle of space, collapses three dimensions into two, alters scale, often reduces color to black and white, and distorts tonal relationships. Most important, it incorporates the photographer's subjective biases in numerous decisions from the choice of film to camera angle, distance, framing, and instant of shutter release. Even the camera and lens system, the theorists point out, is biased toward a Western way of organizing spatial perceptions, known as Renaissance perspective. Digital photography and its ability to alter content without detection have added ammunition to the theorists' argument. For many, these mediations are sufficient to deny any truth-value to all photographs.

Central to postmodernism is an assault on the European Enlightenment tradition of rationality, including positivism's notion of scientific progress. In contrast to objectivity, for example, postmodern thinkers insist on the photograph's subjectivity. In contrast to scientific knowledge of reality, they argue that all human knowledge is constructed and, thus, can never match the real world. If knowledge is constructed inside each knower's mind, there can be no certainty of absolute truth.

Cultural theorists differ from traditional historians about what should be studied. Instead of focusing on important photojournalists, theorists believe the social, economic, and cultural forces that determined them are the proper areas of study. Instead of important images, they emphasize the contexts in which those images are produced and the ideologies they advance. The photographs are important only as evidence of those contexts and forces. Caroline Brothers, for example, argues that historians should not look at the surface contents of photographs, but at their underlying ideologies and how the circumstances of their production and publication shaped those ideologies. In her book on photography from the Spanish Civil War, Brothers "seeks to explore images of conflict not for what they literally depict so much as for how they were used, how their meanings were structured so they became elements of and stakes in the struggle instead of just witnesses to it."[4] Instead of a canon, or list determined by consensus, of the most important photographs, theorists challenge the politics of determining such a canon. In a hierarchy dominated by white males, they point out that the contributions of women and minorities are neglected.

Most pertinent to the thesis of this book, many postmodernists dispute the photograph's role as a witness to history. They argue that photographs lack a fixed meaning. Instead, their meanings are shaped by the captions and stories that accompany them. As time passes, these meanings change to match the beliefs and needs of the current culture. To believe otherwise is to deceive oneself. To state otherwise is to lie to one's audience. Despite making such arguments—often vehemently—for almost forty years, the theorists have persuaded few people outside academe.

Even those nonscholars who accept postmodernism's fundamental tenet of relativism are still likely to give special credence to the photograph. In the era of digital photography, most people realize photographs can be easily manipulated. They are not so naive as to accept the old adage "The camera never lies." Nonetheless, they persist in believing there is a connection between the reality in front of the camera and the resulting photograph, and that it can offer them some understanding of that reality. They do not construe the fact that some photographs are manipulated to mean that all are. Without denying subjectivity, they understand the medium can be used in objective ways, including scientific applications. They understand it is impractical to conduct one's life according to a theory that denies any connection between what's in front of the camera and the image produced. They trust the X-rays taken by their dentist.

The second tradition—the use of photography as a weapon for social reform—began near the end of the nineteenth century, when photography aligned itself with the Progressive Movement, which sought to correct a broad spectrum of problems. Jacob Riis, a New York newspaper reporter, was the first to wield photography to improve the lives of his fellow Americans. When his stories about the depredations in health and morality caused by poor housing conditions on the Lower East Side of New York failed to stir readers, Riis taught himself photography in order to demonstrate the problems visually. During the 1880s and 1890s, he documented workers in sweatshops, homeless people sleeping in basements and police stations, and street urchins stealing food from vendors. He projected the photographs as lantern slides to illustrate his lectures and published them in his book, *How the Other Half Lives.* They raised public awareness about a situation largely invisible to upper-class New Yorkers. Theodore Roosevelt, as police commissioner of New York City, attempted to correct the problems Riis identified. As a result, many of the worst tenements were torn down and replaced by buildings with light and ventilation. Public parks were developed, schools improved, and safe water made available.

In the same reformist spirit, Lewis Hine, working for the Child Labor Committee, photographed girls working in textile mills, boys in coal mines, and small children picking cotton or hawking newspapers late at night. His pictures helped pressure Congress to pass laws regulating child labor. Both Riis and Hine demonstrated that, in a democracy, using photographs to expose social problems can help mobilize the public will to correct them.

This tradition continued with Dorothea Lange's portrayals of Depression victims, Charles Moore's photographs of the civil rights movement, Donna Ferrato's images of spousal abuse, and Eugene Richards's project on crack cocaine. The social documentary approach, with its promise of improving the lot of less-fortunate people, motivates many contemporary photojournalists to produce picture stories and long-term projects that expose a spectrum of social ills.

What constitutes a hallowed tradition to photojournalists is considered an ideology by many theorists. The major critique of the social documentary tradition comes from Marxism. Building on ideas of the German writer Walter Benjamin, Susan Sontag propounds this position in her 1973 book, *On Photography*. She argues that in a capitalist economy all images, including those intended to promote social reform, are items for consumption. This happens, she says, because in the dialectic between truth and beauty, photographs always beautify even the most horrific conditions:

> Contrary to what is suggested by the humanist claims made for photography, the camera's ability to transform reality into something beautiful derives from its relative weakness as a means of conveying truth. The reason that humanism has become the reigning ideology of ambitious professional photographers ... is that

it masks the confusions about truth and beauty underlying the photographic enterprise.[5]

One effect of this beautifying is that photography serves the dominant class—those who control the capital—by helping to distract the lower classes from their discontents. "A capitalist society requires a culture based on images," she writes. "It needs to furnish vast amounts of entertainment in order to stimulate buying and anesthetize the injuries of class, race and sex."[6] Sontag altered her perspective in her 2003 book, *Regarding the Pain of Others.* In it, she seemed to acknowledge that photographs can affect viewers' emotional responses to horrific situations and social inequities— that in some cases they do more than merely beautify.

Other critics contend that photographers who profess to be helping the less fortunate are in fact rationalizing their true motivation—advancing their careers. They exploit and objectify the people they photograph instead of empowering them to improve their own lives. A third position maintains that a steady diet of social documentary images leads to "compassion fatigue."[7] When viewers are flooded with emotional images of war, natural disaster, poverty, and injustice without any way to help correct those problems, they tune out the messages.

Although many reformist photographers use humanism as a strategy, the third tradition—capturing the human condition— gained its definitive articulation in the 1955 exhibition The Family of Man, curated by Edward Steichen at the Museum of Modern Art in New York. As it traveled the world in the late 1950s, more than nine million people saw it. Its book version, still in print, spread humanist photography to millions more. From Steichen, succeeding generations of photojournalists learned to see all subjects as sharing in a common humanity and dignity. While it is easy to catch people in unguarded moments when their expressions, gestures, or surroundings ridicule them, most photojournalists reject such pictures, treating their subjects with respect. Many go beyond this, capturing human touches that invite viewers to empathize and identify with the subjects.

There is a second dimension to Steichen's humanism. The Family of Man organized the human condition into a set of universal experiences. Around the globe all people undergo birth and death; between these events they work, play, worship, buy and sell, teach and learn, make music, dance, and love. These themes inspire photojournalists, whether covering an event, searching for a feature picture, or pursuing a documentary project.

From its inception, The Family of Man exhibition generated a storm of criticism that continues to the present. Marxists labeled its underlying humanism as a diversion from the contradictions of capitalism. Perhaps the strongest rebuttal came from Barthes, who argued The Family of Man was one more example of capitalist ideology being used to conceal repressive economic and political conditions by portraying them as natural.

Developing alongside these three major traditions was the rapid and continuous evolution of photographic technology. Daguerre's and Talbot's inventions spawned a host of improvements leading to smaller cameras, faster lenses, and more sensitive film, printing paper, and chemicals. Artificial lighting, color film, and numerous other refinements, including digital photography, followed. Each development made new kinds of photographs possible. "Technology drives the medium" has become a shorthand phrase for how technical advances broaden the repertoire of possible images.

Of the many developments, three have fundamentally transformed photojournalism. The first was a development in printing production that made photojournalism possible. In 1880, the half-tone process permitted photographs to be engraved and published in newspapers and magazines, but inertia caused publishers to retain woodcut engravings for several decades. The first photo-oriented tabloid newspaper appeared in 1904. By World War I, such mainstream newspapers as the *New York Times* used photomechanical reproduction to publish photographs of the war. By the 1920s and 1930s, picture agencies began transmitting news photographs by wire, which brought the remaining American newspapers into the photomechanical era.

The 35 mm camera changed the way photojournalists see and work. Before its introduction in the 1920s, they used the Speed Graphic, a heavy, bulky camera with film holders that allowed two exposures each. To save on expensive film, photographers typically posed their subjects, which produced static pictures. The 35 mm Leica—light, inconspicuous, and offering a roll of thirty-six exposures—made it possible to capture the spontaneous action and multiple images necessary for picture stories. This spontaneity eventually led to an ethical stance against posing subjects.

In the third advance, digital photography has transformed photojournalism since the early 1990s. Although the optical and mechanical aspects of photography remain, electronics has replaced chemistry. This dovetailed with the computerization of the publishing process and brought numerous advantages to photojournalism. It allows photographers to cover events much closer to printing deadlines and transmit them to their newsrooms in time for publication. And it has facilitated photojournalism on the Internet through such formats as the audio slideshow.

For all its advantages, digital photography raises ethical issues. Most result from the fact that images can be manipulated in ways that are almost undetectable. Critical theorists use this as additional ammunition to deny the truth-value of the photographic image. This book argues that credibility does not reside in the medium of photography but in individual photojournalists and editors who employ digital technology ethically.

Implicit in postmodernism's critique of scientific progress is a deep suspicion of the claim "technology drives the medium." Theorists diminish the importance of the developments in photographic technology, arguing that cultural determinants had a greater influence on changes in imagery. Kevin Barnhurst maintains that the traditional model of the evolution of picture making, characterized as progress toward photographic realism, is too simplistic. "Instead of a tale of progress toward truth," he writes, "newer critics recount the history of picture making as ideological, the story of an idea that became dominant."[8] Like all stories, he implies, this account is shaped by the biases of its tellers.

The history of photojournalism has generally followed approaches in the larger history of photography. Barnhurst suggests five major approaches in writing that history: (1) the technical, which emphasizes the development in cameras, lenses, film, chemical processes, and other innovations; (2) the authorial, which focuses on important individuals; (3) the aesthetic, which considers changes in imagery, such as preferences in composition; (4) the social, which explores the ways institutions shape photography and how people use it; and (5) the cultural-critical approach, which foregrounds "the values and myths of the cultures in which the scenes take place, the status of the photograph as information, the political and economic power of the players, and the ethics of the exchanges among them."[9]

In the history of photojournalism, biographies of important photographers like Robert Capa, Margaret Bourke-White,

W. Eugene Smith, and Gordon Parks represent the authorial approach. Instead of aesthetics, many photojournalism books focus on historically important photographs, such as Joe Rosenthal's shot of marines raising the flag on Iwo Jima. Books such as John Faber's *Great News Photos and the Stories Behind Them* devote a page or two to the photographer, the photograph, the circumstances behind its making, and its significance. A few authors expand their scope to more traditional narratives of photojournalism's origins and development. Michael Carlebach's two-volume history, which traces American photojournalism from the origins of photography in 1839 through the 1930s, exemplifies this genre. Several cultural-critical theorists have studied specific issues, but there is not yet an overview of photojournalism from the cultural-critical perspective.

A traditional history of photojournalism would present the what, who, and when: what events and developments occurred, what notable images were taken, who took them, and when. Without neglecting these elements, this book emphasizes the how and the why. The evolution of photographic technology, which determines both the kinds of images that are possible and their distribution, constitutes the how. The why—photojournalists' motivation—is this book's primary theme.

Three large ideas—the desire to witness and record historical events and important people, the belief in photography's power to advance social justice, and the embrace of a universal humanism—have become the defining traditions of the profession. They constitute the value system of most photojournalists. To see photojournalism as merely the recording of daily news events misses its essence. Recognizing the motivational role of the three traditions is essential to understanding the flood of images produced each day by newspaper, agency, and freelance photojournalists.

These traditions have been promulgated through photojournalism courses at universities and workshops, as well as contests sponsored by the National Press Photographers Association and other organizations. They have become such an integral part of the culture and ethic of contemporary photojournalism that many photojournalists have internalized them without recognizing them or examining them critically. Without embracing the postmodern perspective, this book presents its critique in hopes of stimulating such an examination.

TWO

FROM PHOTOGRAPHY'S INVENTION
TO PROTO-PHOTOJOURNALISM

Travel in a time machine back to the America of September 19, 1839. The country is slogging through a six-year depression, following the Panic of 1837. The Battle of the Alamo, fought in 1836, remains fresh in people's memory. Even more vivid is the rebellion of slaves aboard the Spanish ship *La Amistad* on July 2, 1839, which will shake the foundations of slavery. Martin Van Buren, a Democrat, is nearly three years into his one-term presidency. The Second Great Awakening, a revival of religious fervor, is sweeping New England and western states. Among its objectives are the abolition of slavery and the promotion of temperance. The song "Annie Laurie" delights many Americans.

In the sixty-three years since the Declaration of Independence, the states have doubled to twenty-six. They fill the eastern side of the continent, and a column of states extends down the west side of the Mississippi River. West Virginia has not yet split off from Virginia. Florida, Iowa, and Wisconsin are still territories. Texas remains an independent republic. It will not add its 268,601 square miles to the Union until 1845. Because of the Louisiana Purchase, the government owns much of the continent west of the Mississippi, but vast regions remain unexplored and unsettled.

When the 1840 census is taken, the nation will number 17.07 million inhabitants,[1] but not all are citizens; 2.48 million are slaves, with the greatest concentrations in Virginia, the Carolinas, Georgia, and Alabama. New York leads in population with 2.4 million people, followed by Pennsylvania with 1.7 million, Ohio with 1.5 million, and Virginia with 1.2 million. Delaware, at 78,085, has the smallest state population. The Wisconsin Territory numbers only 30,945.

Although the Industrial Revolution is under way, the United States remains an agrarian economy, with 3.7 million employed in agriculture. By comparison, only 789,359 report they are in manufacturing and skilled trades; 117,351 in commerce; 65,051 in the learned professions and engineering; and 15,162 in mining. Commerce has been stimulated by the construction of three thousand miles of railroad track and, in the Northeast, more than three thousand canals. Even so, the economy is not healthy. The effects of the crash of 1837 persist at the national and individual levels.

There are 135 daily newspapers. New York State leads with 34, followed by Pennsylvania with 12, Louisiana with 11, Massachusetts with 10, and Ohio with 9. Weeklies and other periodicals bring the total to 1,614. Some 11,247 people work in the newspaper industry.

Literacy among free whites is high. The 1840 census will be the first to ask whether respondents can read and write. Among the 6.4 million free whites over the age of twenty, only 548,660, or 8.54 percent, report they cannot. Literacy ranges from a high of 99.7 percent in Connecticut to a low of 73 percent in North Carolina. Most citizens who buy newspapers did not learn to read them in public schools. It will be another thirteen years before Massachusetts becomes the first state to institute compulsory education, requiring children from eight to fourteen to attend publicly financed schools for at least three months a year. Most states will not adopt similar laws until after the Civil War.[2] In higher education, 171 colleges and universities enroll sixteen thousand students.

The level of visual literacy is also solid. Ordinary Americans have the opportunity to see a variety of images, although people with relatively more wealth who live in cities have greater exposure than farmworkers in rural areas or settlers on the western frontiers. Even in the West, however, such popular publications as the *Crockett Almanac* illustrate their fanciful stories with equally fanciful woodcuts. *Godey's Lady's Book* magazine publishes engravings of the latest women's fashions. Religious tracts and political pamphlets are illustrated with melodramatic woodcuts. In the cities, shops sell engravings and lithographic copies of paintings by old masters and modern painters. Illustrated books are also available. Among the most sumptuous is *The Birds of America,* illustrated with fifty-one colored etchings based on watercolors that John J. Audubon made from 1827 to 1838.

Although publicly sponsored art museums are rare, there are annual exhibitions of paintings at art schools, such as the National Academy of Design in New York and the Pennsylvania Academy in Philadelphia. For workers, there are "mechanics' fairs" that exhibit art in addition to showing crafts and technology. Prominent painters regularly send their masterpieces on tour around the country to be exhibited to the public. Affluent Americans hire miniaturists to paint their portraits from locket size up to a few inches. Silhouette artists serve less wealthy patrons. Whatever their level of wealth, literacy, or visual sophistication, on September 19, 1839, few Americans are prepared for a new method of picture making that seems perfection itself.

The inventor and artist Samuel F. B. Morse was one of the few Americans who already knew about Daguerre's new invention that preserved images created by exposing metal plates to light. Morse, who was in Paris seeking a patent for his telegraph, received a personal demonstration from Daguerre in early March, not long after he announced his discovery to the French Academy of Sciences on January 9. Morse described the process in a letter to his brother, who loaned it to the *New York Observer* for publication. Better known in his own day as a painter, Morse expressed enthusiasm for the exquisitely minute delineation of this new method for making images. He described a daguerreotype of a street scene with a distant sign. "The eye could just discern that there were lines of letters upon it," he wrote, "but so minute as not to be read with the naked eye. By the assistance of a powerful lens ... every letter was clearly and distinctly legible."[3]

As an artist, he considered the tonal quality of the daguerreotypes as "Rembrandt perfected." As an inventor, he was even more impressed by the scientific application of the new process. Describing a picture of a spider that Daguerre had taken with a microscope, he predicted the new discovery would "open a new field of research in the depth of microscopic nature" that would give naturalists "a new kingdom to explore as much beyond the microscope as the microscope is beyond the naked eye."[4]

On September 20, the steamship *British Queen* docked in New York, carrying news of Daguerre's invention. On board were copies of the *London Globe,* containing an article describing the process. In the days before wire services, editors freely lifted articles from other newspapers. *The Globe's* account was quickly reprinted in New York, Philadelphia, Baltimore, and Washington, D.C.

Several people immediately began experimenting, and by September 27, D. W. Seager succeeded in making the first daguerreotype in America. It showed St. Paul's Unitarian Church in New York. Under the headline "The New Art," a reporter for the *Morning Herald* told of seeing "a very curious specimen of the new mode, recently invented by Daguerre in Paris, of taking on copper the exact resemblances of scenes and living objects, through the medium of the sun's rays reflected in a *camera obscura*."[5] Calling the daguerreotype a "remarkable gem," he said, "It looks like fairy work, and changes its color like a chameleon." Emphasizing Seager's historical achievement, he concluded, "It is the first time the rays of the sun were ever caught on this continent, and imprisoned, in all their glory and beauty."[6]

In less than a week, Seager advertised that he would give a public lecture. "The process is rapid and simple," the ad stated, "but requiring delicacy, and a certain adherence to rules which will be explicitly laid down, as well as the particular minutiae to be observed to insure a certainty of success."[7]

Although Daguerre's process was faster and easier than making a drawing or painting, compared to contemporary photography, it was hardly "rapid and simple." Building on the work of his deceased partner, Joseph Necephore Niepce, Daguerre revitalized an old instrument, the camera obscura (Latin for "dark room"). The principle that light rays traveling through a small opening form a picture on the opposite wall was first recorded by the Chinese philosopher Mo-Ti in the fifth century B.C.E. Across the centuries, the camera obscura was used primarily in science and astronomy. In the 1500s, it was reduced from a full room to a large wooden box. A lens was inserted into the aperture, which improved the image quality, and a mirror was added to reflect the image onto a horizontal glass surface. By 1558, a drawing manual by Giovanni Battista Della Porta described how artists could put paper on this glass and trace the pictures.[8] In the 1830s, Niepce and Daguerre succeeded in making the camera obscura's ephemeral images permanent. On August 19, 1839, when Daguerre presented his process to the French Senate, it voted him an annual pension for offering it freely to the world.

The process began by coating a copper plate with silver and highly polishing it. It was held over boxes emitting fumes of iodine and bromine, which reacted with the silver, making the plate sensitive to light. To protect it from premature exposure, the plate was placed in a holder, then fitted into the back of the camera. When ready to make the picture, the daguerreotypist removed a protective slide from the holder. Because exposure times were very long, shutters were not necessary. Instead, operators took a cap off the lens, counted out the seconds—sometimes minutes—and replaced the cap and the slide.

The latent image needed chemical development to make it visible. Working in a darkroom, the operator placed the exposed plate over a metal box containing heated mercury. Its fumes reacted with the silver plate, causing the image to appear. When the development was complete, the operator bathed it in hyposulfite of soda, which became commonly known as hypo or stop bath, to remove any silver that had not been activated during the exposure. Many people considered the pale silver finish to be ghostly and unaesthetic, so operators often bathed plates in gold chloride to give them a warm, brownish tone. Because the delicate surface was easily scratched, they protected daguerreotypes with glass-covered frames.

Daguerre's original process was too slow for portraits. The first table of recommended exposures ranged from five minutes at midday in bright, sunny conditions to fifty to seventy minutes after 3:00 P.M. on a "quite cloudy" day.[9] Almost immediately, innovators began searching for ways to shorten exposures. Two improvements were especially important: "Faster" lenses with wider apertures were designed to let more light reach the plates. The Petzval lens, produced in Vienna, Austria, soon dominated the field. Accelerators, called "quicks," made the chemicals more sensitive.[10] Exposure times dropped to a few seconds, and eventually to half a second.

On October 7, ten days after Seager made the first daguerreotype in America, Alexander S. Wolcott made the world's first photographic portrait. Wolcott, a New Yorker who manufactured optical and scientific instruments and supplies for dentists, posed his business partner John Johnson in profile. Wolcott fitted a camera obscura with a concave mirror that concentrated the light rays onto the silver plate. He received the first photographic patent in the United States for his innovation.[11] Wolcott and Johnson also developed a system of mirrors to concentrate sunlight on the subject's face. Because the light was so intense, they interposed a glass container filled with blue liquid to protect the sitter's eyes. In March 1840, they opened a portrait studio at Broadway and Chambers streets in New York.

Having a portrait made during this period was not a pleasant experience. Besides the intense light, client's heads were wedged into cast-iron braces to hold them steady while the lens was open. They were instructed not to blink or budge. Some operators dusted their sitters' faces with white powder to make them reflect light better. Little wonder their expressions were universally dour. The results were not entirely satisfactory for other reasons. Some colors registered faster than others, giving an uneven result. John W. Draper, another early portrait maker, wrote in a scientific paper published in 1840 that "persons whose faces are freckled all over give rise to the most ludicrous results, a white, mottled appearance with just as many black dots as the sitter had yellow ones."[12]

Despite such drawbacks, hundreds of studios soon opened. Americans had caught what French wags ridiculed as daguerreotypomania. Demand for the portraits was strong, and many out-of-work Americans saw an opportunity to rebound from the depression by launching a new career. From New York and Washington to smaller cities like Cincinnati, Daguerreian studios enjoyed a thriving business. Itinerant portraitists traveled to small towns that couldn't support a full-time studio, setting up temporary operations in rented rooms. In the 1850 census, 938 Americans listed their occupation as daguerreotypist. An additional 1,000 worked in the support industry, manufacturing cameras, plates, chemicals, frames, and other supplies.

In Paris, the poet and art critic Charles Baudelaire ridiculed the vanity that he saw driving such portraiture. "A revengeful God has given ear to the prayers of this multitude," Baudelaire wrote of middle-class Parisians eager to have their portraits made. "Daguerre was his Messiah. Our squalid society rushed, Narcissus to a man, to gaze at its trivial image on a scrap of metal."[13] Previously, the primary means of having one's portrait made was to hire a painter. The lengthy time required and the painter's skill made the cost too expensive for all but royalty, nobility, church prelates, and the extremely wealthy. American egalitarianism saw no reason to criticize people for their desire to have a portrait, particularly when there was profit to be made. The mechanical nature of photography made portraits affordable for the middle class and, as advances in technology and mass production brought prices down, eventually for people of modest income. The earliest portraits were made as experiments, for which the sitters, who were family members, friends, or business associates, paid nothing. The price for commercial portraits depended on the size of the plate. A full-size daguerreotype measured 6½ × 8½ inches. Robert Taft, author of the first history of American photography, writes that in the early 1840s such a portrait cost $5, a considerable sum. Smaller sizes, down to 2¾ × 3¼ inches were proportionally cheaper. As American industry geared up to mass-produce the plates and chemicals, prices dropped, and by the gold rush of 1849, miners typically paid $2.50 for a portrait. By 1853, two extremes in price had been established. The mammoth size, which measured 15 × 17 inches, cost $50. Operators serving the lower classes advertised daguerreotype portraits for 25¢ in the New York newspapers.[14]

Many of the first American operators learned their craft from Morse, who was professor of arts and design at New York University. Some were mediocre at best. For others, Daguerreian portraiture was a sideline to augment their primary businesses. James F. Ryder, a Cleveland photographer, noted how "watch repairers, dentists," and other businessmen made daguerreotypes "on the side!" "It was possible," he quipped, "to have a horse shod, your boots tapped, a tooth pulled, or a likeness taken by the same man."[15] Such dabblers routinely blamed the sitter for their own shoddy work, but many studio operators were professionals who devoted their careers to mastering the craft and producing quality portraits. Among the best were Albert Southworth and Josiah Hawes, partners in a Boston studio. They combined technical excellence with the ability to move beyond a mere likeness to suggest the inner character of their sitters.

John Plumbe Jr. was the first to establish a chain of photographic studios, opening branches in more than a dozen cities, including Boston, New York, Philadelphia, Baltimore, and towns as far west as Louisville and St. Louis. He was one of the first to exploit the mass production and sale of images based on photographs. He hired lithographers to copy his daguerreotypes, calling the reproductions plumbeotypes. Among his most famous is an 1846 view of the U.S. Capitol, still lacking its cupola. He exhibited a collection of plumbeotypes at the National Fair in Washington in 1846 and published them in *Plumbe's Popular Magazine* and in the *National Plumbeotype Gallery.*

The foremost photographic entrepreneur in the middle decades of the nineteenth century was Edward Anthony, who was a twenty-one-year-old civil engineer when news of the daguerreotype arrived in New York. With financial backing from Dr. J.W. Chilton, a prominent physician and chemist, Anthony opened a studio in New York. He scored an early coup in 1843, when he and his partner, J. M. Edwards, photographed all the U.S. congressional representatives. They exhibited these and other portraits of Washington notables at their New York studio under the title National Daguerrean Gallery. These historically important images were destroyed by fire in 1852. A portrait of President John Quincy Adams was the only one to survive.

Through the early 1840s, daguerreotypists had to make their own plates and mix their own chemicals. By the second half of the decade, there were enough studios to support a supply industry. In 1847, Anthony switched from photographing to importing daguerreotype materials from France and selling them to American operators. Five years later, he brought his brother Henry into the business as a partner. They began manufacturing the supplies themselves, including cameras, chemicals, cases for finished daguerreotypes, and albums for paper prints. The Anthonys dominated the photographic-supply industry for almost half a century.

During the same period, a photographic press developed. On November 1, 1850, Samuel D. Humphrey launched the *Daguerre-*

ian Journal, the world's first magazine devoted to photography. On its first cover was an engraving of Daguerre and a notice that it would be published semimonthly for a subscription of three dollars per year. A subtitle explained it was "Devoted to the Daguerrean and Photographic Art. Also, embraces the Sciences, Art, and Literature."[16] Two months later, H. H. Snelling began a competing publication, the *Photographic Art Journal.*

Daguerre's process permeated American consciousness. *Daguerreian* began to be used as an adjective to describe anything considered especially true to life. In New York, a men's clothing store advertised that it would affix daguerreotype portraits of its customers into the linings of their hats at no extra charge. The owners would have the advantage of being able to recognize and claim their own covering from a group of similar-looking hats.[17] An 1846 article in the *Christian Watchman* predicted the new means of picture making would insinuate its way into every dimension of existence: "For our own part we are unable to conceive any limits to the perfection of this art. On the contrary, it tasks the imagination to conjecture what it will *not* accomplish." With tongue-in-cheek hyperbole, it declared, "A man cannot make a proposal or a lady decline one—a steam boiler cannot explode, or an ambitious river overflow its banks—a gardener cannot elope with an heiress, or a reverend bishop commit an indiscretion, but straightway, an officious daguerreotype will proclaim the whole affair to the world."[18]

In popular culture, Nathaniel Hawthorne made the protagonist in his 1851 novel *The House of the Seven Gables,* known only by his last name, Holgrave, a daguerreotypist. Hawthorne offers insights into contemporary attitudes about photography, particularly the belief it had the power to capture the sitter's inner essence. When Phoebe Pyncheon learns of Holgrave's occupation, she expresses her dislike for daguerreotype portraits because they are "so hard and stern" and their subjects look unfriendly. "Most of my likenesses do look unamiable," Holgrave acknowledges, "but the very sufficient reason, I fancy, is, because the originals are so." He insists that "heaven's broad and simple sunshine" goes beyond surface appearances to bring "out the secret character that no painter would ever venture upon, even if he could detect it. There is, at least, no flattery in my humble line of art."[19] As the novel unfolds, Holgrave's unflattering daguerreotypes of Judge Jaffrey Pyncheon prove to be true indicators of the old man's evil character. Although the daguerreotype process remained dominant in the United States for almost two decades, it was eventually eclipsed. The primary limitation was that only one version of a daguerreotype existed. This was not a drawback for portraits intended for private use. But daguerreotypists who wanted to reach wide audiences had to make copies or hire engravers to reproduce them.

Another process offered a solution. When the British gentleman William Henry Fox Talbot heard the announcement of Daguerre's process, he quickly wrote a paper about his own experiments. He presented "An Account of the Art of Photogenic Drawing or the Process by Which Natural Objects May Be Made to Delineate Themselves Without the Aid of the Artist's Pencil" to the Royal Society on January 31, 1839. Among other accomplishments, Talbot was a philosopher, linguist, mathematician, physicist, philologist, and Egyptologist. Seemingly, he was good at everything except drawing. In 1833, while on his honeymoon at Lake Como near Milan, Italy, he tried drawing the scenery with a mechanical drawing aide called the camera lucida. Frustrated with the results, he switched to the camera obscura, putting tracing paper on the glass. The pressure of his hand jarred the camera, and he could not get the paper back in register with the scene. Out of his frustration,

Talbot wrote, "the idea occurred to me . . . how charming it would be if it were possible to cause these natural images to imprint themselves durably and remain fixed on the paper!"[20]

In August 1835, he succeeded in making his first image, showing an ornate window in his mansion near Stonehenge in southern England. He marveled that two hundred panes of glass could be counted without requiring a magnifying glass. He called his images calotypes, after the Greek word for beauty. His friend Sir John Herschel combined the Greek words for light and writing and called the process "photography." Herschel, a mathematician and astronomer, also coined the terms *negative* and *positive* and made the essential discovery that hyposulphite of soda would stop the development of unexposed silver, thus preventing the images from turning dark when exposed to additional light.

Unlike the unique daguerreotype, Talbot's process produced a negative in which the black and white tones in the scene were reversed. From it, a potentially unlimited number of positive copies could be printed. In 1844, Talbot published *The Pencil of Nature,* which was illustrated with photographic prints that were pasted onto the pages. While many of his photographs show artistry, Talbot promoted the practical side of his invention. In *The Pencil's* text, he listed several utilitarian applications, including making visual inventories of valuable possessions, scientific observations of leaves and other botanical specimens, and facsimile copies of lithographs and printed texts. Talbot described his process as ideal for preserving minute detail that would be too laborious and time consuming for an artist to record. "It has often been said . . . that there is no royal road to learning of any kind," Talbot wrote. "But the proverb is fallacious: for there is, assuredly, a royal road to *Drawing.* . . . Even accomplished artists now avail themselves of an invention which delineates in a few moments the almost endless details of Gothic architecture which a whole day would hardly suffice to draw correctly in the ordinary manner."[21]

Despite the advantages of the negative-positive system, Talbot's process was not immediately adopted for two reasons. His negatives and prints were made with paper bathed in silver salts. Instead of sitting on top of the surface, the sensitive material was embedded in the paper's fabric. This produced images that sacrificed detail for broad masses of tones similar to charcoal drawings. Many artists found them pleasing, but nonartists compared them unfavorably to the minute detail of the daguerreotype. The second impediment was financial. While France made Daguerre's process freely available to the world, Talbot patented his. He charged heavily and vigorously enforced his patent. Few Americans were inclined to pay when the daguerreotype pleased their clients better.

The situation changed in the late 1840s when the English sculptor Frederick Scott Archer invented a process that combined the daguerreotype's detail with Talbot's negative-positive capacity for unlimited prints. Instead of soaking paper in a solution, Archer dissolved the silver in collodion suspended in ether and alcohol, then spread the mixture onto a glass plate. Archer did not seek a patent and made his process freely available, even describing it in *The Collodion Process on Glass.* Although he died in poverty three years later, his process remained dominant until 1880. It spread quickly to the United States and supplanted the daguerreotype by the Civil War.

Collodion had one major drawback. When it dried, the silver emulsion was insensitive to light. Photographers had to coat the glass plate, insert it in a holder, put the holder in a camera, make the exposure, remove the holder, and develop the negative, all before the collodion dried. To make photographs outside their studios, they had to carry a portable darkroom with chemicals, glass plates, and negative holders in a wagon or backpacks.

Because of insensitive materials, long exposures, and cumbersome equipment, the vast majority of photographs taken during the 1840s and 1850s in America were studio portraits. Even so, almost from the beginning, some photographers did photograph events and locations in the larger world. In almost all cases they were motivated by a desire to communicate information visually. Often they recorded information about the physical nature of the land. In 1842, for example, Anthony was commissioned to make daguerreotypes in northern Maine that helped settle a dispute with Great Britain about the boundary between the United States and Canada.

At other times, they photographed news. In what Carlebach calls "one of the earliest attempts to make a spot news picture in America," the brothers William and Frederick Langenheim photographed the 1844 military occupation of Philadelphia following riots against Roman Catholics.[22] In July of the following year, they became the first to photograph Niagara Falls, which most Americans had not seen. In the realm of science, Josiah Hawes photographed one of the earliest operations performed with anesthesia, which took place at Massachusetts General Hospital in Boston in 1846.[23]

In 1853, when several grain mills caught fire in Oswego, New York, George N. Barnard, a local portraitist, photographed the conflagration. Two daguerreotypes that survive at the George Eastman House museum in Rochester demonstrate how Barnard worked the situation as it unfolded. The earlier picture shows the timber framework of one building like a skeleton against the bright flames (see figure 1). Next to it a second mill still has its facade, but smoke and flames appear along its roof. For this picture,

Barnard positioned himself directly across the Oswego River from the buildings. In the foreground, several men on a barge watch the fire. For his second picture, showing the mills reduced to a pile of timber and smoke, Barnard moved upriver several blocks and apparently climbed up in a building to get an elevated angle. Barnard copied his daguerreotypes and, according to advertisements in the Oswego newspapers, offered them for sale for the next several months. He continued photographing newsworthy events, covering the Civil War and photographing the devastation caused by the Great Chicago Fire in 1871.

Daguerre's original motivation found its realization in America. He began his career painting scenic backdrops for Parisian theaters. In 1822, he invented the diorama, which became one of the city's most popular entertainments. Dioramas were huge paintings on translucent linen, some measuring up to seventy-two feet long by forty-six feet high. They were painted with highly illusionistic scenes on both sides. By shifting the lighting, Daguerre caused images on the back to appear as those on the front faded. Music and sound effects enhanced the theatrical experience. To continue attracting crowds, Daguerre and his assistants painted at least twenty of the huge canvases between 1822 and 1839. His primary motivation for inventing photography was to make quick sketches for his diorama paintings. Although Daguerre did not pursue this application of his invention, many American photographers did. They used daguerreotypes as sketches for panoramic scenes of the unsettled West, which were popular with eastern audiences.

John Banvard opened the first American panorama in Boston, in December 1846. The painting moved across a stage, unrolling from one spool and being taken up on another, offering ticket holders a twelve-hundred-mile trip from the headwaters of the

Mississippi to New Orleans. Banvard spent four hundred days making sketches for his three-mile-long panorama. Six years later, John Wesley Jones opened his *Pantoscope of California, Nebraska, Utah, and the Mormons* in the same theater. In his advertisements, Jones emphasized that instead of basing his painting on sketches, he painted from some fifteen hundred daguerreotypes his crew had taken in northern California and the Rocky Mountains. The photographic sources invested it with great credibility. The antislavery crusader Henry Ward Beecher wrote, "In accuracy it probably exceeds any, as the daguerreotype has been used to give exactness to its delineations."[24] Unfortunately, once the painting was completed, Jones disposed of the plates. For him, their value was as a record of visual information, not as works of art to exhibit in their own right. "Jones, for all his entrepreneurial savvy, could not imagine any other way to find a market for his daguerreotype views," historian Martha Sandweiss wrote. "In a world crowded with other forms of visual representation, his daguerreotypes did not win instant acclaim; they were the means to a more dramatic and enthralling end."[25]

Other panoramas based on photographs included one of the Mississippi River by Leon Pomarede and one of the overland trail by James F. Wilkins. Their popularity with ordinary Americans was reflected in the praise that newspaper reviewers heaped on them. One writer in the *St. Louis Weekly Reveille* called them a "wonderful invention for annihilating time and space," and continued to point out their many advantages over actual travel: the traveler "may now, comfortably seated in a pleasant room, and, without being subjected to the annoyance of railway porters, disagreeable traveling companions, and the perpetual losses of trunks and carpet bags, enjoy all the varieties of scenery, and revel in all the riches and beauties of nature."[26]

Entertainment was not the only motivation for western photography. Both the government and businesses commissioned teams to explore and map unknown regions. Expedition leaders frequently took along artists and photographers to record discoveries. In 1853, when Col. John Charles Frémont made his fifth and final trip across the Rocky Mountains, searching for the best route for a railroad to the Pacific Ocean, he hired Solomon Nunes Carvalho of Charleston, South Carolina, to photograph and sketch the terrain. Carvalho suffered greatly from the weather and rough frontier conditions but succeeded in producing a set of daguerreotypes that were turned into wood engravings and circulated.

Whatever their educational, entertainment, or business value, such panoramas and daguerreotypes played into a consuming American ideology. They arrived during the era of Manifest Destiny, the period between the War of 1812 and the Civil War, when the nation expanded to possess the continent from the Atlantic to the Pacific. The impulse to create visual narratives of the West grew out of the ideology that the United States had a divinely given right and duty to settle the continent. That ideology fed interest in the West, motivating many easterners to migrate.

Portraying the West as a land of opportunity spurred Manifest Destiny. Most dramatic was the discovery of gold in northern California. While the gold rush of 1849 seduced men of all classes and occupations, daguerreotypists in the San Francisco area were the one group guaranteed to prosper by making portraits of the miners. Many daguerreotypists left their studios to record conditions in the fields. They documented solitary prospectors and crews of miners at large operations, with their tents, camp life, log cabins, and rude stores.

However newsworthy a mill fire might seem, it hardly compared to war in its power to motivate photographers. While England's

Roger Fenton is often credited with making the first war photographs during the Crimean War in 1854, that distinction belongs to an anonymous American, who preceded him by seven years. Several daguerreotypes were taken during the Mexican–American War in 1847 by one or more operators whose names are now lost.

Despite a treaty ceding Texas to the United States, Mexico continued to regard it as a rebel territory that it still owned. When it was finally admitted as a state in 1845, President James Polk tried to buy the land, but Mexican popular opinion prevented the government from accepting his proposal. Early in 1846, Polk sent American troops under General Zachary Taylor to an area north of the Rio Grande claimed by both Mexico and Texas. Mexican cavalry attacked and killed a patrol, and Mexican artillery shelled a fort Taylor had built. A fierce battle at Resaca de la Palma followed. At Polk's urging, Congress declared war against Mexico on May 13, 1846. The United States won easily and added 1.2 million square miles of land to its size, including Texas, California, New Mexico, Arizona, Nevada, and Utah.

Two sets of images from the war, totaling fifty daguerreotypes, survive. Pictures showing American troops embarking for Mexico were made at Fort Marion and St. Augustine, Florida. The rest were taken in or around Saltillo, Mexico, about two hundred miles west of what is now Brownsville, Texas. Their uniform size (2¾ × 3¼ inches) and shared location suggests they were all by the same photographer. By current standards they appear muddy and static. The most significant one shows General John Wool, with his staff and a guard of dragoons, mounted on horseback (see figure 2). As they pause in Saltillo's Calle Real to allow the photographer to make his exposure, a stray dog turns to survey the invaders and a woman leans out a window to watch.[27] Other images show American troops in the streets, views taken from the rooftops, pictures of an artillery battery, and close-ups of the church of Santiago. The operator made two daguerreotypes of the grave of Lieutenant Colonel Henry Clay Jr., youngest son of Henry Clay, the Kentucky senator known as the Great Compromiser. Sandweiss offers an illuminating comparison between one of these images and a lithograph by James Cameron purporting to show Clay's death. Its title, "Death of Lieut. Col. Henry Clay, Jr., of the Second Regiment Kentucky Volunteers at the Battle of *Beuna Vista* Feb. 23d, 1847," reads like a caption.[28] The lithograph shows a dragoon supporting Clay as he pushes himself up from the ground and gestures toward the soldiers to disregard him and continue fighting. Palm trees and other tropical vegetation frame the scene. In the midground, Clay's horse, eager to return to battle, personifies the spirit of its fallen rider. In the background, the U.S. dragoons in shakos and white sashes fire at a cluster of Mexicans. With its theme of heroic self-sacrifice, the lithograph romanticized Clay's death in battle.

By contrast, the daguerreotype is barren of symbolic meanings. In a dusty, rock-strewn foreground, a cross stands at the head of an open grave. Behind the grave an adobe vault stands out against a dark background. Instead of palms, scraggly, leafless trees dot the cemetery. One casts its shadow across the vault like rude calligraphy. These daguerreotypes were neither exhibited nor reproduced. As Sandweiss explains, "They met with a fate of utter indifference," which may explain why their maker remains anonymous.[29] Americans welcomed pictures such as Cameron's fictionalized reconstruction of Clay's death. One example was a book of twelve hand-colored lithographs created by the French artist Carl Nebel, who was not present during the war. Published in 1851 under the title *The War Between the United States and Mexico Illustrated,* it carried written descriptions by George Wilkins Kendall, a reporter for the *New Orleans Daily Picayune* who did witness some of the action. One writer praised Nebel's battle scenes as showing "the faithfulness of a daguerreotype reflection."[30]

The depictions by Nebel and other artists were prized precisely because they were not faithful. They were artistic inventions, based on a romantic tradition of battle painting. Stock conventions had developed over hundreds of years, including dead bodies in agonized postures, rearing horses, overturned cannon, gallant officers brandishing swords or waving flags as they led their troops into the battle's inferno, and backgrounds with the battered walls of forts emerging through billowing smoke. Cameron's image of Clay mimicked a popular theme of the dying hero, uttering his final words to comrades.

By the time of the Mexican-American War the state of the press and of visual culture had created an expectation for illustrated news. Morse's telegraph brought accounts of battles with great speed. With hundreds of paintings to imitate, nineteenth-century illustrators had no need to witness a battle firsthand. They merely substituted the face of the current military hero onto a generic body and matched details to accounts of the battle. Daguerreotypes could not compete, partly because their long exposures and cumbersome equipment made spontaneity impossible, but primarily because they could not match the illustrators' romanticized version of war. By the Civil War, the situation shifted as the veracity of photographs riveted viewers. Even so, for several decades, publishers exploited the best of both systems; they gave their readers romanticized engravings while claiming accuracy with the credit line "From a photograph."

The most famous daguerreotypist of the mid-nineteenth century was Mathew B. Brady. He combined high standards of quality, an entrepreneurial spirit, and a flare for self-promotion. He also had a historical consciousness and understood the value that a visual record of his era would hold for future generations. Brady's contributions fall into two chapters. The first was his portraitures of prominent politicians and cultural figures. As one indication of his commitment to documenting history, he photographed nineteen presidents, every one from John Quincy Adams through William McKinley except for William Henry Harrison, who died after one month in office.[31] The second chapter, his coverage of the Civil War, came after he had switched from daguerreotypes to negative-positive photography. While he exhibited and sold the photographs during the war, he envisioned this project as historical documentation.

The son of immigrant parents from County Cork, Ireland, Brady was born in 1822 near Lake George, New York, about sixty miles north of Albany. In the fall of 1839, he traveled to New York City, intending to study painting with Morse. Instead Morse's enthusiasm for the daguerreotype steered him toward photography. Brady supported himself by working as a clerk at a department store owned by A. T. Stewart, and in 1844, Stewart advanced him the capital to open his studio and gallery. A lithograph from a daguerreotype shows the twenty-two-year-old Brady with thick, wavy hair, a sharp nose, and an intense expression. Sporting a silk cravat, a double-breasted coat and vest, and wire-frame spectacles, he exudes the air of a dandy.

Brady and the bustling metropolis were meant for each other. "The luster of his subjects seemed to rub off on him," wrote Carlebach, "and he became America's unofficial, self-appointed court photographer."[32]

The Daguerreian portrait business was highly competitive in New York. An 1844 business directory listed ninety-six studios.

When Brady launched his gallery, at the corner of Broadway and Fulton Street, he was determined to outclass the others. He hired the best camera operators, offered a private entrance for famous clients and fine ladies, and was not above flattering his sitters. Most important he operated on a grand scale, impressing clients with sumptuous decor and furnishings. A writer in *Humphrey's Journal* spared no adjectives describing Brady's gallery. Its carpet was of "superior velvet," its walls covered with "gold paper," its curtains of "the most costly needle worked lace." From its frescoed ceiling hung "a six-light gilt and enameled chandelier." Its window shades were "commensurate with the gayest of palaces, while the golden cornices, and festooned damask, indicate that Art dictated their arrangement."[33] Brady's gallery was not merely a business purveying portraits but a gathering place where the upper middle class, whose aspirations matched the décor, came to socialize and be seen. Visitors could mingle freely with no obligation to sit for a likeness. Portraits of prominent Americans that covered the walls played an educational role but also served to advertise the quality of Brady's work. He understood that photographing important people would bring lesser ones into his studio. He avidly pursued presidents, senators, congressmen, singers, performers, and other luminaries. His sitters included the writers Edgar Allan Poe, Washington Irving, Nathaniel Hawthorne, and James Fenimore Cooper; the politicians Henry Clay, Daniel Webster, and John C. Calhoun; and people from other professions, such as General Winfield Scott, commander of U.S. forces in the Mexican-American War; Jenny Lind, the famous "Swedish Nightingale"; Horace Greeley, editor of the *New York Tribune,* best known for advising a generation of young men to go west; Thomas Nast, the political cartoonist; Napoleon III, emperor of France; His Royal Highness Edward, Prince of Wales; and a young actor named John Wilkes Booth, who would gain infamy as the assassin of President Lincoln. Some clients were sent to him by his friend, P. T. Barnum, the showman whose museum of oddities was just across Broadway from Brady's gallery.

Whatever the quality of his work, Brady's genius was in self-promotion. An advertisement for the opening of his second gallery in 1850 featured a woodcut of a palatial room filled with elegant women in bonnets, shawls, and floor-length dresses, conversing with men in tails and top hats. The walls were hung with framed pictures, and others were arranged on tables. The nature of the business was reduced to a tiny figure of an operator with a camera in the far left background. Noting "many improvements" over the previous gallery, the ad declared, "The proprietor has no hesitation in claiming advantages possessed by no similar establishment either in this country or in Europe. The facilities for the production of First-class Pictures are unrivaled." Of the portraits on exhibition, the ad continued: "This Gallery contains a matchless collection of EUROPEAN AND AMERICAN CELEBRITIES, unrivaled on this continent."[34]

Seven years into his career, Brady could also brag about the numerous medals he had won for his daguerreotypes. He was not above using snob appeal to attract wealthy clients. In an ad published in a New York City newspaper, he decried the "cheap pictures" some competitors were offering for twenty-five and fifty cents. The ad declared that Brady was "unwilling to abandon any artistic ground to the producers of inferior work," desiring instead to appeal "to an enlightened public" that preferred pictures of the quality appropriate to "men of talent, science, and application." Declaring that he wanted to preserve and perfect the photographic art, Brady accused the competition of causing it to "degenerate by inferiority of materials which must correspond with the meanness of the price."[35]

Borrowing an idea from Anthony's 1843 National Daguerrean Gallery, Brady decided in early 1845 to photograph a pantheon of prominent Americans. One example of his determination was his efforts to secure a portrait of the dying Andrew Jackson, victor at the Battle of New Orleans and the nation's seventh president. When Brady learned Jackson was seriously ill, he traveled to the Hermitage, Jackson's estate near Nashville. Disregarding the advice of his physician and the concerns of his family, Jackson dressed in a suit and cravat and sat for Brady's camera on April 15, 1845, two months before his death on June 8.

In 1848, Brady opened a branch studio and gallery in Washington, D.C., where he persuaded politicians of all parties to pose for him. He gave important sitters a free portrait, keeping extra images to exhibit and copy for sales. Brady planned to publish and sell images from his Gallery of Illustrious Americans. He hired François D'Avignon, considered the world's best lithographer, to translate the daguerreotypes, paying him one hundred dollars per image. He originally intended to include twenty-four subjects, but because of financial constraints, only twelve portraits were lithographed. Published in January 1850, the book was elegantly bound and gilded. Despite lavish praise by reviewers, the fifteen-dollar book sold poorly in the United States. It was one of several financial setbacks Brady would experience.

Americans gained an international reputation for the quality of their photography. The World's Fair of 1851, held at the Crystal Palace in London, included a competition for daguerreotypes. Against practitioners from England and several European countries, Americans took all three medals. "On examining the daguerreotypes contributed by the United States," the jurors wrote, "every observer must be struck with their beauty of execution, and the broad and well toned masses of light and shade, the total absence of all glare, which render them so superior to many works of this class." M. M. Lawrence won praise for his 12½ × 10½ inch portraits. "Notwithstanding their large size, they are, throughout, perfectly in focus and are beautifully finished in all details," the jurors wrote. The Boston inventor John Adams Whipple won a medal for his daguerreotype of the moon taken with the telescope at Harvard College. The judges considered Whipple's photograph "as indicating the commencement of a new era in astronomical representation." The medal for general excellence went to Brady, who sent forty-eight portraits.[36]

Brady attended the fair and then traveled several months in Europe. He photographed prominent Europeans, including Emperor Napoleon III of France and Princess Charlotte of Belgium. His most important new contact was not royalty, but a Scottish photographer and chemist named Alexander Gardner. When Gardner came to the United States in 1856, he brought two important technological developments with him: the collodion process and enlargement. The collodion process, developed by Archer in 1851, began the shift from daguerreotypes to the negative-positive process. With enlargement, not only could multiple copies be printed from glass negatives, their size could be increased by projection. Brady hired Gardner to manage his operations, and soon his studios were selling 11 × 17 inch enlargements, called the imperial size. The prints used the albumin process, in which a silver emulsion was suspended in egg whites.

Brady made his most famous portrait, of Abraham Lincoln, at his New York studio on February 27, 1860, a few hours before the Illinois congressman made the most important speech of his political career (see figure 3). Lincoln was scheduled to speak that night at Cooper Union, a school for working men and women. Invited by the Young Men's Central Republican Union, he delivered a seven-thousand-word speech demonstrating that the framers of the Constitution believed the federal government had the right to forbid slavery in the territories and newly admitted states.

Lincoln was not handsome. An old friend, Ward Hill Lamon, described his large ears, flabby cheeks, "thick lower lip," and long, blunt nose that was "slightly awry towards the right-hand side." "There was a large mole on his right cheek," Lamon wrote, "and an uncommonly prominent Adam's apple on his throat."[37] Previous portraits made in Illinois and other western locations were so unacceptable that Lincoln's wife, Mary Todd Lincoln, would not allow them to be circulated. On the morning of the speech, Richard C. McCormick and other members of the Republican group took Lincoln sightseeing. They visited Brady's studio, then at Broadway and Bleecker. After looking over the gallery, which included Stephen Douglas, who had bested Lincoln in the 1858 race for senator from Illinois, Lincoln went upstairs to the sitting room.

Brady's eyesight was already failing, so he left the camera operation to his employees, but on this occasion he took charge of posing Lincoln, determined to show him to best advantage. The resulting photograph exemplifies Brady's skill. At six feet four inches, Lincoln's height was his most distinctive feature. Brady decided to emphasize it by posing him standing instead of in the typical seated pose. He framed Lincoln with two props: a false column on his right and a table with two books on which Lincoln rested his left hand. He arranged his hair to cover the tops of his large ears and pulled down his right shirt cuff to conceal the fact that his coat sleeve was too short. "I had great trouble in making a natural picture," Brady recalled in an interview late in life. "I asked him if I might not arrange his collar, and with that began to pull it up. 'Ah,' said Lincoln, 'I see you want to shorten my neck.' 'That's just it,'" Brady replied, "and we both laughed."[38]

Lincoln gazed directly into the lens and pressed his lips together, which produced a serious expression but also minimized his lower lip. Brady succeeded in giving the unkempt, unsophisticated westerner a distinguished air. The picture was forgotten for several weeks. Lincoln himself didn't immediately get a copy. It was only after he was nominated for president at the Republican National Convention on May 16, 1860, that it resurfaced and was widely circulated.

Lincoln's Cooper Union speech was published verbatim in many newspapers, but the photograph had an equal influence in propelling Lincoln into the presidency. It was reproduced in both *Frank Leslie's Weekly* and *Harper's Weekly,* the most prominent illustrated publications of the time. The *Harper's* engraver embellished the picture (see figure 4). Behind the books, he added an ink well and some sheets of paper. In the background, he added a large window framed with patterned drapes. In the deep background, beyond a terrace and vine-covered balustrade, a herd of buffalo offered a reminder of Lincoln's western roots. As with all engravings drawn from photographs, the published image was reversed from left to right.

The 1860 campaign marked the first time photography played an important role in presidential politics. Lincoln's image formed the basis of a poster and other campaign imagery, plus numerous political cartoons. Card-size copies were sold to thousands of supporters. The artist Silas Hawley had trouble selling his drawn portrait of Lincoln. "The country is flooded with the pictures of Lincoln, in all conceivable shapes and sizes, and *cheap,*" he lamented. "It is in the medal form, it is on envelopes, it is on badges;

it is on cards; it is, indeed, on everything, and everywhere. And all for a *few cents!*"[39]

Two years after the Cooper Union picture, when Lincoln went to sit for another portrait at Brady's Washington studio, someone offered to introduce him to the photographer. They needed no introduction, Lincoln insisted. "Brady and the Cooper Union speech made me president!"[40]

While *Leslie's* and *Harper's* led the trend, many other publications exploited the veracity that photography gave to news illustrations. Although engravers still took considerable license, the phrase "From a daguerreotype" assured readers the image was true to life. The most famous and frequent such credit line was "From a photograph by Mathew Brady." Using *magazine* in its original meaning of a storehouse, Brady said, "My gallery has been the magazine to illustrate all the publications in the land. The illustrated papers got nearly all their portraits and war scenes from my camera."[41] Others concurred. Frank Leslie, who published many of Brady's pictures, said Brady's "national Gallery of Daguerreotypes has been of signal importance to publishers throughout the Union."[42] The Cleveland photographer James Ryder stated, "I think Brady stands at the head as to prominence. He has taken portraits of more public and prominent people than any of his rivals. Presidents, senators, governors, congressmen, ambassadors, statesmen of all degrees, notables of all countries have sat [for] him."[43]

The photographic historian Taft considered Brady's portraiture more important than his coverage of the Civil War. "In addition to the notables of Washington," he wrote, Brady photographed "explorers, merchants, engineers, the military, philanthropists, medics, editors, college presidents, poets, lawyers, prima donnas, chess players, actors and actresses, ship-builders, seamen, firemen, foreign visitors of note, impresarios, and clergymen." Taft credited the photographer "with being one of the foremost historians of his day."[44] The assessment would have pleased Brady, who also thought of himself as a historian. Late in life he told an interviewer, "From the first I regarded myself as under obligation to my country to preserve the faces of its historic men and mothers."[45]

Historical events as momentous as war never have a single cause. At its deepest level, the Civil War was rooted in contradictions that dated to the birth of the nation. The same founders who declared, "All men are created equal," compromised on slavery to persuade the southern colonies to enter the Union. Although the Constitution does not contain the words *slave* or *slavery,* articles 1 and 4 permitted importing slaves until 1808 and provided that slaves who escaped to free states must be returned to their owners. After 1808, plantation owners were still allowed to breed and sell slaves. In declaring that no person could "be deprived of life, liberty, or property without due process of law," the Fifth Amendment considered slaves not as persons entitled to such liberty, but as subhuman property that their owners had a Constitutional right to possess.

After Eli Whitney invented the cotton gin in 1794, slavery became very profitable for the owners of cotton plantations. Southerners considered slavery essential to their economy. During the 1850s, numerous developments caused them to fear for the survival of their "peculiar institution": Southern representatives were outnumbered in the House, Congress passed tariffs on foreign goods, effectively making the South a captive market for Northern industry, and the abolitionist movement agitated for the emancipation of slaves on moral grounds. In March 1857, the Supreme Court affirmed the fugitive provisions of the Constitution, ruling that Dred Scott, a slave, had no standing to sue his owner for freedom.

While the decision favored the Southern position, it galvanized abolitionists to increase their efforts. Stephen Douglas's doctrine of popular sovereignty, which challenged the Missouri Compromise of 1820, had a similar effect. Perhaps the most chilling development occurred when John Brown and his followers seized the U.S. arsenal at Harper's Ferry, West Virginia. Brown's call for the slaves to rise up and join him in rebellion against owners stoked the fears of Southern whites.

Among those opposing slavery was Lincoln, a one-term congressman from Illinois who had broken with the Whigs to join the Republican Party, founded in Ripon, Wisconsin, in 1854. Although he lost the Senate race to Douglas in 1858, their debates earned him a national reputation as a champion of the Republican cause. The party's 1860 platform affirmed states' rights but opposed extension of slavery into the western territories. The platform and Lincoln's repeated assurances that he would not attempt to abolish slavery failed to mollify many Southerners. In December 1860, South Carolina became the first state to leave the Union. Mississippi, Florida, Alabama, Georgia, Louisiana, and Texas quickly followed. On February 4, 1861, they formed the Confederate States of America. In the waning days of his presidency, James Buchanan made no move to oppose the secession. Lincoln, who valued the Union above all, insisted during his inaugural address on March 4, 1861, that he would not abolish slavery in the South and said he would welcome the seven states back into the Union. But the momentum toward war was too strong. When the Union forces tried to supply a garrison at Fort Sumter, South Carolina, Confederate artillery shelled the fort on April 13. The war had started. Rather than respond to Lincoln's call for troops, Virginia, Arkansas, Tennessee, and North Carolina also seceded and joined the Confederacy.

Photographic technology had progressed greatly by the summer of 1861, when it was called on to record the Civil War. The collodion process, with faster emulsions and glass-plate negatives that could make unlimited albumin enlargements, had replaced the daguerreotype's long exposure, small size, and unique image. Lenses had improved in speed and came in a variety of focal lengths. Despite these advancements, cameras were still too heavy to be handheld; tripods were essential. Negatives were still plates in holders, and the collodion chemistry still required that a plate be developed immediately. The optical-chemical process was still not fast enough to stop movement, as evidenced by many images where a soldier who moved his face during the exposure appears ghosted or a horse's legs dissolve in a blur. Unable to capture spontaneity, photographers chose static subjects or halted the action of lively ones.

These technical limitations combined with conventional ways of seeing and the repetitive nature of warfare to channel Civil War photographs into well-defined categories. From a distance of 150 years, they appear predictable, but to viewers in the 1860s they were astonishingly fresh. Numerically the largest category comprised portraits of officers and soldiers. Just as the public craved images of politicians and cultural figures before the war, it now wanted to see the generals mentioned in news dispatches. Photographers competed to portray military leaders, then exhibited and sold the resulting prints.

The impetus for the ordinary soldier to have his portrait made arose from a sadder reality. Many understood that they would not return home alive, and they wanted to leave their image with families and sweethearts. The Cleveland photographer James Ryder took such portraits pro bono. He advertised: "All young men going to the front not having a photograph to leave with their mothers should . . . come and get one free of charge." He refused other photographic commissions, putting his "patriotic obligation to serve the boys before all others."[46] Many less selfless photographers reaped large profits by following the armies into the field and setting up temporary studios.

The process of choice in the field was the tintype, also called a ferrotype because of its iron base or a melainotype for its black background. Either term was more accurate than *tintype,* since it contained no tin. The process involved coating a thin sheet of iron with black lacquer to produce a glossy surface. Just as with a glass-plate negative, a collodion emulsion was applied to the metal surface, the exposure made, and the image developed. Because the image was on a black background, instead of a glass plate, it appeared as a positive. Like daguerreotypes, there was only one version of a tintype. The lack of copies didn't bother the soldiers, who liked them because they were light and easy to mail. The process remained popular for the rest of the century, entering vernacular language in the expression "not on your tintype."

Beyond portraits, the most common subjects during the Civil War included buildings, especially houses that had been commandeered as headquarters for generals and their staffs; military logistics, from pontoon bridges, trains, and field kitchens to the stringing of telegraph wire; equipment (batteries of cannon proved an especially popular motif); soldiers posing in formation, relaxing in camp, occasionally training, and often demonstrating camaraderie; navy officers, sailors, ships, and cannon; battle sites and their aftermath, especially slain soldiers; and the destruction and devastation of civilian property. The ruins created by General William T. Sherman's scorched-earth march from Atlanta to Savannah, Georgia, are notable examples.

Photographs were only one kind of picture in a larger visual culture of the war. Others included woodcuts in the illustrated press, lithographs made for sale by illustrators such as Currier, and paintings by accomplished artists. Winslow Homer created numerous oil paintings of soldiers in the Union camps, while W. L. Sheppard executed similar scenes in watercolor on the Confederate side.

Southern photographers tried to work along the same lines as their Northern counterparts, but naval and rail blockades soon made it difficult for them to obtain supplies, which were manufactured in the North. Among the few who continued to operate was Andrew David Lytle, who opened a studio in Baton Rouge, Louisiana, in 1859, to make portraits of the Confederate soldiers. After Union forces captured the city on May 9, 1862, Lytle began portraying them, and military authorities let supplies through to him. A loyal Confederate, he used the supplies to make reconnaissance photographs of Union positions from tall buildings.[47]

Approximately three hundred permits to photograph combat operations were issued by the Union army. Many recipients remained anonymous, but the most famous included Brady, Gardner, Timothy O'Sullivan, and Captain Andrew J. Russell.

Brady cultivated his legend at the Battle of Bull Run, the first major land engagement of the war. Although Lincoln began mobilization immediately after Fort Sumter, it took several months for troops to arrive in Washington and become organized into an army. Despite objections that the men were not ready, Lincoln pressured General Irvin McDowell to advance into Virginia. Spirits in the capital were optimistic, and numerous Washingtonians, including congressmen on horseback and ladies in carriages, followed the army as if on a picnic outing. Among the throng was

Brady with two wagons outfitted with cameras, glass plates, and chemistry.

On July 21, 1861, McDowell's army made contact with the Confederate forces near Manassas Junction, about twenty-five miles southwest of Washington, and the attack began. At first Union soldiers succeeded in pushing back three brigades. Finally, they were stopped by the Virginia brigade under Thomas J. Jackson, who earned his nickname "Stonewall" that day. Volleys from Jackson's men broke the advance of the Union soldiers, who turned and fled. Retreat became a rout as soldiers abandoned their weapons and fled their units. An overturned wagon blocked a bridge over Bull Run Creek, and the mayhem intensified as civilians vied with soldiers for space on the dirt roads.

When Brady made it back to Washington, he had himself photographed, wearing a straw hat and a white duster, with a saber projecting from its bottom. He captioned the picture "Brady the Photographer returned from Bull Run/Photo taken July 22nd 1861" and circulated it to the photographic press.[48]

Reports of his successes were glowing. The *New York Times* reported he accompanied a Union column "into the action, and was caught in the whirl and panic which accompanied the retreat of our Army." The article placed Brady in the thick of the action "at every point, before and after the fight, neglecting no opportunity and sparing no labor in the pursuit of his professional object."[49] The photographic magazine *Humphrey's Journal* went even further, declaring that "the only reliable records at Bull's Run" were Brady's photographs. "The correspondents of the Rebel newspapers are sheer falsifiers; the correspondents of the Northern journals are not to be depended upon, and the correspondents of the English press are altogether worse than either; but Brady never misrepresents."[50] The writer should have included himself among the "sheer falsifiers." Neither Brady nor any other photographer succeeded in making a photograph at Bull Run. All images purporting to show the battle were made the following March after the Confederates withdrew from Manassas. Carlebach points out that Brady never listed any images from Bull Run in his catalogs. "These glowing testimonials were based on Brady's account of events rather than a firsthand look at his pictures," Carlebach explains. The "stirring story of his bravery under fire and the success of his mission" was Brady's fabrication.[51] In an account, given many years later, he said, "I went to the first battle of Bull Run with two wagons. . . . We made pictures and expected to be in Richmond the next day, but it was not so, and so our apparatus was a good deal damaged on the way back to Washington."[52]

A little more than a year later, Brady's employee, Gardner, took horrific images at the Battle of Antietam, near Sharpsburg, Maryland. On September 17, 1862, when General George McClellan's forces engaged General Robert E. Lee's Army of Northern Virginia, the fighting produced almost twenty-three thousand casualties, more than in any other one-day battle in the nation's history, including D-day in World War II. After the fighting, Gardner and his assistant, James Gibson, moved onto the field, photographing the Confederate dead. A week later, when Brady exhibited the photographs at his New York gallery, they evoked a strong response from the press.

Photographs of slain soldiers on the battlefield had never been seen before, and despite their horrific contents, they captivated the public's interest. "Of all objects of horror one would think the battle-field . . . should bear the palm of repulsiveness," a *New York Times* reporter wrote. "But on the contrary, there is a terrible fascination about it that draws one near these pictures, and makes him loath to leave them. You will see hushed, reverend groups standing around these weird copies of carnage, bending down to look in the pale faces of the dead, chained by the strange spell that dwells in dead men's eyes." The reporter went on to voice an ethical concern that continues today: "We would scarce choose to be in the gallery when one of the women bending over them should recognize a husband, a son, or a brother in the still, lifeless lines of bodies that lie ready for the gaping trenches."[53]

A more anguished response came from Dr. Oliver Wendell Holmes, who had journeyed to Antietam to search for his son, Oliver Wendell Holmes Jr., who had been shot in the neck.[54] In an *Atlantic Monthly* article, the elder Holmes meditated on the power of photographs to rekindle his firsthand experience: "It was so nearly like visiting the battlefield to look over these views, that all the emotions excited by the actual sight of the stained and sordid scene, strewed with rags and wrecks, came back to us." Holmes believed that the war was justified to cut out "the disease of our nation," but he was appalled by its inhumanity: "The sight of these pictures is a commentary on civilization such as a savage might well triumph to show its missionaries." As for his personal reaction to the photographs, Holmes said, "We buried them in the recesses of our cabinet as we would have buried the mutilated remains of the dead they too vividly represented."[55]

Brady did not make most of the thousands of images that went out over his signature. His eyesight had been poor for many years, and he left the camera operation to employees. Because he paid them salaries, Brady considered their work his and did not give them credit lines. Brady's contribution was seeing the historical importance of documenting the war and staking his financial resources on underwriting the operation. He outfitted nineteen teams, each typically comprising a camera operator and an assistant, with a wagon containing cameras, tripods, glass plates, and chemistry. He built supply bases, directed assignments, and arranged with the military for credentials. "I had men in all parts of the army, like a rich newspaper," he said.[56]

Brady was motivated by a desire to record history. "My wife and my most conservative friends had looked unfavorably upon the departure from commercial business to pictorial war correspondence," he recalled. In the face of such advice, he persisted because of an internal compulsion: "I can only describe the destiny that overruled me. . . . A spirit in my feet said, 'Go,' and I went."[57]

As one example of his historical consciousness, he photographed the Confederate commander, Robert E. Lee, the day after he surrendered at Appomattox. "It was supposed that after his defeat it would be preposterous to ask him to sit," Brady recalled much later, "but I thought that to be the time for the historical picture." Acknowledging that Robert Ould and Mrs. Lee helped him persuade the general, Brady said, "He allowed me to come to his house and photograph him on his back porch in several situations. Of course I had known him since the Mexican war when he was upon Gen. Scott's staff, and my request was not as from an intruder."[58] Brady demonstrated three traits that still serve photojournalists well: he did not withhold his request on the assumption it would be rejected, he enlisted help from intermediaries, and he exploited past ties with the subject.

Brady's Civil War coverage cost more than one hundred thousand dollars, plunging him deeply in debt to the Anthony brothers for supplies. He misjudged the public's interest in war photographs. While people flocked to see them during the war, once the fighting ended, they were eager to put the war behind them. He could not sell individual prints, and his efforts to sell the entire collection to the government dragged on for several years. He lost his business, was forced to sell investments, and descended into alcoholism. He gave many of his plates to the Anthony brothers in partial payment of his debt. Others were sold as scrap; their emulsions were scraped off, and the glass was used in greenhouses. In 1875, Congress finally bought the remaining negatives for twenty-five thousand dollars. They form the core of the Library of Congress's visual record of the war. Brady gave the money to his creditors, but it was not enough to erase his debt. He returned to New York City, where at the age of seventy-five he was still working, taking portraits in a studio. In 1894, a carriage struck him, breaking his leg and accelerating his decline. He died in a hospital ward for indigent patients on January 15, 1896.

In May 1863—probably because of the issue over credits but perhaps because he felt he could do better on his own—Gardner quit Brady, set up his own studio in Washington, and began photographing the war. He hired away many of Brady's best operators, including Timothy O'Sullivan, James Gibson, George Barnard, and David B. Woodbury. He gave credit lines to these photographers and to the technicians who made the prints. The Battle of Gettysburg, which raged from July 1 through July 3, 1863, was the turning point of the war. Gardner, O'Sullivan, and Gibson trekked seventy-seven miles from Washington to the small Pennsylvania town and were the first photographic team to arrive. William Frassanito, whose *Gettysburg: A Journey in Time* remains the most thorough study of the photographs, calculated the team made about sixty negatives. About 75 percent of them showed "bloated corpses, open graves, dead horses, and related details of wholesale carnage." Because Gardner's photographs of dead soldiers at Antietam had attracted an enthusiastic interest, he probably chose his subject matter based on its potential for sales. Frassanito says Gardner had to race against the crews burying the slain soldiers.[59] Gardner and his team shot with both 8 × 10 inch and stereo cameras. Stereoscopic views had a greater sales value than large prints.

Gardner's photographs are moving, but at least one is a fabrication. Comparing photographs to the actual site, Frassanito determined that Gardner and O'Sullivan moved the body of a slain Confederate soldier about forty yards in order to construct a storytelling picture (see figure 5). Working in the area called Devil's Den, the photographers discovered a small stone wall the Confederates had constructed between two huge boulders as a sniper's position, but there were no bodies present. To construct a narrative, they carried a young Confederate soldier's body from a nearby field, positioned it near the wall, placed a knapsack under his head, and propped a rifle against the wall beside him. Although Frassanito points out that the rifle was "definitely not the type used by sharpshooters,"[60] Gardner titled the picture "Home of a Rebel Sharpshooter." He invented a dramatization to accompany the picture:

> The sharpshooter had evidently been wounded in the head by a fragment of shell, which had exploded over him, and had laid down upon his blanket to await death. There was no means of judging how long he had lived after receiving his wound, but the disordered clothing shows that his sufferings must have been intense. Was he delirious with agony, or did death come slowly to his relief, while memories of home grew dearer as the field of carnage faded before him? What visions, of loved ones far away, may have hovered above his stony pillow! What familiar voices may he not have heard, like whispers beneath the roar of battle, as his eyes grew heavy in their long, last sleep![61]

While false to the situation, the caption says a great deal about Gardner's attempt to romanticize war and his perception of the sentimentality of his audience. *Gardner's Photographic Sketch Book of the War,* elaborately bound in two volumes with fifty tipped-in prints each, suffered the same failure as Brady's work. By one estimate only about two hundred copies were made, and at $150 each, they sold poorly.

Captain Andrew J. Russell was the first soldier-photographer and the only one to serve in the Civil War. Assigned to document the work of the U.S. Military Railroad Construction Corps, he recorded the building of railroads and pontoon bridges. He also photographed battlefields, burial details, the camp life of generals and privates, forts, prisons, and numerous naval scenes. The last Civil War photographs did not show battle scenes but the execution of the conspirators in the assassination of Lincoln. Gardner photographed the convicted males in prison and recorded the hanging of Mary Surratt, Lewis Powell, David Herold, and George Atzerodt on July 7, 1865 (see figure 6).

The end of the Civil War launched a period of rapid industrial growth and territorial expansion. Under Manifest Destiny, the western territories were taken from American Indians and populated by European Americans between 1865 and the end of the century. But first the land had to be explored. Congress sent several scientific expeditions to complete the mapping that had begun before the war. Photography's status as a scientific tool for making objective descriptions ensured it was included in these explorations. Many photographers who gained prominence during the Civil War found second careers on these expeditions. As part of the Geological Exploration of the Fortieth Parallel in the late 1860s, O'Sullivan made memorable photographs at the Carson Sink in Nevada and the Cañon de Chelle in New Mexico. William Henry Jackson's photographs of the natural wonders of Yellowstone helped convince Congress to designate it the nation's first national park in 1872.

In the private sector, the construction of a transcontinental railroad had been a major goal for decades before the war. Russell photographed that effort, producing more than two hundred 10 × 13 inch glass-plate negatives and more than four hundred stereo views. When the two crews—one building from the east, the other from the west—met at Promontory Summit, Utah, on May 10, 1869, Russell's photograph of the handshake after the driving of the golden spike became an iconic symbol of Manifest Destiny (see figure 7). His picture also demonstrates a Eurocentric point of view. The Chinese laborers who did much of the construction work are not shown.

Because of its accessibility by ships, the western edge of the continent was settled long before the Great Plains and Rocky Mountains. Following the gold rush, some photographers turned to the grandeur and natural beauty of northern California. Carlton Watkins and Eadweard Muybridge photographed the Yosemite Valley, which later became a national park. Although their photographs are now regarded as art, their primary motive was to sell pictures to an audience eager to gain visual information about the nation's physical grandeur.

In the twenty-first century, we understand photojournalism as not just taking newsworthy photographs but also reproducing them in mass-circulation publications. By this definition, most of the nineteenth century must be seen as an era of proto-photojournalism. The absence of photomechanical reproduction did not discourage early photographers from exploiting the new medium's potential for visual communication. They immediately saw it as qualitatively different from previous methods of making pictures by hand. They harnessed it to record and communicate data from science, exploration, medicine, criminology, and current events. The term *photojournalism* would not be coined until the mid-twentieth century, but many nineteenth-century photographers understood they were reporting visual information to their fellow citizens on the important people, events, and places of their times. Many, including Brady, understood they were also preserving history for future generations.

THREE

THE PRESS PHOTOGRAPHY
INDUSTRY EVOLVES

Rapid development transformed America after the Civil War. The Great Plains and Rocky Mountains were settled. The Second Industrial Revolution saw new inventions and rapid improvements in agriculture, manufacturing, and transportation. Spurred by electricity, the internal combustion engine, and the assembly line, business and industry expanded rapidly. The economy shifted from agrarian to industrial, enticing much of the population from farms to cities, and Europeans immigrated to the United States, seeking a better life.

A variety of demographic and technological developments helped newspapers participate in this expansion. From 1865 to 1900, the population of the United States doubled. Education increased, cutting the rate of illiteracy from 20 percent to about 10 percent. With the rise of industry, the population in cities tripled. Urban workers were a natural audience for afternoon newspapers, and the increasing availability of electricity let them read after nightfall. The first transatlantic cable was laid in 1866, making news dispatches from Europe fast and plentiful. Newsprint became cheaper. Linotype machines replaced printers who set type by hand. Fast rotary presses made large press runs practical, and color printing became possible by the early 1890s. Daily newspapers increased from about six hundred in 1865 to about twenty-four hundred in 1900. Daily circulation rose from 2.6 million to 15 million, propelling advertising revenues.[1]

Photography was part of the growth. A series of technical advances from the early 1870s to the end of the century combined to make what we now recognize as photojournalism possible. Improvements continued in the optical and chemical aspects of photography, including replacing the collodion process. Richard Maddox, a British doctor who used photography in his medical practice, suspected the ether and cyanide used in collodion was damaging his health. In 1871, he published instructions for a process that suspended silver salts and cadmium bromide in an emulsion of gelatin. Besides its safer chemicals, Maddox's emulsion could be used dry. Other researchers increased the emulsion's sensitivity to light. Within a decade, entrepreneurs were manufacturing dry plates and papers.

Maddox's gelatin silver process, which is still used in black-and-white photography, revolutionized the practice of photography in the field. Instead of having to carry portable darkrooms, photographers could buy dry plates from a store. Handheld and novelty cameras, including tiny "detective cameras" that could be concealed behind a necktie or in a walking cane, appeared. In 1884, the plates were changed from glass to cellulose, allowing roll film to be introduced.

Among optical developments, the first anastigmatic lens, which combined two lenses to correct for problems in refraction, was invented in 1884. Production started in 1890 at the Bausch and Lomb optical factory in Rochester, New York. Faster lenses and more-sensitive film made the old method of removing the lens cap and counting off the exposure impractical. In the 1880s, Edward Bausch patented a diaphragm shutter in the lens, based on the way the iris in the human eye expands and contracts. In 1891, the British optical manufacturer Thomas Dallmeyer invented the first telephoto lens.

Two new cameras, the Kodak and the Graflex, affected the practice of news photography. In Rochester, New York, amateur photographer George Eastman quit his job as a bookkeeper at a bank to open a photography-supply business. Eastman was an entrepreneur whose primary insight was to recognize the potential for making photography available to the masses. Complicated, expensive processes had confined photography primarily to people in the portrait business and a small number of amateurs whose wealth allowed them unlimited materials and time. Eastman brought photography to a mass market by a greatly simplified process, modern assembly-line production, and brilliant marketing.

He applied a gelatin emulsion to long strips of cellulose wound in rolls of one hundred exposures. He sold inexpensive cameras already loaded with this film. When customers finished their pictures, they mailed the cameras back to the company, where employees developed and printed the negatives, inserted a new roll of film, and mailed the package back. Emphasizing its simplicity, Eastman advertised his camera with the slogan "You push the button, we do the rest," which quickly entered popular speech.[2]

Naming his camera Kodak was another marketing coup. Unrelated to any person or thing, the name was chosen because the *k* sound at the beginning and end made it easy to remember. Suddenly making pictures was available to the masses. Everyone could be a photographer. Camera clubs sprang up to help these new shutterbugs learn to make better pictures. Bicycle outings to the countryside were organized so members could photograph nature.

The Kodak had two major effects on press photography. Although many professionals insisted on using large cameras that required tripods, some tried the smaller, handheld, roll-film cameras made by Kodak and its competitors. Typically they carried them as a second camera for occasions when they wanted to work spontaneously. More important, the Kodak encouraged many thousands of Americans who would never have attempted the cumbersome, expensive processes to try photography. Few became professionals, but collectively they constituted an audience with a higher appreciation for photographs. Photographically literate, they became an important base of readers of illustrated newspapers and magazines.

The second camera, the Graflex, was developed by William Folmer in 1898, and it soon became the standard press camera. It was handheld at chest level and had a leather hood on its top that operators sighted into to focus and compose their pictures. This let them dispense with the dark cloth that view camera operators used to shut out extraneous light.

As important as these developments were, it took an invention in printing technology to make true photojournalism possible. For the first forty years of photography's existence, people who wanted to use photographs as illustrations had two choices: book publishers made prints and pasted them into the publication, while newspapers and magazines hired engravers to make woodcuts or steel engravings based on the photographs.

After lengthy experimentation, Stephen Horgan, a photographer and technician for the *New York Daily Graphic,* developed a method for reproducing photographs on newspaper presses. He incised a plate of glass with a grid of horizontal and vertical lines and then rephotographed the image through it. This broke the image into thousands of tiny dots that simulated the tonal scale from black through grays to white. Two names have been applied to his discovery: the halftone process, because it simulates halftones, or grays, and photomechanical reproduction, because it replaced a human craft with a photographic process. Just as the camera eliminated the artist's bias in drawing, photomechanical reproduction eliminated the engraver's liberties and inaccuracies.

Horgan's invention permitted true photojournalism, the reproduction of actual photographs on the same page with headlines, stories, and captions. Photographs were finally compatible with newspapers' production systems. In the late 1890s, Horgan revised his process to fit the new, faster rotary presses.

Despite its potential to revolutionize newspaper content and production, it did not become widely accepted in America until World War I. It seemed destined to be a dead-end innovation. Cameras could not compete with the drama of woodcuts. Publishers believed their readers preferred fictionalized engravings and that they would consider halftone reproductions a cheap substitute for handcrafted woodcuts. In addition, they were trapped by the system that had developed around woodcuts. Newspapers had engravers on their staff—in 1891, they numbered about one thousand nationwide—but halftones had to be sent out to specialists. The time required made them impractical for deadline stories. All these reasons made editors and publishers slow to adopt photomechanical reproduction.

Magazines led the transition. With days or weeks of lead time, they were free from the newspapers' deadline constraints. *The Illustrated American,* launched in 1890 by Lorillard Spencer, was typical in publishing multiple pictures. It described its purpose as providing a pictorial chronicle of contemporary history. Other magazines that regularly published halftones during the 1890s included *Collier's, Cosmopolitan, Harper's Weekly, Leslie's Weekly, McClure's, Munsey's,* and *Scribner's Monthly* (later, the *Century*).

Among newspapers, Joseph Pulitzer's *World* published its first halftone in 1893. The *New York Tribune* followed in 1897. Several newspapers adopted the process during the Spanish-American War in 1898, but after the war they relapsed to a limited use of pictures. By 1900, many newspapers still did not have staff photographers, relying instead on picture agencies.

The *Daily Mirror,* a tabloid launched in London in 1904, was the first to style itself as a picture newspaper. America did not have a comparable one until after World War I, when the *New York Daily News* was founded in 1919. By then, halftones were produced in-house, making them faster and cheaper than woodcuts.

Readers had come to expect photographs. The Spanish-American War and World War I had shown publishers how photographs could build circulation among mass audiences. With this increase in photographic reproduction, an argument against images resurfaced—an argument as old as the parable of the shadows on the cave wall from Plato's *Republic.* In the 1840s, the British poet William Wordsworth criticized newspapers' use of woodcuts as infantile: "A backward movement surely have we here / From manhood—back to childhood . . . / Avaunt this vile abuse of pictured page!"[3]

Wordsworth's claim that pictures would diminish reading was sounded again at the end of the century. In a letter to the *New York Evening Post* in 1898, Professor Royal Amidon, of Columbia Medical College, surveyed the state of New York newspapers and found a "low literary standard and the blunting of moral refinement," which he believed contributed to illiteracy. He predicted a mindlessness in which "the editor can substitute more pictures for the small amount of reading matter now presented."[4] *The Nation,* a weekly magazine of news and opinion that did not publish illustrations, characterized the use of photographs in daily newspapers as succumbing to immaturity: "The childish view of the world is, so to speak, 'on top.'"[5]

Among those defending the halftone was its inventor, Horgan, who argued that a "picture is the quickest and most agreeable method of conveying an idea or impression."[6] The country's two leading newspaper publishers openly acknowledged their use of photographs to attract readers. "I had a small newspaper, which had been dead for years, and I was trying in every way to build up its circulation," said Pulitzer, recalling the origins of photography in his New York *World.* "What could I use for bait? A picture, of course. . . . We showed on the upper-right-hand section of our first page the picture of a statesman, a blushing bride, a fugitive absconder, or a murderer on occasion—whoever was most prominent in the day's doings. Circulation grew by the thousands."[7]

Pulitzer's rival William Randolph Hearst explained in a letter to his father why he planned to increase the number of photographs in the *San Francisco Examiner:* "Illustrations embellish a page," he wrote. They "attract the eye and stimulate the imagination of the masses and materially aid the comprehension of an unaccustomed reader and thus are of particular importance to that class of people which the *Examiner* claims to address."[8]

Critics also attacked photography's role in yellow journalism. The term has become an epithet for sensationalism, pandering, and an often reckless disregard for the truth. It was coined in 1897 in reference to the Yellow Kid, the protagonist in a popular comic called *Hogan's Alley.* Created by Richard Outcault, it began appearing in Pulitzer's *World* in 1895. The Yellow Kid appeared to be about four years old, with huge ears, a bald head, and a broad grin. He wore a loose nightshirt, which the *World* began printing in bright yellow. The color became the symbol for newspaper excesses during the era.[9] Yellow journalism's practitioners were criticized for undue attention to crime, scandal, catastrophes, high society, and celebrities at the expense of serious, substantive news. They also used anonymous sources, engaged in self-promotion, and used headlines and photographs that spanned multiple columns.

Charlotte Perkins Gilman, a prominent San Franciscan, criticized the exploitation of her divorce by Hearst's *Examiner* with an elitist argument frequently applied to photographs. She accused it of "harping on those themes which unlettered peasants find attractive."[10] Press historian W. Joseph Campbell, in arguing for a reconsideration of the stereotypes about yellow journalism, disputes charges such as Gilman's that it pandered only to poorly educated masses. Characterizing "yellow journalism as appealing principally or exclusively to downscale readers is not only elitist: It misrepresents the broad appeal of the genre," Campbell writes. Emphasizing the complexity of journalistic practice, he argues the negative connotations of yellow journalism must be balanced by the investigative journalism practiced during the Progressive Era when crusaders sought to reform government, politics, and big business. "Yellow journalism reflected the brashness and the widely perceived hurried pace of urban America at the turn of the twentieth century," Campbell writes. "It was a lively, provocative, swaggering style of journalism well suited to an innovative and expansive time."[11]

Photographs played a large role in yellow journalism's sensationalism, illustrating stories about scandal, crime, sex, and war. During a period when Victorian mores were still dominant, Hearst regularly published pictures of women modeling lingerie fashions.

In January 1897, one critic labeled Hearst's practices as "nude journalism."[12] The following month, the library in Newark, New Jersey, banned Hearst's *Journal* and Pulitzer's *World* as indecent. Other libraries, YMCAs, and organizations joined the boycott.

Scruples about the invasion of privacy did not get in the way of building circulation. Photographs of corrupt politicians and prominent people involved in personal scandals were expected, but in 1884, Pulitzer moved beyond covering hard news to print what later would be called human-interest features, intended to entertain more than inform. Under the title "Brooklyn Belles," he published woodcuts of debutantes from prominent families. Among the fiercest critics of this move was the *Journalist,* a trade journal. Pictures of "criminals, of politicians . . . or any one who is either thrust forward or pushes himself before the public" were acceptable, it editorialized. But it found no justification "for a newspaper to invade the sanctity of the home circle and hold up to public gaze and mayhap ridicule the portraits of young ladies who in nowise court publicity, and in whom the public has no interest except as they are pretty women."[13]

Despite this moralizing, Pulitzer and others continued publishing such pictures and expanded the range to include candid photographs taken in public places. "It behooves every man, woman and child to walk circumspectly while on the streets," warned the editors of *Anthony's Photographic Bulletin,* "for it is impossible to tell when they may be confronted with a photograph showing them in some ridiculous or embarrassing position."[14]

During the yellow journalism era and the newspaper wars between Pulitzer and Hearst, photojournalists established most of the basic categories of news pictures still in practice today: catastrophes, celebrities, ceremonies, sports, people and events from the political and military realms, technology, spectacles, and novelties.[15]

For sheer spectacle, nothing could match war for exciting the public's imagination or boosting newspaper circulation. Historians debate how big a role American newspapers played in pushing President William McKinley into launching the Spanish-American War. Campbell disputes the standard view that Hearst, Pulitzer, and others fomented public sentiment to the point where war was inevitable. Whatever their effect, it is clear the New York newspapers published numerous articles against Spain, that they enjoyed sizable circulation gains during the short-lived war, and that photography played a key role in their coverage of the war.

Once the world's largest colonial power, Spain had lost all of its American colonies except Puerto Rico and Cuba by the middle of the 1800s. Cuban rebels fought for independence from Spain in the 1870s and again in the 1890s. Their leader, José Martí, founder of the Cuban Revolutionary Party, was killed in 1895. American business had invested some fifty million dollars in the sugar industry in Cuba, and American newspapers urged support for the Cuban revolutionaries in their fight for freedom from Spain. As the Spanish commander General Valeriano Weyler imposed harsh conditions on the Cuban people, McKinley sent the battleship *Maine* to the harbor in Havana in January 1898.

On February 15, 1898, a powerful explosion destroyed the ship; 260 sailors and marines were killed immediately, and another 6 died later. An investigation by the U.S. Navy concluded a mine caused the explosion but did not speculate on who placed it. Later studies argued that spontaneous combustion of coal dust ignited stores of gunpowder, but the cause remains unresolved. Newspapers in New York, especially Hearst's *Journal,* immediately concluded that the Spanish had attacked the ship, and they began to foment American public opinion toward war. Although McKinley opposed it, Congress declared war on Spain in April.

The first published images were fanciful drawings of flying debris and shouting sailors. A small group of American correspondents and photographers went to Havana, but it took more than a week for them to take and develop photographs and ship them by sea to New York. The photographs hardly compared to the artists' inventions. Only a mast and the ship's stern remained visible above placid waters.

As calls for war intensified, journalists, anticipating an invasion of Cuba, flocked to Florida. They included Frederic Remington, painter of the American West; Stephen Crane, author of the Civil War novel *The Red Badge of Courage;* and Richard Harding Davis, considered the nation's top war correspondent. Among the photojournalists were Burr McIntosh, photographing for *Leslie's Weekly;* James Burton and William Dinwiddie, both with *Harper's Weekly;* and John Hemment, of Hearst's *Journal.* Hemment enjoyed the best working conditions. He rode a horse, had an assistant, and lived on Hearst's personal yacht in the Havana harbor, where he processed his plates. Hemment practiced a conservative approach to photography, working with glass negatives and large cameras on tripods. To his credit, he recognized the limitations of his approach and predicted that future wars would be photographed on film with small cameras. "A camera not larger than five by seven [inches] is the most convenient to use," he concluded.[16] He also complained that, because of advances in military technology, the war was not as picturesque as previous ones. "The pictures made nowadays do not convey to the reader the same romantic spectacle that one is accustomed to seek and find in past war pictures," he wrote, "for the use of smokeless powder has taken away the effect of clouds of dense smoke."[17]

Photojournalists using handheld cameras also found it difficult to capture action in battle. Most were limited to pictures of artillery units firing their cannon, soldiers in the trenches, and the bodies of slain soldiers. They shared the frustration James Burton expressed to his editors at not being able to capture the intense experience of combat under fire. "I found it impossible to make any actual 'battle scenes,' for many reasons—the distance at which the fighting is conducted, the area which is covered, but chiefly the long grass and thickly wooded country," he wrote.[18] The photographers were also plagued by sand and water damage to their cameras and by the intense heat, which frequently caused the emulsion on their negatives to shrivel.

Among the best photojournalists covering the Spanish-American War was Jimmy Hare, who went on to make a career in war photography. Born in England, he came to America in 1890. He had difficulty supporting himself as a camera maker and switched to photographing, primarily for the *Illustrated American*. In early 1898, the magazine's building caught fire, destroying his equipment. A few weeks later, after the sinking of the *Maine,* Hare went to Robert J. Collier and proposed he send him to Cuba to photograph for his magazine, *Collier's Weekly.* "The *Maine* blew up, and Jimmy blew in," Collier said later.[19] Were it not for Hare, he joked, he would never have had to worry about profits. With Hare's coverage, *Collier's Weekly* flourished, increasing from fewer than 50,000 subscriptions at the beginning of 1898 to 250,000 in 1900. Its advertising lineage increased two and a half times during 1898.[20]

During the war, many correspondents and photographers affected swashbuckling behavior and took foolhardy chances. James Creelman, a reporter for Hearst's *Journal,* was shot while trying to recover a fallen Spanish flag at the battle of El Caney. "There was a gratuitous bravery that smacked of posturing and affectation," wrote Susan Moeller, a historian of war photography. "Photographers and journalists feared that if they did not flagrantly risk their lives . . . the exhilaration of war would have passed them by."[21]

Hare, who was in his forties when he covered the war, was not afraid to take risks, but he did not engage in bravado. Crane described a situation when he and Hare were under fire: As the air whistled with bullets, Crane said Hare's "face [was] bloodless, white as paper." He recalled the photographer asking, "Say, this is pretty hot, ain't it?" When Crane confirmed it was, indeed, serious, Hare responded, "All right." He took "[my] assurance with simple faith," Crane said, "and deported himself with kindly dignity as one moving amid great things. His face was still as pale as paper, but . . . the main point was his perfect willingness to be frightened for reasons."[22]

Hare understood what all war photographers know: the reporter can reconstruct a battle story from official reports, interviews, and observations after the event, but the photographer must be present to get pictures. After the battle of Kettle Hill, one soldier told him, "You must be a congenital damn fool to be up here. I wouldn't be unless I had to!" "Neither would I," he replied, "but you can't get *real* pictures unless you take some risk!"[23]

Hare worked with a handheld camera, but like Burton he was not able to capture the actual fighting. His best photograph shows six soldiers carrying a wounded comrade to the rear during a battle at San Juan. Assessing the overall coverage of the war, Moeller is sharply critical of the narrow range of images and the lack of pictures showing what battle was like for the individual soldier. "Few photographs of the Spanish-American War gave the public back home the opportunity to learn the intimate details of war," she wrote. Acknowledging the limitations of camera technology, she still faults the photographers for not making "a more imaginative attempt to capture the full range of emotions and experience of the conflict on film." Because of this shortcoming, she concludes, "the United States entered World War I with all its naïveté [about war] intact."[24]

The war boosted the circulation of those newspapers and magazines that gave it prominent coverage. Hearst's *Journal* increased nearly 100 percent to 1.5 million copies a day, and "*McClure's* magazine gained 100,000 a month."[25] E. L. Godkin, editor of *The Nation,* expressed the common wisdom when he wrote, "Newspapers are made to sell; and for this purpose there is nothing better than war. War brings daily sensation and excitement. On this almost any kind of newspaper may live and make money.... It follows from this, it cannot but follow, that it is only human for a newspaper proprietor to desire war."[26] Godkin mistakenly equated circulation with profit. Many newspapers lost money covering the war. The salaries and expenses of keeping reporters and photographers in the field were substantial, and the logistical costs were enormous. Dispatch boats took stories from Cuba to Key West, Florida, and other ports in the Caribbean, where they were cabled back to New York. Photographs were sent by ship. By one estimate Hearst spent $500,000 on the war. Production costs also increased as newspapers engaged in fierce battles for street sales by replating their presses for extra editions whenever a new story arrived. On top of such costs, advertising revenue declined sharply during the war.[27]

Secretary of State John Hay called it a "splendid little war"— with good reason. On August 12, 1898, after less than two months of actual fighting, the Spanish gave up. About three thousand American soldiers died—almost 90 percent of them from tropical diseases instead of combat. The war cost the country $250 million. Victory marked the beginning of U.S. imperialism. Spain ceded the United States most of its remaining colonial possessions, including Puerto Rico in the Caribbean and Guam in the Pacific. It sold the Philippines to the United States for $20 million. Cuba was given its freedom, but under strict U.S. controls. Despite the isolationist tendencies of most Americans, the United States became a world power with wide-flung colonial possessions. As with the Civil War, the end of the Spanish-American War launched an economic boom. The lingering Panic of 1893 gave way to prosperity, population growth, and technological innovations that ended only with the stock market crash in 1929.

Although stars such as Hare, Burton, and Hemment helped improve circulation, after the war only the large-circulation metropolitan newspapers continued to employ staff photographers. Most papers bought whatever photographs they published from picture services that were part of larger syndications of news stories. As early as 1872, the Western Newspaper Union began distributing fictional stories and columns by Robert Louis Stevenson, Mark Twain, Jack London, and other well-known writers. The Associated Press (AP) started in 1846 when five New York newspapers cooperated to get news from the Mexican War. In a few months, they spread their costs by telegraphing the dispatches to other newspapers in Boston, Albany, Buffalo, and Philadelphia. Among the AP's chief competitors was United Press (UP), founded in 1882. The AP signed exclusive contracts with European agencies, including Reuters, forcing UP into bankruptcy in 1897. When a court ruled it a monopoly in 1900, the AP reorganized as a nonprofit cooperative with member newspapers sharing stories and photographs. In technological innovations, the AP switched from transmitting stories by telegraph to using the telephone in 1910 and the teletype in 1913.

One of the first important picture agencies was started by a former reporter, George Bain. When the *St. Louis Post-Dispatch* assigned him to its Washington bureau, Bain began taking photographs to illustrate his stories. He used a handheld camera, which yielded relatively candid pictures of the politicians he was writing about. Enthusiastic reaction from editors and readers confirmed Bain's belief in the value of news pictures. He became manager of the United Press's Washington bureau, expanding his photographic operation from a single newspaper to the agency level. When UP went bankrupt, he started the Bain News Service, which thrived for almost forty years.[28] Using his lucrative series of candid photographs of Mark Twain as a base, he started his own picture service in 1901. Like Brady, he primarily handled the organization and business, hiring better-qualified photographers to take the pictures.

In 1905, George Harris and Martha Ewing launched the Harris and Ewing service in Washington. Their operation grew to more than one hundred employees with international branches. Besides such relatively small operations, several agencies and big newspapers also started picture services, including Hearst's International News Photos and Scripps-Howard's News Enterprise Association. In 1919, the *New York Times* began Wide World Photos, and two years later the *Chicago Tribune* and the *New York Daily News* started Pacific and Atlantic Photos.

Newspapers and magazines were not the only means of circulating pictures of important people, places, and events. Businesses such as Griffith and Griffith, the H. C. White Company, the Keystone View Company, and Underwood and Underwood sold the public photographs of celebrities, politicians, and the American West well into the early twentieth century. They produced popular stereoscopic views that gave the illusion of three dimensionality, and they added a new format, the picture postcard.

Created by an economics professor in Germany, postcards began to be illustrated with drawings in the 1870s. They caught the

imagination of the American public during the World's Columbian Exposition in Chicago in 1893 and were officially approved
by Congress for use in the mail in 1898. Stereographs and postcards
of major events such as the Spanish-American War and the San
Francisco Earthquake sold in massive numbers. Entrepreneurial
photographers in small towns turned their pictures of local news
events and scenes into postcards. Other developments increased
their popularity: Kodak began offering photographic printing
paper on card stock cut to postcard size. The U.S. Postal Service
approved rural free delivery. And a traveling salesman invented a
revolving steel rack that allowed stores to display them. The postal
service delivered some 668 million postcards in 1908. By 1913, the
number had grown to 968 million. Carlebach has emphasized the
importance of the postcard as a means of visual communication
during an era when many small-town newspapers still did not
publish halftones because their conservative editors "refused to believe pictures were either serious or useful." He wrote, "Postcards
were inexpensive to make, and in the absence of any competing
medium of visual communication, profit was practically guaranteed. During the first two decades of the twentieth century, local
photographers who recorded hometown news were most likely to
sell the images in the form of postcards."[29]

Although men dominated in number, photography was open to
women. The British photographer Julia Margaret Cameron was
one of the best portraitists of the nineteenth century. The pic-
torialist movement, which won the recognition of photography
as a fine art, included Gertrude Kasebier, Anne Brigman, and
Zaida Ben-Yusuf as prominent members. As amateur photography expanded, many women joined its ranks. The *New York Times*
noted in an 1893 article, "Ladies also use the camera nowadays." Its

reporter added they were not just taking family snapshots but producing work that was being displayed and sold in art galleries.[30]

Women entered photojournalism as well, despite editors who thought the work was too coarse for ladies. In 1901, one newspaper editor wrote to the *Ladies' Home Journal,* "I would rather see my daughters starve than that they should have ever heard or seen what women on my staff have been compelled to hear and see."[31] Nonetheless, women were willing to endure the crude language and harsh competitiveness of daily journalism, and Canadian-American Jessie Tarbox Beals is credited with being the first. Beals's story offers an early example of the energy, ingenuity, and determination of women in photojournalism but also the challenges they faced in trying to balance a career with the competing claims of family.[32]

Born in 1870 in Hamilton, Ontario, Beals moved to Williamsburg, Massachusetts, at age eighteen and began teaching school to support herself. After winning a primitive camera in a competition, she became fascinated with photography and soon traded up to a twelve-dollar Kodak. She used it to supplement her income by operating a small portrait business and by photographing Smith College students. In 1897, she married a machinist, Alfred Beals, and taught him to do her darkroom processing. Together, they traveled around Massachusetts, photographing fairs and other large gatherings and selling the pictures to the subjects.

In 1899, one of Beals's photographs was published in the *Boston Post* but was miscredited. In 1900, the *County Reformer* and the *Phoenix* in Brattleboro, Vermont, published photographs with her credit, establishing her as the first American woman photojournalist. In another first, Beals went from freelance status to become the first woman staff photographer when the *Buffalo Inquirer and Courier* hired her in 1902. She soon established a reputation for

competitiveness and determination. When a judge barred photographers from covering a murder trial, she did not let her cumbersome clothes or the weight of her large-view camera stop her.
She climbed a bookcase and photographed the court proceedings
through a transom window, earning a five-column display on the
front page. Beals lectured frequently about her work and encouraged other women to consider it, but she was candid about the
requirements: "If one is the possessor of health and strength, a
good news instinct ... a fair photographic outfit, and the ability
to hustle, which is the most necessary qualification, one can be
a news photographer," she said. Besides hustle, she also demonstrated a toughness born of having to support herself, as evidenced
in her assessment of female contemporaries: "Mere feminine, delicate, Dresden China type of women, get nowhere in business
or professional life," she wrote. "They marry millionaires, if they
are lucky."[33]

Hustle and the vision of something better led Beals to quit the
Buffalo newspaper in 1904 to cover a huge fair called the Louisiana
Purchase Exposition. Once she overcame the difficulties of getting
credentials, she became the event's star photographer, recording its
multiple facets but gaining special attention for her coverage of the
fledgling aviation industry. The exposition gave her a gold medal
for her aerial photography. She sold her work to *Leslie's Weekly,* to
numerous newspapers, including the *New York Herald* and *New York
Tribune,* and to the exposition's publicity department.

Like Brady, she had an instinct for promoting herself and par-
layed her success at the fair into an invitation to photograph
President Theodore Roosevelt and his fellow Rough Riders from
the Spanish-American War at a reunion in 1905. That same year,
she and Alfred moved to New York City, where she launched a
portrait business and continued to freelance for newspapers and

magazines. One of her specializations was taking portraits of artists and writers, which she sold to magazines that catered to the arts community. At the age of forty, Beals had a daughter, Nanette. The child was frequently ill, and Beals suffered the anxiety and stress that many working mothers experience. When Nanette was old enough, Beals enrolled her in a boarding school in order to have the freedom to work. Her marriage was under strain—Alfred was not Nanette's father—and in 1917, Beals left her husband, divorcing him several years later. During this same period she began writing poetry, which she published in her 1928 book *Songs of a Wanderer,* and specialized in photographing the Bohemian scene in New York's Greenwich Village. While she continued to sell to publications, an increasing portion of her income came from selling postcards that featured her New York and Boston scenes and her portraits of such luminaries as Mark Twain. After an interlude living and photographing in California, she was forced to return to New York when the stock market crashed in 1929. The Great Depression, her age, and competition from other women photographers all weighed hard on Beals during the 1930s. Impoverished, she died in Bellevue Hospital's charity ward in 1942. But her work and legacy live on, preserved at the New York Historical Society and celebrated in a 2000 exhibition entitled Jessie Tarbox Beals: On Assignment.

Frances Benjamin Johnston was another prominent woman photojournalist at the turn of the century. Educated in a Roman Catholic convent, she announced her intentions to reject Victorian values in an 1896 self-portrait (see figure 8). The thirty-two-year-old former art student managed to break several taboos in a single picture: Seated on a box in front of a fireplace, she wears a Bohemian outfit with a man's cap. In her left hand she holds a beer stein; in her right, a cigarette. In the equivalent of thumbing her nose at society's conventions, she lifts her skirt above her knees exposing her petticoat and legs. Her most flagrant flouting of conventions occurred outside of photographs: she refused to marry, supporting herself and enjoying her independence.

Johnston grew up in Washington as the only child of a socially prominent family. Her mother had covered Congress as a reporter for the *Baltimore Sun*. When Johnston returned from studying art in Paris in the mid-1880s, she abandoned painting for photography and gained a reputation for her portraits of political and cultural figures. Her clients included Susan B. Anthony, Mark Twain, George Washington Carver, Joel Chandler Harris, and Admiral George Dewey. She earned the title "photographer to the American court" by photographing the families of five presidents: William Henry Harrison, Grover Cleveland, William McKinley, Theodore Roosevelt, and William Howard Taft. She is best remembered for her 1899 pictures of the progressive educational practices at the Hampton Institute (now Hampton University) in Virginia. Her photographs of African and Native Americans in academic classrooms and vocational-training settings were featured prominently in The American Negro exhibit at the World Exposition in Paris in 1900. In an 1897 article for the *Ladies' Home Journal* titled "What a Woman Can Do with a Camera," Johnston advised her readers, "Photography as a profession should appeal particularly to women, and in it there are great opportunities for a good paying business."[34]

In the next generation, Consuelo Kanaga worked as a photographer for the *San Francisco Chronicle* and the *San Francisco Daily News* from 1915 to 1922. During the 1920s, she moved from photojournalism to documentary work. She is best known for portraying African Americans as individuals instead of stereotypes. "One thing I had to say in my photography," Kanaga commented, "was that Negroes are beautiful and that poverty is a tender and terrible subject to be approached on one's knees."[35] Despite these three, the number of women in photojournalism during the early decades of the twentieth century was exceedingly small.

Among the many technological innovations spawned by photography in the late 1800s was a new form of entertainment called motion pictures. Soon the medium expanded to record news and public figures. Newsreels, which were shown in movie theaters before the feature films, established the foundation for television news a few decades later.

Motion pictures do not move. Instead a sequence of still photographs, each slightly different from the previous, simulates motion through persistence of vision, a principle of human vision first described by Aristotle about 300 B.C.E. When still pictures advance faster than twenty-four per second, human perception blends them together, creating the illusion of movement. In 1867, William Lincoln patented the zoetrope, the first device for animating drawings. A strip of paper with sequential images was put in a shallow metal drum. Slits in the paper were aligned with corresponding ones in the drum. As it spun, a viewer looking through the slits saw the illusion of motion.

A decade later, British photographer Eadweard Muybridge moved the technology forward by substituting photography for the drawings. Leland Stanford, the former governor of California, hired Muybridge to settle a dispute over whether a galloping horse lifted all four legs off the ground. In June 1878, using a series of twelve cameras to photograph one of Stanford's horses, he demonstrated there was a point when all four hooves left the ground. His pictures also disproved the "hobbyhorse" pose, an artistic convention of painting galloping horses with their legs thrust forward and back. Muybridge adapted the zoetrope into his zoo-praxiscope, which projected his animal locomotion studies and led to motion pictures.[36]

When celluloid film became available, William Dickson, an employee of Thomas Edison, put emulsion on a long strip of cellulose. What took Muybridge numerous cameras to record could now be done with one camera using continuous film. Motion pictures were born. The Edison laboratory also developed the Kinetograph, a camera for photographing moving pictures, and the Kinetoscope, a device for projecting them in a small cabinet. Both inventions were introduced at the World's Columbian Exposition in Chicago in 1893. Soon Kinetoscope parlors appeared in large cities, showing fifty-foot films that looped continuously. Early offerings, photographed in studios, showed a man sneezing, acrobats performing, and boxers in action. Independently, the French brothers Auguste and Louis Lumière developed the cinématographe, which combined the functions of camera, film processor, and projector in one machine. They announced their invention in 1895, and that same year their father Antoine Lumière began projecting short films to paying audiences in Paris.

Early films were of two types: those staged and photographed in studios and those taken outdoors in real settings with little or no direction. The latter were called "actualities," a reference to their realism. Two examples from 1896 included the derby horse race at Epsom Downs in England and a parade featuring William McKinley campaigning for the presidency. Charles Pathé launched the first newsreel business in 1908. One of four French brothers who oversaw a conglomerate of interests in records, camera manufacturing, film making, and movie theaters, Pathé produced news films to show in his theaters before the featured dramas. By 1911, distributors sent out fresh Pathé newsreels to American theaters every Thursday. By 1914, the company employed thirty-seven cameramen, who shot about fifteen thousand feet of film each week for its American audience. That same year, it began offering the Pathé Daily News, mailing a fresh newsreel daily. The scarcity of film during World War I ended this service. American firms began competing with Pathé. During the early twentieth century, Gaumont Animated Weekly, Kinograms, and the Vitagraph Monthly of Current Events began operating. Fox newsreel was affiliated with UP news service. Hearst entered the newsreel arena when his employee Edgar Hatrick filmed the inauguration of President Woodrow Wilson in 1913. Hearst earned three thousand dollars on the film, which cost only about three hundred dollars to film and edit. Later that year, Hatrick joined William Selig of the *Chicago Tribune* to launch the Hearst-Selig News Pictorial. In October 1914, it made a dramatic film of Louvain, a Belgian city that had been bombed by the Germans near the beginning of World War I. After the United States entered the war in 1917, the government got involved in newsreels. Photojournalism was heavily censored, but the Committee on Public Information produced a newsreel called the Official War Review, which gave the government's version of the war. Much of the footage came from Army Signal Corps soldiers, but Hearst-Selig assigned Joe Hubbell, one of its best cameramen, to shoot for Official War Review.

Until the mid-1920s, films were silent. Theaters hired piano players, organists, and even small orchestras to play music that evoked the mood of the flickering pictures. Subtitles provided dialogue for some films, and live narrators explained others. When technology made synchronizing sound with moving film possible, the industry quickly adopted the innovation. In 1927, Warner Brothers' *The Jazz Singer* was the first film to synchronize dialogue and singing with moving pictures. It was a huge success, and within two years, almost all Hollywood films were produced with sound. Newsreels joined the "talkies" craze. Although they included interviews and natural sound, most of their sound came from narrators such as Edwin C. Hill, Jean Paul King, Graham McNamee, Harry von Zell, and Westbrook Van Voorhis. Their voice-over commentaries, delivered in stentorian tones, gave newsreels an air of authority that few viewers thought to question.

The newsreel industry consolidated during the 1920s and 1930s into six major firms. The March of Time, produced by Henry Luce's Time, Inc., was the only one not associated with a major movie company. The others were Movietone News, a subsidiary of 20th Century Fox; News of the Day, Metro-Goldwyn-Mayer; Pathé News, RKO Pictures, and Warner Brothers; Paramount News, Paramount Pictures; and Universal Newsreel, Universal Studios.

From the first decade of the twentieth century onward, still photographers and newsreel cameramen worked side by side at many events. Often, the same person shot still photographs and film. Both newspapers and newsreels saw the news in the same conceptual categories: disasters, politicians, celebrities, sports, war, and oddities.

While still photojournalism survived competition from television, newsreels did not. For a period during the 1950s and early 1960s, newsreels had the advantage of color, but their relatively slow distribution could not match the immediacy of the day's events shown on television in the viewer's home. After a long industry decline, the last newsreel was released in December 1967.

World War I was horrific in its devastation and duration. Military technology contributed to the suffering and death. The introduction of the machine gun turned the traditional tactic of an assault by infantry soldiers into carnage. When tactics shifted to trench warfare, the introduction of poisonous gas meant soldiers were not safe in the trenches either. The tank helped break the trench lines toward the end of the war. Airplanes revolutionized reconnaissance and bombing. With rain, snow, freezing temperatures, and unsanitary conditions compounding the soldiers' misery, cynicism was hardly surprising. Their common term for the battle lines on the western front was the "sausage grinder," an allusion to the way it chewed them up. Estimates put World War I military deaths at 9.7 million with additional millions wounded. Censorship and military control hampered reporters and photojournalists during World War I. A consensus for censorship had been growing in the military for years. American officers who observed the war between Japan and Russia in 1904–5 admired the Japanese army's total control of journalists and recommended the U.S. Army adopt similar restrictions.[37] The immediate precedent for censorship occurred during the Mexican civil war. In the early years of the war, photographers moved freely, covering both sides. After Francisco "Pancho" Villa staged a raid into New Mexico in March 1916, the United States entered the war, and journalists' freedom of movement ceased. General John J. Pershing established three important precedents: First, the Army Signal Corps began taking and distributing photographs to American newspapers, substituting its own perspective for that of independent photojournalists. Second, the army restricted press photographers from witnessing many events. And finally, military censors reviewed all photographs by military and civilian photographers alike. A year later, when the United States entered World War I, Pershing, who commanded the American Expeditionary Force in Europe, implemented these protocols even more stringently. As Carlebach writes, during the twentieth century "no conflict was more rigidly censored than the First World War."[38]

In early 1917, Major Douglas MacArthur, who gained fame during World War II and the Korean War, was the army's chief censor. He believed "the success of the Cuban expedition" during the Spanish-American War "was seriously menaced" by news reports of the mobilization in Tampa, which reached the Spanish command as well as American newspaper readers. He also resented reporters with no military expertise who "cry for and obtain new Generals and new plans of campaigns." Calling for total censorship, he wrote, "The army and navy are the only agencies of the Government by which it can obtain its desired ends." Thus, he argued, "Every utility and influence within the country [including the press] should be brought to their aid."[39]

President Wilson seemed ready to accept his recommendation, but George Creel, a prominent journalist who had supported Wilson's election, persuaded him to moderate it. Wilson created the Committee on Public Information (CPI) and made Creel its director. It functioned as a propaganda operation to generate public support for the war. Although not as draconian as MacArthur proposed, the CPI still controlled the press and censored its war coverage. In addition to reviewing all prints and film footage, it gained agreement from the news media not to publish any photographs without the official stamp "Passed by the Committee on Public Information, Washington." As a final measure of its control, the committee could veto applications for credentials to cover the war, denying access to photographers who tried to circumvent its control. Among the prohibited images were those with military intelligence implications, such as troop movements, identification of units and their locations, and those showing war materiel. Also forbidden were photographs that might harm the morale of soldiers at the front or civilians at home. The latter included photographs of dead and wounded American soldiers and other situations that would "cause unnecessary and unwarranted anxiety to the families of men at the front."[40] Although they complained, most photographers internalized the rules so completely that they rarely took such pictures, and the censors had to reject relatively few photographs. This self-censorship meant many photographs that might have been historically important after the war were never taken. Wythe Williams, a *New York Times* reporter writing in *Collier's Weekly,* complained, "If we have a story about the American expeditionary force that is any good, it is a safe bet that it will not be allowed to pass, so why write it?"[41] This "What's the use?" attitude extended to photographers as well.

Censorship by European authorities predated American involvement in World War I. French military authorities still blamed the country's defeat in the Franco-Prussian War of 1870 on the press.[42] They believed that stories and especially photographs of any military location or operation gave intelligence to the enemy that would be used against them. They also wanted to prevent criticism of their conduct of the war and treatment of their troops. Photographers attempting to practice their profession were likely to be blacklisted or arrested as spies.

Among those suffering such censorship was Hare, who had distinguished himself in the Spanish-American War. Commissioned by *Leslie's Weekly,* Hare left for England shortly after hostilities began in August 1914. British authorities refused to let him photograph at London's Paddington Station. In France, he was "detained near Soissons and sent back to Paris." He succeeded in reaching Antwerp, Belgium, where he photographed the city being shelled by the Germans, but he soon left after being warned on November 1, 1914, "that all the reporters and photographers are to be rounded up and arrested tomorrow."[43] After the fighting descended into trench warfare, all journalists were confined to rear areas, where their activities were tightly controlled. Hare, who had experienced censorship during the Russo–Japanese and the Mexican wars, was particularly frustrated by his inability to photograph significant events and felt his time and expenses were wasted. "Photographs seem to be the one thing that the [British] War Office is really afraid of," he commented.[44]

Photographs that did get published were often fake representations of combat. In one famous case, a picture purporting to show a Canadian soldier thumbing his nose at the Germans as he and his comrades attacked, shows rifles with their breech covers still on (see figure 9). This safety practice was used in training camps, not combat.[45] Generals were happy to stage such operations for photographers who would aggrandize them. In committing such fabrications, many photographers aggrandized themselves as well. They concocted stories for their home publications about the dangers they endured to "get the picture" for the readers back home.

Despite the censorship, World War I boosted newspaper circulations. *New York Times* publisher Arthur Ochs responded to the war with two initiatives: the New York Times News Service, which circulated the paper's Pulitzer Prize–winning war coverage and the *Mid-Week Pictorial,* a rotogravure magazine launched to publish photographs of the war.[46] *Mid-Week*'s images were often static, posed, and heavily retouched. In Moeller's assessment, 90 percent of World War I photographs failed to capture "the reality of war as the soldiers lived it. . . . The war in the published pictures was not the war as fought in Europe."[47]

Following World War I, picture journalism expanded with the advent of tabloid newspapers. Although it has become synonymous with sensationalism, *tabloid* originally referred to the publication's size. The typical tabloid was 11 × 17 inches, while a broadsheet measured about 14 × 22 inches. The smaller size made tabloids easier for commuters to read on subways and buses. After conversations with the publisher of London's *Daily Mirror,* Joseph Medill Patterson launched America's first tabloid, the *Daily News,* on June 26, 1919, as a subsidiary of the *Chicago Tribune. The Daily News,* which billed itself as "New York's Picture Newspaper," was selling more than one hundred thousand by its first anniversary and topped one million by 1925. It displayed a large news picture on its front page and a sports picture on its back. Its success prompted numerous publishers to launch tabloids in cities across the country.

As with yellow journalism, much of the criticism against the tabloids was class oriented. In theory, broadsheets catered to the middle and upper classes, while tabloids targeted working-class readers. Critics argued that tabloid publishers used pictures to pander to a semiliterate class interested in crime, gossip, scandals, celebrities, and sex instead of serious news. The humorist Will Rogers quipped that if tabloid readers "saw a half-page picture of a pretty woman they felt that she was either a murderess or a movie divorcée; if it was a full-page, she might be both."[48] In 1926, Silas Bent wrote in *The Nation* that pictures "are a throw back to the intelligence which communicated by means of ideographs, before the alphabet was invented." They appealed to "the lowest mental common denominator," he said, entering "consciousness over the lowest threshold."[49] Bent also criticized press photographers for their aggressiveness, writing, "The photographs which the newspapers regard as best would never be obtained if the camera men were polite enough to ask permission before taking them."[50]

The reality was more complex. Contrary to such associations of photographs with low income and intelligence, researcher Simon Bessie demonstrated that in 1937, 80.4 percent of *Daily News* sales were in middle-class neighborhoods, 10.8 percent in upper-class neighborhoods, and only 8.8 percent in lower-class neighborhoods.[51] The appeal of photographs extended more broadly than critics recognized.

One photographer who enjoyed a lucrative career supplying New York tabloids with crime photographs was Arthur Fellig, who styled himself as Weegee. The name was his phonetic spelling of the Ouija board, the popular fortune-telling game. He chose it to promote his claims that he was the first photographer to the scene of a crime and that he often beat the police. Instead of psychic powers, his success stemmed from having a police radio in his car. In 1938, he became the first photographer in New York granted such a privilege. Weegee did not merely fit the stereotype of the brash, flamboyant, cigar-chewing press photographer with a crumpled fedora, rumpled suit, and ever-present Speed Graphic—he helped invent it. He claimed to have photographed more than five thousand murders, undoubtedly an exaggeration since official estimates of gangland slayings during the era range from seven hundred to one thousand. Born in the Ukraine as Usher Fellig, he moved with his family to Manhattan's Lower East Side in 1910. Through hard work and chutzpah, he achieved the American dream, scoring success in the New York tabloids and later becoming a celebrated author through such books as *Naked City*. His photographs, preserved in museum collections, are now considered art.

Two events, an execution and a kidnapping trial, represent the complex practices of press photography during the tabloid era. After a trial that filled front pages with details of a love triangle, Ruth Snyder was convicted of murdering her husband and sentenced to be executed in the electric chair at the state prison in Ossining, New York. Public executions had ended in America in the 1860s, but the *Daily News* resolved to show Snyder's death. Because prison officials would recognize its staff photographers, it brought in Tom Howard of the *Chicago Tribune's* picture service. Posing as a reporter, he entered the execution chamber with a miniature camera strapped to his ankle. When the electrocution occurred, Howard lifted his pants leg and squeezed a cable release that opened the shutter. The next morning, Friday the thirteenth, 1928, the *Daily News* filled its front page with his photograph. It created a sensation not only for breaking the taboo against pictures of executions but also for its sensational content. Howard opened his shutter twice, for a total of five seconds.[52] The multiple exposures combined with the movement of Snyder's body dramatized her death.

In 1932, the kidnapping and killing of Charles Lindberg Jr., the infant son of the famous aviator Charles Lindberg and his wife, Anne Morrow Lindberg, provided a diversion from the Great Depression. Richard "Bruno" Hauptmann, an immigrant carpenter who lived in the Bronx, was charged with the kidnapping. His trial in Flemington, New Jersey, drew more than three hundred reporters, including gossip columnists, mystery novelists, and such famous writers as Walter Winchell, Edna Ferber, and Damon Runyon. Press photographers were falsely accused of creating a circus atmosphere during the trial. In fact, Judge Thomas W. Trenchard forbade photographing during the trial, and only three pictures were taken—all surreptitiously and without disrupting the proceedings. Trenchard did permit photographing during recesses in the trial, however, and photographers contributed to the lack of decorum by aggressively pursuing their subjects. Empathy for the Lindberg family fueled the criticism. Many readers felt the perceived indignity of the trial coverage intensified their suffering over the death of their son.

Following Hauptmann's conviction and death sentence, the American Bar Association (ABA) created a committee to work with representatives of the American Newspaper Publishers Association and the American Society of Newspaper Editors to resolve the issues of free press and fair trial that the Lindberg trial coverage had raised. Photographers became the scapegoat for the transgressions of the entire media. At its 1937 convention, the ABA instructed its press-bar committee to continue negotiating with the journalists to resolve disagreements, but three days later its Committee on Professional Ethics proposed Canon 35, which was adopted without public discussion. It read:

> The taking of photographs in the courtroom during sessions of the courts, or recesses between sessions and the broadcasting of court proceedings are calculated to detract from the essential dignity of the proceedings, degrade the court and create misconceptions with respect thereto in the mind of the public, and should not be permitted.[53]

Although the ABA had no power to impose the rule, most judges were ABA members, and most courts adopted Canon 35.

Joseph Costa, a founder of the National Press Photographers Association (NPPA) and a lifelong crusader to allow cameras in the courts, argued convincingly that photographers did not disrupt the Hauptmann trial and that their conduct outside the courtroom was colored by the actions and stories of the writers. On the former point, he cited *New York Times* trial stories that repeatedly noted the deep silence in the courtroom. After the trial both the prosecution and defense attorneys were accused of cultivating publicity for their sides, and writers were accused of printing rumors calculated to convict Hauptmann. Photographers were barely mentioned in this post-trial coverage. Costa, who covered the trial, noted that reporters were just as aggressive in chasing witnesses for interviews as photographers were for pictures. Due to the efforts of Costa and the NPPA, many states, beginning with Florida in the 1970s, have abandoned Canon 35's prohibitions.

The end of World War I unleashed major advances in photographic technology. During the 1920s and 1930s, more sensitive film and improved lenses let photographers use faster shutter speeds and work in lower light. Small, light cameras made capturing spontaneity possible. Artificial lighting let photojournalists work at night and indoors.

In America, the Speed Graphic, introduced by the Graflex company in 1912, became the dominant press camera. In Europe, the small, hand-to-eye 35 mm Leica, which was invented in 1914, was finally marketed in the mid-1920s. Its light weight, inconspicuous size, fast lenses, and thirty-six-exposure roll film made spontaneous photography possible and helped launch modern magazine photojournalism. The two cameras required different working methods and produced different results. Beginning with *Life* magazine in the mid-1930s, they coexisted in America, but 35 mm photography replaced the Speed Graphic by the mid-1960s.

One measure of the Speed Graphic's popularity was Weegee's advice to would-be press photographers in *Naked City*. He told them to buy a Speed Graphic because "the cops will assume that you belong on the scene and will let you get beyond the police lines."[54] Over the years, there were several models with improved features and a variety of film sizes, but the most popular used 4 × 5 inch sheet film. It gave photographers choices of three sighting devices and two shutters: in the lens or at the focal plane. Models made after 1928 allowed for interchangeable lenses. After World War II, the company introduced the Grafmatic film holder, a magazine of film sheets that permitted exposing six negatives before reloading.

At six pounds, the camera was light enough to be handheld but heavy enough to discourage candid shooting. It proved adept at capturing sports action, especially football, but often these pictures were taken from the press box with tripod-mounted cameras and telephoto lenses with focal lengths up to sixty inches. For news and feature assignments, most photographers posed their subjects or made exposures when motion was temporarily suspended. Freezing action, which became a major part of the 35 mm aesthetic, was not part of the Speed Graphic approach. Dickey Chapelle, a prominent photojournalist, said of the camera, "It is so big that snap-shooting, or making a picture casually, can't be done."[55]

Film was expensive and, during wartime, scarce. Film discipline was bred into apprentice photographers. Instead of hoping the law of averages would yield one good picture from many grab shots, photographers worked to capture the essence of a situation in a single frame. John Bushemi, who was killed during World War II while working as a combat photographer for *Yank* magazine, proudly claimed such discipline in his nickname, "One Shot."[56] In most cases press photographers controlled their subjects; this ranged from carefully posing them with setting and props to asking them to "Hold still, please!" or to wait for a second shot with "One more, please!" President Harry Truman once introduced the White House photographers as the "Just One More Club."[57]

Flash was another technical development that exerted a huge impact on press photography. From the 1890s to the mid-1920s, artificially lighting a scene required pouring magnesium powder in a tray and igniting it. After an intense flash of light, the room filled with acrid smoke, choking the subjects and preventing a second exposure for several minutes. The powder also injured many photographers. Jacob Riis burned himself more than once and on one occasion would have lost his sight had he not been wearing glasses. The German Paul Vierkötter invented the flashbulb in 1925. Based on the technology of the incandescent light bulb, his device involved sealing magnesium wire—later foil—in a vacuum bulb. The first flashbulbs were marketed in Germany as Vacublitz. General Electric began selling them in the United States in 1930.[58]

Photographers quickly adopted the new technology, and one publisher played a role. George Sheldon, a staff photographer for the *San Francisco Examiner,* was severely burned by magnesium powder while photographing his employer, Hearst. "The following day Hearst ordered all photographers throughout his chain to stop using powder and switch to [flash] bulbs," Carlebach notes.[59] Weegee endorsed using flashbulbs during the day as well as at night, and by the 1932 Republican National Convention, photographers "with safe new flashlamps were permitted to ply their trade up and down the aisles."[60]

Flash added its own look to the Speed Graphic aesthetic. Photographers typically left the flash attached to the camera, which meant the lighting hit the subject from the camera's angle. This eliminated almost all shadows, making subjects' faces look flat. While the illumination was brilliant, it dropped off rapidly after about twelve feet, producing brightly lit subjects against darker backgrounds. John Szarkowski, director of photography at the Museum of Modern Art, characterized flash as "profoundly artificial, intrusive, and minutely descriptive." But he added, "In the hands of a photographer who understands it, it produces pictures of startling graphic economy and force."[61]

What seemed normal during the era is easily recognizable now as the Speed Graphic aesthetic—static, posed situations, illuminated by artificial lighting. The contents of the photographs were also determined by their era, a time when most cities and even modest-sized towns had two or more competing newspapers. Assignments typically came from word editors on the city desk. Good photographers added their imagination and skill to improve them. Even so, the work fell into predictable categories. Frank Scherschel, chief photographer of the *Milwaukee Journal,* identified the following: spot news, sports, story illustrations for the society and fashion sections, the rotogravure magazine, and routine assignments. Scherschel estimated that routine assignments made up 80 percent of the work.[62] They included staged publicity photos, cute kids, oversized vegetables, and oddities of all sorts. Other hackneyed ideas included the second-day reaction shot. In one example, a photographer for the *St. Paul Pioneer Press* was sent to photograph the widow and children of a slain police officer looking at the story of his murder in that morning's newspaper.[63] It would take until the 1960s and 1970s for visual journalists to gain control of the assignment process at most American newspapers and eliminate such cliché assignments.

Technology also revolutionized the transmission of photographs. By 1933, about fifty photographic news services operated in New York City alone, including the *New York Times'* Wide World Photos, Hearst's International News Photos, Scripps-Howard's News Enterprise Association, Pacific and Atlantic Photos, and the AP's News Photo. They distributed their photographs by courier to clients in the city and by mail to those outside. Kent Cooper, general manager of the AP, envisioned "the day when we will be sending pictures over our own leased wire system, just as we now send the news."[64] He contracted with Bell Telephone to develop facsimile technology to transmit photographs. With it, a technician mounted a photograph on a rotating drum. As it turned, a pin-point light scanned the photograph tones, transforming its tones into electronic signals that were transmitted over telephone lines. At the receiving end, the signals were converted into a cellulose negative or a paper positive. The process took about eight minutes. The AP launched the service to 40 member newspapers in 1935; by 1949, it had expanded to 350.[65] Cable and wireless connections eventually linked Europe and Asia into the system so that a news photograph from anywhere in the world could reach a picture editor's desk within minutes.

Figure 1. During the era of proto-photojournalism, George N. Barnard used the daguerreotype process to capture the fiery destruction of several grain mills in Oswego, New York, in 1853.
INTERNATIONAL MUSEUM OF PHOTOGRAPHY AT GEORGE EASTMAN HOUSE

Figure 2. Among the first war photographs is this anonymous daguerreotype of General John Wool and his staff, pausing to be photographed during the Mexican-American War in 1847. It was not until 1936, almost a century later, that photographic technology had evolved sufficiently to capture combat action. YALE COLLECTION OF WESTERN AMERICANA, BEINECKE RARE BOOK AND MANUSCRIPT LIBRARY

Figure 3. Mathew B. Brady posed Abraham Lincoln and adjusted his clothing and hair to minimize his physical flaws in this famous portrait made on February 27, 1860, a few hours before Lincoln's Cooper Union speech. **Figure 4.** After Lincoln won the Republican nomination for the presidency, Brady's portrait provided the basis for several engravings, including this one on the cover of *Harper's Weekly*. The engraver embellished the austere setting, and the engraving process caused the image to appear reversed.

Figure 5. Historian William Frassanito determined, based on a visit
to the site of the Battle of Gettysburg, that Alexander Gardner and
Timothy O'Sullivan moved the body of this slain Confederate soldier
about forty yards in order to construct this story-telling picture.
Gardner titled the picture "Home of a Rebel Sharpshooter," but
the rifle was not the kind used by snipers during the Civil War.

Figure 6. On July 7, 1865, at the Old Arsenal Penitentiary in Washington, D.C., Army Captain Andrew J. Russell documented the executions of the conspirators convicted of assassinating President Lincoln. The glass base of Russell's negative broke, creating the cracks in the emulsion in the lower left corner. LIBRARY OF CONGRESS

Figure 7. Andrew J. Russell's photograph of the celebration of two crews meeting to complete the first transcontinental railroad at Promontory Summit, Utah, in 1869 helped promote the spirit of Manifest Destiny that swept the nation after the Civil War. But his picture excludes the Chinese laborers who did much of the construction. UTAH STATE HISTORICAL SOCIETY

Figure 8. By smoking, drinking, and exposing her petticoats and legs, Frances Benjamin Johnston, one of the first women photojournalists, flouted the conventions of polite society in this self-portrait made in the late 1800S. LIBRARY OF CONGRESS

Figure 9. This World War I photograph, purporting to show a Canadian soldier thumbing his nose at the Germans as he and his comrades attack, was probably taken in a training camp, not during combat. LIBRARY AND ARCHIVES CANADA

Figure 10. Newspaper reporter Jacob Riis taught himself photography in order to document the wretched living conditions of the denizens of New York's Lower East Side, including this weary tailor about to break a loaf of challah in his home, a coal cellar. MUSEUM OF THE CITY OF NEW YORK

Figure 11. In his photographic crusade against child labor, Lewis Hine chose a very shallow depth of field to emphasize the expression of this girl working in a North Carolina cotton mill. Comparing her height to the buttons on his vest, which he had premeasured, he noted that she was fifty-one inches tall. LIBRARY OF CONGRESS

Figures 12 and 13. The plaintive expressions and penetrating gazes of Floyd Burroughs and his wife, Allie Mae, express the hopelessness created by the Great Depression and the exploitative sharecropping system they labored under. Walker Evans, a member of the Farm Security Administration's photography team, and writer James Agee lived with the Burroughses and two other families in Hale County, Alabama, in 1936. TOP: LIBRARY OF CONGRESS; BOTTOM: INDIANA UNIVERSITY ART MUSEUM, HENRY HOLMES SMITH ARCHIVE, #200.X.12.8, IMAGE FURNISHED BY MICHAEL CAVANAGH AND KEVIN MONTAGUE

Figure 14. Under the title "Migrant Mother," Dorothea Lange's photograph of Florence Thompson and three of her seven children has come to symbolize the Great Depression and its impact on ordinary Americans. Thompson later criticized Lange for the photograph, which she made in 1936 near Nipomo, California. LIBRARY OF CONGRESS

Figure 15. In 1957, Will Counts put a human face on racism as he captured Hazel Bryan shouting at Elizabeth Eckford, who had just been prevented from integrating Little Rock High School by Arkansas National Guard troops. **Figure 16.** Forty years later, Counts and his wife, Vivian, arranged a reconciliation between Elizabeth Eckford and Hazel Bryan Massery and photographed them in front of the school. Massery, who did not want her life to be defined by a single moment, was grateful for the chance to apologize to Eckford. BOTH: WILL COUNTS COLLECTION, INDIANA UNIVERSITY ARCHIVES

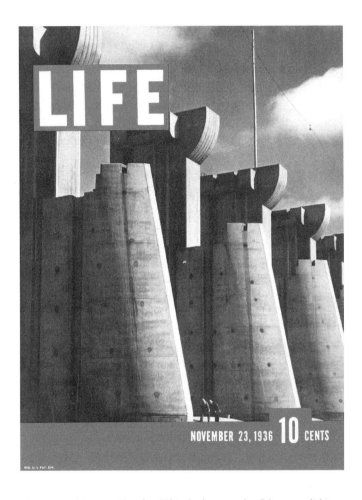

Figure 17. Margaret Bourke-White's photograph of the monolithic spillway of a dam under construction at Fort Peck, Montana, was the cover for the inaugural edition of *Life* magazine on November 23, 1936. TIME/LIFE, GETTY IMAGES

Figure 18. In 1948, *Life* magazine's editors introduced W. Eugene Smith's story on Dr. Ernest Ceriani, the sole physician for the Rocky Mountain town of Kremmling, Colorado, with this photograph. In twenty-three days of shooting, Smith rejected *Life*'s system of photographing situations predetermined by editors in New York in favor of capturing candid moments. TIME/LIFE, GETTY IMAGES

Hello, Everybody!
This Is the Voice of the Press Photographer

EDITORIAL

Greetings to All in the Craft of Press Photography:

With this issue is born a voice, one that has been mute much too long. It may sound a little weak at first, but with your help it will gain in volume, tore and authority to become, we are confident, within the very near future, the official voice of Press Photography in the United States.

Sounds big—doesn't it? A little on the boastful side, perhaps? Not at all! It's high time we did a little shouting! For more years than we should care to admit we've been taking a pushing around. And what have we done about it? Nothing, absolutely nothing! True, in the privacy of a ramp darkroom we've been known to give vent to our feeling to the extent of kicking the trash can or delivering the snappy comeback that should have been aired on the job. But officially, we've been as silent as a politician ducking an embarrassing question.

If you would believe the movie scenarists and short story writers, we're just the roughest, toughest gang of men outside of prison walls. Actually, we'll have to admit, we'd qualify much better as collective Caspar Milquetoasts.

But all that is in the past. We're no longer going to permit ourselves to be relegated to the position of unwelcome, but necessary, step-children of the Fourth Estate. We've got a voice, finally, and we're going to make use of it. No false modesty. No muffling of that voice under a barrel. We're going to yell so loud—when the occasion demands, and not just for the fun of hearing ourselves shout—that those in this country who have been injuring us with scant courtesy will begin to realize that here is a new force to be reckoned with. We'll show neither fear nor favor. And, in the process, we'll not spare ourselves, either.

EDITORIAL   (Cont. on page 10)

HAVE YOU JOINED THE NATIONAL?

Vol. I   BOSTON, MASS., APRIL, 1946   No. I

New York Skyscrapers

Due to the fact that BOB CRANSTON, who usually handles matters of this kind, is guiding about the globe to Rome, Florida, tr., the task of reporting the doings in Manhattan falls to me. I will try to do the best I can.

First, al'ow me to say that the New York PPA is indeed flattered by the choice of JOE COSTA as first President of the National Press Photographers Association. I don't think we would be human if we did not feel deeply honored and allow our chests to swell a bit. We are certain, knowing Joe's record as past President of the New York Association and his untiring efforts in other capacities, that the National Association is off to a good start in being headed by him.

SKYSCRAPERS(Cont. on page 10)

NOTICE

If your Local Association has a monthly bulletin it will help me in getting out shorts for this 'National Monthly". . . Please put me on your mailing list.

The Editor.

National Association Gains Momentum

News Photographers All Over U. S. Rush to Join

For the sleepy-heads and the die-hards our heartfelt sympathy . . . for the alert and the wise . . . congratulations.

Elsewhere (perhaps we should apologize and say everywhere) in this First Edition of the National Press Photographer you will find many notes from various people extolling the fine qualities of our first President, Joe Costa . . . you will also find expressions of confidence in the outcome of the National Association. These fine letters are but a few of the many that have come into the hands of Joe Costa, Burt Williams and Charlie Mack, whose latest photo greets you below.

| BURT WILLIAMS | JOE COSTA | CHARLIE MACK |
| National Secretary | National President | National Treasurer |

Our offer of sympathy to the sleepy-heads and die-hards is engendered by reporters and press-men . . . we really mean it. For many years the News Cameramen have allowed themselves to be led...

Figure 19. In April 1946, the first issue of *National Press Photographer* magazine proclaimed that press photographers finally had a national voice. "We're going to yell so loud," wrote Joe Costa, president of the newly formed National Press Photographers Association, that photographers' critics "will begin to realize that here is a new force to be reckoned with." COPYRIGHT © NATIONAL PRESS PHOTOGRAPHERS ASSOCIATION

Figure 20. The National Press Photographers Association's first president, Joe Costa (*far left*), was a natural at public relations. He, secretary Burt Williams (*second from left*), and treasurer Charles Mack (*far right*) watch President Harry S. Truman autograph a gavel, which he gave the association in return for being presented the ceremonial first copy of *The Complete Book of Press Photography* in 1950. COPYRIGHT © NATIONAL PRESS PHOTOGRAPHERS ASSOCIATION

Figure 21. Both supporters and critics of the 1955 Family of Man exhibition have overlooked a key photograph, which was not in the accompanying book, and thus have missed curator Edward Steichen's message against nuclear war. Steichen's assistant Wayne Miller photographed his family in front of the mural-sized color transparency of a hydrogen bomb explosion. PHOTOGRAPH BY WAYNE MILLER; COURTESY OF MAGNUM PHOTOS

Figure 22. Army Specialist Sabrina Harman took numerous photographs of the mistreatment that members of the 320th Military Police Battalion inflicted on Iraqi detainees in 2003 at the Abu Ghraib prison. This one, showing an Iraqi who was told he would be electrocuted if he fell off the box, has come to symbolize the abuses. The Internet now allows anybody with a digital camera and a modem to bypass both censors and journalistic gatekeepers.

FOUR

PHOTOGRAPHY AS A TOOL
FOR SOCIAL REFORM

The 1890 census officially declared the American frontier no longer existed; the American continent was settled from coast to coast. In July, Idaho and Wyoming joined the Union, bringing the number of states to forty-four. The census listed the population at 62.6 million, an increase of 24.8 percent since 1880. Immigration added to the increase. Of the total population, 9.3 million residents, or 14.8 percent, were born in foreign countries; 1.7 million could not speak English. Twenty-eight cities numbered more than one hundred thousand, and three—New York, Chicago, and Philadelphia—exceeded one million. Despite growth in urban population, almost 71 percent of Americans still lived in rural areas.[1]

The census failed to include one statistic about economic class: 1 percent of the population owned more than 50 percent of the nation's wealth.[2] As the nation experienced massive economic growth after the Civil War, wealth concentrated in the hands of a few. An extreme gap separated the richest Americans, who controlled industry, transportation, and banking, from the workers, who provided cheap labor. Many Americans used the term *robber baron* to describe John D. Rockefeller, Andrew Carnegie,

Cornelius Vanderbilt, J. P. Morgan, and others, who used ruthless tactics against workers and competitors alike to control the oil, steel, railroad, and finance industries. They were aided by a government policy of laissez-faire, an absence of regulation, which allowed corporations to exploit workers as they pleased.

Among their tactics were wage manipulation and union busting. Because the capitalists supported politicians financially, they had government on their side. When workers tried to form unions or go on strike, the owners of mines and factories could count on the National Guard or the U.S. Army to take their side. Typically, leaders were arrested, unions were heavily fined and disbanded, and strikers were turned out of their jobs.

In New York and other large cities, the conditions in the poorest neighborhoods rivaled those in Charles Dickens's *Hard Times* or Victor Hugo's *Les Misérables.* Poor residents, many of them first-generation immigrants, crowded together in squalid living conditions and worked in sweatshops for starvation wages.

Between the high capitalists and the exploited laboring class stood a group of middle-class reformers determined to improve conditions for the poor, clean up government corruption, and correct unfair business practices. These reformers, who believed in the power of science and rational thought to redress problems, gave the period from 1890 to World War I its name, the Progressive Era.

The widely accepted veracity of the photograph made it an ideal tool for reform-minded photographers of the era who campaigned for the improvement of social conditions. They subscribed to the faith that in a democracy, exposing social problems through photography would help create the political will to solve those problems. The tradition they launched, called social documentary photography, is still widely practiced.

It began in the 1880s with John Thomson's pictures of the London slums and Thomas Annan's of those in Glasgow, Scotland. The first American to apply photography to social problems was a newspaper reporter. Beginning in 1890, Jacob Riis photographed the poverty, crime, filth, sweatshops, and unsafe housing on New York City's Lower East Side. His photographs, articles, and slide lectures eventually prompted city officials to improve sanitation and education and replace some of the tenements.

Riis empathized with the impoverished residents, most of them recent immigrants from Europe, because he had been one of them. In 1870, with his native Denmark in recession, the twenty-one-year-old Riis left for America. He soon found himself homeless and penniless and, as he recalled later, "joined the great army of tramps, wandering about the streets in the daytime with one aim of somehow stilling the hunger that gnawed at my vitals, and fighting at night with vagrant curs or outcasts as miserable as myself for the protection of some sheltering ash-bin or doorway."[3] Working as a carpenter, he experienced the exploitation that he would later expose in the sweatshops of the Lower East Side. He was paid by the piece, and as he produced more, his employer cut the rate per piece.

Drawing on his youthful experiences helping his father do newspaper reporting, Riis decided to become a crusading reporter. "It seemed to me that a reporter's was the highest and noblest of all callings," he wrote, because "no one could sift wrong from right as he, and punish the wrong."[4] His first job as a general assignment reporter for the New York News Association paid ten dollars a week. Eventually he moved up to police reporter for the *New York Tribune,* a job which thoroughly acquainted him with the wretched conditions of tenement dwellers, especially those around Five Points and Mulberry Bend on the Lower East Side.

Riis wanted to illustrate his stories with photographs, but the technology was too slow to photograph indoors or at night, when the problems were most visible. In 1887, the development of flash powder made photographing in the dark possible. Riis enlisted friends who were amateur photographers, and they set out to photograph in the slums. By February 1888, he had succeeded in publishing twelve drawings based on the images. His larger purpose was to produce "magic lantern slides, showing as no mere description could, the misery and vice that he had noticed" in ten years as a police reporter.[5] He accumulated photographs to illustrate a lecture on the ills of poverty, which he planned to deliver at churches. When his friends tired of the nightly forays, he paid twenty-five dollars—then, a week's salary—for a 4 × 5 inch camera and accompanying gear and taught himself photography. He understood that photographs would convince his audiences where written stories had failed.

Many churches turned down his request to lecture, because they owned slum buildings as investment properties. Finally, the Broadway Tabernacle gave him a venue, and he raised $143.50 for the City Mission Society. Soon he was lecturing at a variety of churches. The editor of Scribner's magazine invited him to write a story for his magazine and devoted eighteen pages of its Christmas 1889 issue to the article. Riis expanded the article into a book, How the Other Half Lives, published in 1890. The first book in America to use photomechanical reproduction extensively, it published seventeen photographs and an additional eighteen engravings based on photographs.

It was an immediate success. Ministers quoted it in their Sunday sermons, newspapers reviewed it favorably, and it soon went into extra editions. But some critics saw it as sensationalist, and others disliked its unrelieved bleakness, notably Riis's assessment that "life [in the slums] does not seem worth the living."[6] Among its readers was Theodore Roosevelt. Riis described how he arrived at work one day and found Roosevelt's business card on his desk. He had written on the back, "I have read your book and I have come to help." A few years later, when Roosevelt became president of New York City's board of police commissioners, he began to make reforms, with Riis as his adviser. Their friendship continued for the rest of their lives: Riis wrote a biography for Roosevelt's presidential campaign, and Roosevelt called him "the most useful citizen of New York."[7] Riis crusaded against the tenement house, which he saw as an incubator of poverty, crime, sickness, and premature death. *How the Other Half Lives* was his challenge for New York's middle and upper classes to join the war. The poor were invisible to comfortable, wealthy New Yorkers who could enjoy their lives without ever noticing the impoverished families who shared their city. Riis was determined to raise public awareness through the power of photographs. He showed flophouses where a sleeping spot cost a nickel a night, hovels that were little more than lean-tos propped against the sides of rotting brick tenements, illegal saloons, street urchins stealing from a fruit vendor's cart, and other children sewing clothing in sweatshops.

His direct, frontal pictures are concerned with information, not composition. In many, the subjects pose, looking into the camera. Their tattered clothing, haggard expressions, and filthy environs document grinding oppression. Just as revealing are the aggregation of details: sagging buildings, rickety pushcarts, planks of wood serving as beds, a blind peddler's empty cigar box, a pile of fabric waiting to be stitched into pants. In one picture, a weary man prepares to break a loaf of challah bread that rests on a grimy tablecloth in the coal cellar that serves as his home (see figure 10). In another, a gang of boys demonstrates for Riis's camera how they rob their victims. A third shows a husband, wife, and young son rolling cigars in their one-room apartment. Running through all his photographs is a sense of the relentless oppression of poverty. The book's text offers a complex verbal argument that parallels the visual one. Beneath a folksy, conversational style, Riis appealed to the fear, guilt, sympathy, justice, patriotism, and curiosity of his wealthy readers. Playing on fear, he began and ended with references to the draft riots of 1863, which in four days killed more than one hundred people, injured at least three hundred, and destroyed property valued at $1.5 million.[8] Although that incident had specific political causes, Riis implied repeatedly that the social injustice festering in the city's slums could provoke an even greater disturbance. "The sea of a mighty population, held in galling fetters, heaves uneasily in the tenements," he wrote. "Once already our city ... has felt the swell of its resistless flood. If it rise once more, no human power may avail to check it. The gap between the classes in which it surges, unseen, unsuspected by the thoughtless, is widening day by day."[9]

To prick his readers' guilt, he noted that tenement owners passed as respectable members of society. He referred to one as "an honored family, one of the 'oldest and best,' rich in possessions and influence, and high in the councils of the city's government."[10] To appeal to their sympathy, he tallied the high mortality rates of children and the pressures on young working women to turn to prostitution because they could not survive on their salaries.

His description of "Bohemian" (Czechoslovakian) cigar makers related a classic pattern of exploitation. The industry was controlled by men who were simultaneously the landlords, employers, and suppliers of the laborers who hand-rolled cigars. They adjusted rents and the cost of raw tobacco upward and pay downward to keep the workers in perpetual serfdom. "The manufacturer," Riis wrote, "charges them outrageous rents, deals them out tobacco by the week, and devotes the rest of his energies to paring down of wages to within a peg or two of the point where the tenant rebels in desperation."[11] Appealing to civic spirit, Riis argued that the poor health and lack of education that persisted in the tenements could not produce citizens fit to vote in a democracy.

Riis shared the prejudices of many white, northern European Americans of his era. Although he wanted to help African Americans, Chinese, Jews, and southern Europeans, his comments about them seem racist and bigoted to a contemporary reader. Moreover, his zeal for his own crusade led him to trespass on property and photograph people without their permission. His inept use of magnesium powder also set fire to some tenements. On several levels, however, Riis's campaign succeeded. He did not eradicate poverty, but he helped raise awareness of the problems and prompt reforms. Roosevelt provided clean drinking water, shut down police lodging houses, and enforced closing times at saloons. Parks and playgrounds were built, and schooling was made available to more children. Many of the worst warrens were demolished. Stifling tenements with few windows were replaced by buildings that had airshafts for ventilation. And the notorious Mulberry Bend, locus and symbol of the worst tenements, was replaced by a new symbol—Mulberry Park. A decade after *How the Other Half Lives,* Riis wrote *A Ten Years' War,* in which he reflected on the struggle for reform. He chronicled accomplishments and acknowledged disappointments, especially the return to power of the Tammany Hall political machine. The root problem, Riis said, was the indifference of good people, which he believed was improving. "Today we see the churches of every denomination uniting ... pleading for parks, playgrounds, kindergartens, libraries, clubs, and better homes," he wrote. "The cry has been answered. The gap in the social body, between rich and poor, is no longer widening." While he saw much more work to be done, he concluded, "I see only cause for hope."[12] Riis stopped photographing in the late 1890s, but his legacy as a social reformer who improved conditions with his camera continues to inspire photojournalists.

Independently of Riis, a social documentarian with a different cause appeared. For a decade, Lewis Hine photographed children working in coal mines, textile mills, cotton fields, and food-processing plants. His photographs of a boy who had lost an arm in an industrial accident, of children as young as five picking cotton or shucking oysters, and of youngsters of eight or nine, grimy with coal dust, were made into posters and published in the *Survey,* a progressive magazine. They exposed the injustice done to working children and accelerated the passage of laws regulating child labor.

The census of 1900 revealed that out of a population of 76.2 million, some 2 million children of all ages were working. Among those between the ages of ten and fifteen, over 18 percent were working. Child labor was deeply entrenched in the American economy. The owners of factories, coal mines, cotton plantations, mills, and other industries were happy to hire children at a fraction of what they paid adult workers. Managers of textile mills valued child employees because their small hands could fit more easily into the looms to replace bobbins. Many parents, caught in a cycle of poverty, needed their children to work. Beyond the oppression of forcing children as young as five to work twelve hours a day or more, the system denied them education, condemning them to a life of manual labor. It also damaged their health. Accidents were common as children used sharp knives to shuck oysters and handled molten glass in bottle factories. Children working in coal mines and textile mills suffered lung damage from breathing coal and cotton dust.

Progressives saw this exploitation as both a moral evil and a social problem that needed to be opposed with the same zeal the abolitionists directed against slavery. In 1904, reformers founded the National Child Labor Committee (NCLC). It hired Hine in 1908.

A native of Oshkosh, Wisconsin, Hine experienced the harsh realities of child labor firsthand. When he was sixteen, his father died, forcing him into a series of menial jobs. Sometimes working thirteen hours a day, six days a week, he took jobs as a laborer in a furniture factory, a woodcutter, a delivery boy, a door-to-door salesman, a janitor, a bookkeeper, and a bank clerk. During this period, he attended night school and saved his wages to continue his education. In the late 1800s, he enrolled at the University of Chicago, where he met Frank Manny, a leader in education reform, who introduced him to other progressive thinkers and activists. In 1904, Manny moved to New York City to head the Ethical Culture School, dedicated to the ideals of social justice and John Dewey's progressive methods of active learning. Manny hired Hine to teach science and soon made him the school's official photographer. Besides recording school functions, Manny assigned him to take photographs for teaching purposes. The two went to Ellis Island, off the lower tip of Manhattan, where Hine photographed immigrants arriving from eastern and southern Europe. Manny wanted the students to have the same respect for Ellis Island and its immigrants as they had for Plymouth Rock and the Pilgrims.

In 1907, Paul Kellogg hired Hine to photograph for a sociological survey of Pittsburgh. The work was published in Kellogg's *Charities and Commons.* As Kellogg changed his journal's name to the *Survey* and later the *Survey Graphic,* he continued to publish Hine's images and writing.[13] Hine quit teaching to work full time for the NCLC.

As an experienced photographer, a researcher who understood social science methods, a teacher with the ability to relate to children, and a man with his own personal history of working as a youth, Hine brought a unique set of skills and attitudes to the job. His personal feelings were in perfect synch with the committee's objective to expose the exploitation of child workers. "For many years I have followed the procession of child workers winding through a thousand industrial communities from the canneries of Maine to the fields of Texas," Hine said. "I have heard their tragic stories, watched their cramped lives and seen their fruitless struggles in the industrial game where the odds are all against them."[14]

He photographed children working in coal mines, textile mills, cotton fields, and food-processing plants. He recorded newsies hawking their papers late at night on the streets of metropolitan cities and telegraph boys whose deliveries took them into houses of prostitution. He documented children who had lost an arm or leg in industrial accidents. He caught oyster shuckers working from 3:30 A.M. to 5:00 P.M., young cigar makers smoking their own products, shoe-shine boys, bowling ally pin setters, fruit pickers, and bottle makers.

Hine's photograph of a girl working in a North Carolina cotton mill is typical (see figure 11). His caption noted that she was fifty-one inches tall, had been working there for a year, and sometimes worked night shifts for forty-eight cents a day. The photograph offers a good example of his technique and approach: Hine positioned his view camera on a tripod close to the girl so she fills much of the frame. He chose a very shallow depth of field with the focus beginning on the machine just in front of her and dropping off just behind her. This shallow focus emphasizes the details of her face, hands, and dress and minimizes the strong pattern of the machine, which might otherwise have competed for attention. Although Hine was experienced in using flash, this photograph is illuminated by natural light coming from windows on the girl's left. It splits her face into dark and light halves. Her hair is in braids, the left one tied with a light-colored ribbon. She wears a dress with a sailor collar and a ruffled front, but it has not been ironed. As if to steady herself, she rests one hand on the loom, the other on the window sill. Her expression is haunting. Her wide eyes and set lips seem to interrogate the viewer. When he asked her age, Hine wrote, "She hesitated, then said, 'I don't remember.'" She added confidentially, "I'm not old enough to work, but do just the same."[15] Many owners and bosses were aware of the crusade against child labor and did not welcome its representatives. Hine fabricated false identities to gain access. As a teacher he had delighted his students by performing theatrical roles, and he used his acting skills to gain access to factories, mines, and fields. He identified himself as a fire inspector, a roving photographer collecting images for postcards, a life insurance salesman, and "a reporter interested in machines and factory construction."[16] His field technique depended on taking extremely careful notes. As powerful as his photographs were, he knew industry representatives would try to discredit them by claiming they were fakes. In preemptive defense, he took detailed notes about the children and their work. In documenting their size, for example, he compared their height to the buttons on his vest, which he had premeasured. He interviewed them, their parents, and their supervisors and combined all the information into captions for each photograph. In one, he identified the photograph's subject as Furman Owens, age twelve, who had already been working in the textile mills in Columbia, South Carolina, for four years. Hine said the boy could not read and did not even know the alphabet. "Yes I want to learn," he told Hine, "but can't when I work all the time."[17] Many people crusaded against child labor, and it is important not to overstate Hine's contribution. Still, his photographs turned an abstract social problem into concrete instances of specific children with names and stories. In the campaign to educate the public and raise political support, his photographs played a key role. Owen Lovejoy, who as general secretary of the NCLC was Hine's supervisor, wrote to him: "The work that you did under my direction was more responsible than any or all other efforts to bring the facts or conditions of child labor employment to public attention."[18]

Although ultimately successful, the campaign moved slowly and suffered many setbacks. The first bill regulating child labor was introduced in the U.S. Senate in 1906, but it did not become law until a decade later. The Supreme Court, however, soon ruled it unconstitutional on the grounds that Congress's powers to regulate interstate commerce did not extend to overseeing labor practices. Another bill was passed and struck down in 1918, but the reformers did not give up. During the 1920s, a proposed constitutional amendment giving Congress the power to regulate child labor stalled when opponents attacked it as part of a communist plot to weaken the United States. Finally, Congress passed the Fair Labor Standards Act in 1938, and the Supreme Court upheld it in 1941.

Hine's work was grueling; some years he traveled as much as thirty thousand miles. In 1917, at the age of forty-three, he told the NCLC he wanted to cut back in order to spend more time with his wife and their five-year-old son. When the committee responded by cutting his salary, he resigned. Within a year he was traveling again, photographing the work of the Red Cross in Europe during the waning months of World War I. Returning to America, he became caught up in the postwar boom of the Roaring Twenties and began making positive images of workers. He explained that he wanted to honor the "men and women that go daily to their tasks in the great industrial structure, [who] fit into life's mosaic as interesting and highly individual units of the pattern we term 'labor.' "[19] Hine cobbled together a series of commissions and assignments, working for the American Red Cross, the Interchurch World Movement, General Electric, *Fortune* magazine, and during the Depression, the Tennessee Valley Authority and the Works Progress Administration. Roy Stryker, head of the Farm Security Administration's photography section, turned down his request for a job. After his child labor work, Hine's greatest project came during 1930–31, when he photographed the construction of the Empire State Building. At the age of fifty-six, he was up on the scaffolding, taking the same risks as the workers. They fixed a special rig that swung him out from the building, one thousand feet above the street. The resulting pictures became the centerpiece of *Men at Work,* a collection of his labor portraits, published in 1932. He died in near poverty in November 1940 at the age of sixty-six. Hine's most published quote captures the dual aspects of documentary photography: "There were two things I wanted to do," he said. "I wanted to show the things that had to be corrected. I wanted to show the things that had to be appreciated."[20]

Although they are now considered reformers, during their era Riis and Hine were part of a movement called muckraking journalism. A reference to stirring up filth, the term was coined by President Theodore Roosevelt to deprecate investigative journalists such as Ida Tarbell, Lincoln Steffens, Upton Sinclair, and Frank Norris, who wrote for socially conscious magazines. Roosevelt had supported the progressives, but when one of them wrote an exposé on corrupt senators who were his political allies, he gave a speech in 1906 that likened them all to a character in John Bunyan's *Pilgrim's Progress.* The investigative journalists, Roosevelt said, were like "the man who could look no way but downward with the muck-rake in his hands; who would neither look up nor regard the crown he was offered, but continued to rake to himself the filth on the floor."[21] Reformist journalists, who believed their work helped elect Roosevelt, felt betrayed. "Muckraking" became an easy way to dismiss their work, and their investigations declined.

Riis and Hine worked as individuals. At the group level, the largest and best-organized social documentary project was the Historical Section of the Farm Security Administration, popularly known as the FSA. Three of this book's themes coalesce in this government project: Its photographs preserve a richer and more coherent visual history of the Great Depression than exists for any other era in our nation's history. The agency succeeded in using photographs to correct social problems, and it relied on humanism to argue its case. The FSA found its reason for being and its subject matter in the Great Depression, the defining experience of the 1930s. Between 1929 and 1932, national income plunged from $105 billion to less than $60 billion. Stocks fell to 20 percent of their pre-crash level. About eleven thousand of twenty-five thousand American banks failed. An estimated twelve million to fifteen million workers—25 to 30 percent of the workforce—were unemployed. From 1929 to 1933, farm prices fell 61 percent. Foreclosures and tax sales forced farmers off their land in record numbers. During the same four years, the nation's suicide rate increased 25 percent. The Depression gripped the national psyche and threatened to unravel the social consensus. President Franklin Delano Roosevelt captured the situation in a memorable sentence: "I see one third of a nation, ill-housed, ill-clad, ill-nourished."[22]

Many Americans could not see the social injustice underlying the Depression. Clouding their perception was the ideology of the American dream. A legacy of the nation's Puritan work ethic and agrarian origins, it promised that in a land of bountiful riches, anyone could be successful through hard work. The corollary, rarely articulated but widely accepted, held that people who were not successful deserved their lot because they were lazy. Instead of recognizing the flaws in the economic system, many Americans blamed the unemployed factory worker and dispossessed farmer for their joblessness. Like most Republicans, President Herbert Hoover believed government should not solve problems for the individual. Extending the concept of survival of the fittest to the economic sphere, social Darwinists welcomed the Depression as a way to eliminate the weakest members of society. Secretary of the Treasury Andrew Mellon, for example, told Hoover the Wall Street crash "will purge the rottenness out of the system," and "enterprising people will pick up the wrecks from less competent people."[23] Others saw the Depression as the result of natural and inexorable laws governing the economic cycle, which government was powerless to withstand.

To the contrary, Roosevelt declared, "We must lay hold of the fact that economic laws are not made by nature. They are made by human beings."[24] Roosevelt and his administration saw the Depression as the result of human mistakes: poor trade policies, unregulated industries, mismanaged markets, poor land use, and overproduction. What stemmed from human causes could be corrected by human action. Social problems were amenable to social remedies. Those remedies were forecast in Roosevelt's 1932 campaign pledge: "A new deal for the forgotten man." The New Deal philosophy maintained that government had the right and duty to regulate the economy in ways that would protect the farmer, laborer, consumer, and small investor.

FSA's Historical Section was charged specifically with helping destitute farmers. Its photographs were intended to inform the public about the plight of their fellow citizens in rural areas, educate them about New Deal programs, and counter Republican opposition to New Deal legislation in Congress. In 1935, Roy Stryker, a Columbia University economics instructor, was appointed to head the agency. He hired, assigned, coordinated, motivated, and taught a shifting staff of talented photographers. His vision—expressed in the shooting scripts, or lists of subjects, he sent the photographers—shaped the collection. He pursued two overriding objectives. His first purpose was advancing the short-term political and social mission of his agency. On a larger level, he wanted to document rural America. "During the whole eight years," he recalled in 1973, "I held onto a personal dream that inevitably got translated into black-and-white pictures: I wanted to do a pictorial encyclopedia of American agriculture."[25]

Besides directing his staff, Stryker was also responsible for getting their work published. By 1940, he was distributing 1,406 photographs per month. The wire services circulated FSA pictures, newspapers and magazines published them, and government agencies used them to illustrate their publications. FSA exhibitions were shown at state fairs. FSA pictures appeared in *Life, U.S. Camera,* and *Survey Graphic* and illustrated numerous books, including Archibald MacLeish's *Land of the Free* and Richard Wright's *Twelve Million Black Voices.* John Steinbeck studied the collection as he gathered material for his novel *The Grapes of Wrath.*

It's difficult to generalize about a vast body of photographs taken by more than fifteen photographers over almost a decade. For the most part, however, they approached their subjects from the tradition of humanism. Unlike the social Darwinists, they believed each individual had inherent worth. They portrayed their subjects as worthy of help, instead of shiftless people who deserved their misfortune. Beneath the tattered, sweat-stained clothes, behind the worried, suspicious expressions, the people in these photographs retain their dignity as individuals. An exchange between FSA photographer Russell Lee and a Minnesota woman reveals this humanism. When she asked why he wanted to take her picture, Lee responded, "Lady, you are having a hard time and a lot of people don't think you are having such a hard time. We want to show that you're a human being, a nice human being, but you're having troubles."[26]

FSA photographers advanced this humanism by controlling the contents of their images. To appreciate this requires recognizing what is not shown. Many people in FSA photographs appear bewildered, despondent, dirty, and disheveled, but never dishonest, abusive, or immoral. Many appear forlorn, but never hopeless. No one appears belligerent, ignorant, lazy, or rebellious. To achieve this consistent portrayal, FSA photographers carefully selected their subjects, framed their compositions, timed their shutters, and edited their film, choosing frames that best matched the agency's purpose. Stryker punched holes in negatives that did not meet his standards.

This humanism made the FSA photographs effective during the Depression and permits contemporary viewers to connect across the decades with the people shown in these pictures. The collection encompasses the major themes of the human condition: childhood, old age, family relationships, the religious experience, education, and work. Stryker summed up his staff's humanistic restraint when he wrote of the collection, "To my knowledge there is no picture in there that in any way whatsoever represents an attempt by a photographer to ridicule his subject, to be cute with him, to violate his privacy, or to do something to make a cliché."[27]

If the FSA photographers' approach was humanist, their style was realist. Following the tenets of straight photography, the dominant movement of the 1920s, many rejected staging their subjects while making the exposure and manipulating the negatives or prints during darkroom processing. Realism dovetailed with the common misconception that a photograph shows viewers what they would have seen if they had been present. Although they took advantage of this naive belief, many FSA photographers neither believed nor claimed their pictures were objective. They acknowledged they were pursing truth from their own subjective points of view. Like many Americans during the era, they believed subjective truth had greater value than objective facts. So long as the photograph got the connotation correct, its denotation need not be literal. FSA photographer John Vachon argued strongly that documentary photographers must bring their own personal perspective and feeling to the subject. "To photograph the American highway, the cameraman must know it, and have an attitude. A definite feeling about it," he wrote.[28] Such personal perspectives did not persuade political critics. Working in South Dakota in 1936, Arthur Rothstein moved the skull of a steer to a patch of parched, cracked earth to dramatize the area's drought. A regional newspaper accused the FSA of fabricating pictures and made it a political issue in Roosevelt's reelection campaign.

FSA photographers included Rothstein, Vachon, Esther Bubley, John Collier Jr., Marjory Collins, Jack Delano, Sheldon Dick, Walker Evans, Dorothea Lange, Russell Lee, Howard Lieberman, Edwin Locke, Carl Mydans, Gordon Parks, Ben Shahn, and Marion Post Wolcott.[29] A few worked throughout the project, but most stayed a couple of years or less. Afterward, many built distinguished careers in photography. Mydans covered World War II for *Life*. Parks also worked for *Life* and became a composer and film director. Rothstein became director of photography for *Look*. Collier pioneered in the field of visual anthropology. Lee became a distinguished professor. Two deserve special discussion.

Of the FSA staff, Walker Evans earned the greatest reputation as an art photographer. While he did not subscribe to the social documentary philosophy, his greatest photographs came from the 1930s, when he worked for the agency. Much has been written about the strained relationship between Evans, who is typically styled as the fiercely independent artist, and Stryker, who is stereotyped as a Washington bureaucrat who sacrificed the personal visions of his staff members to the agency's mission. This plays into the popular myth of the uncompromising artist battling the philistine patron. Evans contributed to this characterization, stating, "I've been particularly infuriated by reading here and there that [Stryker] was 'directing' his photographers. He wasn't directing me; I wouldn't let him."[30]

The men differed fundamentally in objectives. Evans was thirty-two when he took the FSA job in October 1935, and he had immersed himself in modernist art, literature, and ideas during studies at Williams College, a yearlong stay in Paris, and involvement with the artistic avant-garde in New York. Following the tenets of high modernism, he saw photography as an art that should have no other objective than itself and especially should not be used for political purposes. He espoused straight photography and used a view camera with a tripod, black cloth, and sheet film. An admirer of Gustave Flaubert and other French realist writers, he developed a realist style that many viewers perceived as artless. A keen observer of the American scene, Evans called his FSA work an "objective picture of America in the 1930's" and said it "was neither journal-istic or political in technique and intention. It was reflective rather than tendentious and, in a certain way, disinterested."[31]

Stryker's correspondence reveals a deferential tone toward Evans. He sent shooting scripts to other members of his staff but only made suggestions to Evans. His letters did include two recurring themes—Evans's numerically low production of photographs and his penchant for breaking off communication for extended periods while in the field. Evans's reputation, based on several exhibitions, helped him negotiate a higher salary than fellow staffers when Stryker hired him in October 1935.[32] Stryker felt squeezed between Evans's independence and the government's expectations. A 1936 letter captured Stryker's dilemma: "Your monthly expenditures look pretty large and unless I can lay down lots of pictures with your name on them each month, I am afraid I am going to be in for some difficulty," he wrote. The government is paying "you each month a pretty nice sum of money and they have a right to expect certain returns. . . . The way for you to get the opportunity of doing the thing you want is to satisfy them."[33]

Had Evans not been an exceptional photographer, there would have been no dilemma. Stryker would have summarily fired him. But he recognized Evans's photographic vision and protected him from bureaucratic meddling. The images Evans produced for the FSA during a scant two years are the best of his career. The most memorable showed tenant farmers in Hale County, Alabama. In 1936, Evans got a leave of absence from the FSA to work with the writer James Agee on an assignment for *Fortune* magazine. As one of the conditions for granting the leave, the agency retained the rights to his negatives.

Fortune assigned the team to report on the highly exploitive sharecropper system, which permeated Southern agriculture. The landlords owned the land, equipment, and houses. They supplied the seeds and advanced credit for other necessities. For this, they received half of the harvest, plus repayment of the credit. Because agriculture was even more depressed than industry, tenants fell into economic thrall to the owners. Writing of Floyd Burroughs, to whom he gave the pseudonym of George Gudger, Agee explained how he depended on his landlord for land, mule, farm implements, seed, fertilizer, and rations. In return for those things, Agee wrote:

> Gudger pays him back with his labor and with the labor of his family. At the end of the season he pays him back further: with half his corn; with half his cotton; with half his cottonseed. Out of his own half of these crops he also pays him back the rations money, plus interest, and his share of the fertilizer, plus interest, and such other debts, plus interest, as he may have incurred. What is left, once doctors' bills and other debts have been deducted, is his year's earnings. Gudger is a straight half-cropper, or sharecropper.[34]

Evans and Agee lived with the families of Burroughs, Frank Tengle, and Bud Fields for several weeks. Evans's pictures are unblinking statements about the toll the sharecropper system exacted on these families. Almost all are confrontational, in the sense that the subjects look directly at the viewer through the camera. Their expressions are plaintive, their gazes penetrating. Evans portrayed Burroughs in bib overalls, a frayed shirt, and a two-day stubble of beard (see figure 12). His narrowed eyes, tightly set lips, and tilted head express hopelessness. Seated against an unpainted pine door, the thirty-year-old seems burdened by the weight of centuries. It is hard to imagine a more plaintive photograph, until one sees Evans's portrait of Burroughs's wife, Allie Mae Burroughs, with her drawn lips and penetrating eyes that seem to accuse the viewer of complicity in her fate (see figure 13).

The Hale County project offers a good example of what made Evans's work different. While other FSA photographers believed their photographs coupled with New Deal policies could help improve the lives of such farmers, Evans expressed no such optimism, only an unrelenting insistence on the farmers' destitute situation. In these images, we see the meaning of his claim that his work was not political.

The editors at *Fortune* considered the project too bleak and declined to publish it. It finally appeared in 1941 as the book *Let Us Now Praise Famous Men,* but by then America was mobilizing for war, and few were interested in the Depression. The book sold poorly, but as interest in Evans, Agee, and the Depression resurfaced in the 1960s, it became a classic.

Evans resigned from the FSA in September 1937. After a brief period as a writer for *Time,* he worked from 1945 to 1965 as a photographer for *Fortune* magazine. He taught photography at Yale University from 1965 until about a year before his death in 1975.

In contrast to Evans's disinterest, Dorothea Lange was committed to helping the hardscrabble farmers and dispossessed migrant workers she photographed. Based on her contribution to advancing this goal and the humanity of her images, Lange was the best FSA photographer.

Two formative experiences from her childhood shaped her for such humanism. When she was seven, she contracted polio, which left her with a limp for the rest of her life. She credited this disability for her empathy for people and their acceptance of her. "I think [the polio] perhaps was the most important thing that happened to me and formed me, guided me, instructed me, helped me, and humiliated me," she said.[35] On another occasion she said,

"People are kinder to you. It gets you off on a different level than if you go into a situation whole and secure.... My lameness ... truly opened gates for me."[36]

When she was twelve, her father, Henry Nutzhorn, an attorney, abandoned the family. Left with two children to support, Lange's mother moved the family from Hoboken, New Jersey, to her mother's apartment on the Lower East Side of New York. Lange's German immigrant grandmother cared for her and her brother, while her mother worked at the New York Public Library. The experience gave her the role model of a strong, independent woman. It also reinforced her feelings of being an outsider. As the only gentile in a school of Jewish children, she was conscious of not fitting in. She rejected formal schooling, because she felt she could not compete with her ambitious classmates, and decided instead to become a photographer. She worked for several photographers in New York in return for their teaching her the craft.

In January 1918, with World War I still in progress, Lange left New York, intending to travel around the world, supporting herself by photography. On her first day in San Francisco, all her money was stolen, which ended her trip. She took a job in a photography-supply business and joined a camera club to gain access to a darkroom. After several months, friends in the club loaned her three thousand dollars to open a portrait studio on Sutter Street, in the heart of the city. Through the 1920s her business thrived with a clientele of wealthy businessmen and their families. She married the painter Maynard Dixon, and they had two sons.

The Great Depression changed the direction of her life. Dissatisfied with the limitations of her portrait business, she said she "wanted to work on a broader basis. I was still sort of aware that there was a very large world out there that I had entered not too well."[37] She recalled witnessing a poignant scene from her studio window:

> I watched an unemployed young workman coming up the street. He came to the corner, stopped, and stood there a little while. Behind him were the waterfront and the wholesale districts; to his left was the financial district; ahead was Chinatown and the Halls of Justice; to his right were the flop houses and the Barbary Coast. What was he to do? Which way was he to go?[38]

Lange was not indecisive. She moved from the studio to the streets during the winter of 1933. Outside her studio she could see a breadline for unemployed men. With her Graflex she photographed a man in a rumpled overcoat pulled up around his neck, leaning on a wooden rail. His eyes were obscured beneath the brim of his battered hat. His bare hands were clasped together. His forearms protected a tin cup, which would soon contain his ration of soup. His slumped shoulders and downward gaze symbolized the personal malaise the Depression wreaked on many. Asked about the image later, Lange said, "I can only say I knew I was looking at something. You know there are moments such as these when time stands still and all you do is hold your breath and hope it will wait for you. . . . Sometimes you have an inner sense that you have encompassed the thing generally."[39] Lange's street work ranged from breadlines to picket lines, demonstrations, and political rallies. Paul Taylor, a University of California sociologist who specialized in the agricultural sector, saw her photographs at an exhibition and hired her to accompany him to research a lumber mill in Oroville, California, in 1934. It was the beginning of a professional and personal partnership. They divorced their spouses and married each other the following year. Working as a team, Taylor interviewed subjects while Lange, largely unnoticed, photographed them. Their 1935 report about the deplorable conditions of migrant workers in California spurred the federal government to construct camps that provided safe, sanitary conditions. These modest camps, costing only about twenty thousand dollars, were the first government-funded public housing.[40]

One of Taylor's reports found its way to Stryker, who was impressed by Lange's images and hired her in August 1935 as a photographer-investigator. Their relationship was filled with tensions. Lange worked from her home on the West Coast, while the other staffers worked out of the Washington office. Except for an annual visit, her contact with Stryker was limited to slow-moving letters. She wanted control over her negatives and wanted to supply the prints that were circulated. Given the volume, this was not practical. Production was also slowed when she insisted on having her negatives mailed to California to print for special projects. Stryker objected to her hiring her friend Ansel Adams to make prints for the Museum of Modern Art in New York and especially to her having a negative retouched. He saw both instances as pretentious attempts to turn documentary photography into art.[41] In November 1939, when he was forced by the budget office to lay off one staff member, he told Lange her job would end at the first of the year. Karin Becker, a Lange scholar, called it "an unpleasant parting with some bitterness on both sides," but "eventually their mutual respect overrode the tension arising from her termination."[42]

Despite their disagreements, Stryker appreciated Lange's images and considered her effective in the field. Her approach helps explain that effectiveness. First was her belief in herself and her work. On several field trips, she took along as an assistant Rondal Partridge, the teenage son of her friend and fellow photographer

Imogen Cunningham. He quoted her as saying, "When you photograph ... you have every right—must have every right in your mind—to make that photograph."[43] In dealing with people, Lange was never obtrusive or insistent. Her self-confidence and her belief in her cloak of invisibility let her work freely. Of the latter, Taylor commented, "It made her feel that she could go up and do things which otherwise seemed to be intruding on their privacy. It gave her a feeling of confidence in working with the camera."[44] Lange knew how to get natural photographs without directing her subjects. "She did not ask people to hold a pose or repeat an action," Becker wrote, "instead she might ask a question: 'How much does that bag of cotton weigh?' And the man, wanting to give her a precise answer, would lift it onto the scales and Lange would make her photograph."[45]

Lange adopted Taylor's research methods, producing extensive verbal reports to accompany her photographs. When she worked alone, she took copious notes and carefully reconstructed conversations after she finished photographing. Her captions never stated the obvious but provided context that gave her subjects dimensionality. "I don't like the kind of written material that tells a person what to look for or that explains the photograph," Lange said in an interview. "I like the kind of material that gives more background, that fortifies it without directing" the viewer's mind.[46] Typically, that material included information on the subjects' origins and direct quotes from them about their circumstances. When Lange photographed a displaced Nebraska farmer in Calipatria, California, she quoted him as saying he invested in "the good old earth—but we lost on that, too. The finance company caught up with us, the mortgage company caught up with us. Managed to lose $12,000 in 3 years. My boys have no more future than I have, so far as I can see ahead."[47] Stryker considered her captions exemplary and urged other photographers to follow her model. Besides her humanism, the quality of Lange's photographs resulted from her ideas about photography. She was a friend of Adams, Cunningham, Willard van Dyke, and other founders of Group f.64. Although she never joined the group, she embraced its photographic realism and its doctrine of unmanipulated photography. A quotation she posted on the door of her darkroom encapsulated the realist's belief in observation. Attributed to the British philosopher Francis Bacon, it read, "The contemplation of things as they are, without error or confusion, without substitution or imposture, is in itself a nobler thing than a whole harvest of invention."[48] Lange used a Rolleiflex twin-lens reflex camera, which made 2¼ × 2¼ inch negatives on roll film, and Graphic and Graflex cameras, which used sheet film in holders. After her FSA period, she also used the 35 mm camera.

Lange made her most famous picture, "Migrant Mother," in February or March of 1936 (see figure 14). On her way home after a month of photographing, she passed a handmade sign near Nipomo, California, that read PEA PICKERS CAMP. She drove on, but the sign piqued her curiosity about what she might find in the camp. After twenty miles, she turned her car around. By Lange's account, the thirty-two-year-old woman had literally come to the end of her road. Freezing weather had destroyed the pea crop and her chances for work. The family was surviving by scavenging frozen vegetables from the fields and killing birds. She could not leave to search for work, Lange said, because she had sold the tires from her car to buy food. Lange took six exposures on sheet film, including a general view that shows a fourteen-year-old daughter sitting in front of a tent that sheltered the family. In the succeeding frames, she moved steadily closer, but her compositions remained loose, and her framing included distracting contents. In her final exposure she found the angle and distance that positioned the mother against a clean background. In shyness, two of her children turn themselves away from the stranger with the camera as they lean on her shoulders. Her infant rests on her lap. She gazes into the distance, her right hand brushing her cheek. Despite her tentative gesture and seemingly hopeless situation, her expression shows a resolve to overcome her circumstances and protect her family. It is the tension between the woman's determination and her dire straits that makes this photograph the iconic representation of the Great Depression. Stryker praised the picture as embodying the purpose of the FSA: "When Dorothea took that picture, that was the ultimate," he said. "She never surpassed it. To me it was the picture of Farm Security. She has all the suffering of mankind in her, but all the perseverance too. A restraint and a strange courage."[49] Thousands of newspapers, magazines, history textbooks, and Web sites have confirmed his judgment, making it one of the most published photographs ever. Lange said the image took on such a life of its own she felt it no longer belonged to her. The "Migrant Mother," which can be purchased at a nominal cost from the Library of Congress, is one of its most frequently requested images.

Decades later, another side of the story emerged that challenges Lange's account and supports a postmodern judgment that she exploited the woman. In an interview published in 1960, Lange said the woman did not ask her any questions about why she was making the photographs. Lange projected her own attitude onto her subject: "There she sat in that lean-to tent with her children huddled around her, and seemed to know that my pictures might help her, and so she helped me. There was a sort of equality about it."[50]

In 1975, a decade after Lange's death, Florence Owens Thompson wrote to the *Modesto Bee,* identifying herself as the subject of the famous photograph. When the AP interviewed her, Thompson, a Cherokee Indian, said she felt exploited by the picture. "I wish she hadn't taken my picture," she said. "I can't get a penny out of it. She didn't ask my name. She said she wouldn't sell the pictures. She said she'd send me a copy. She never did."[51]

Troy Owens, Thompson's son, disputed Lange's assertion about the tires. "There's no way we sold our tires, because we didn't have any to sell," he told a writer. "The only ones we had were on the Hudson, and we drove off in them." Owen added that he didn't think Lange was lying. "I just think she had one story mixed up with another. Or she was borrowing to fill in what she didn't have."[52]

After the photograph was published, government agents sent ten tons of food and supplies to the Nipomo camp, but Thompson and her family had moved on. Near the end of her life, she did benefit from being photographed. In 1983, she had a stroke and needed medical care that cost over fourteen hundred dollars per week. Her son appealed for help through the *San Jose Mercury News*. A special fund received over thirty-five thousand dollars, mostly in small amounts from people who said they were touched by Lange's photo. Their letters caused Thompson's family to reevaluate their criticism of the photograph. "None of us ever really understood how deeply Mama's photo affected people," Owens said. "I guess we had only looked at it from our perspective. For Mama and us, the photo had always been a bit of a curse. After all those letters came in, I think it gave us a sense of pride."[53]

The downside of producing such a famous image is that the photographer becomes characterized by a single image that overshadows a lifetime of work. Lange's entire body of work rewards the effort of studying it in depth. After her tenure at the FSA, Lange continued her photographic career for another three decades. She documented the Japanese internment camp at Manzanar, California, produced picture stories for *Life,* and photographed foreign trips with her husband. Shortly before she died of cancer in 1965, she oversaw a retrospective of her work for the Museum of Modern Art in New York.

As the Depression gave way to World War II, Stryker tried to save his operation by getting assignments for his staff from the Office of War Information. When opponents in Congress tried to have the FSA collection destroyed, he arranged to have it transferred into the Library of Congress, where it remains a valuable resource for historians, publishers, and all Americans.

In *On Photography,* Sontag charges that all photography is an aggressive act and that photographers who claim to be helping their subjects are rationalizing exploiting them to advance their careers. Extrapolating these ideas, many postmodern theorists criticize the FSA collection as manipulative and condescending. Professor Lawrence Levine from the University of California charges that by portraying their subjects as "perfect victims," the FSA photographers turned them into caricatures and denied their full humanity.[54] Other critics pursue a Marxist argument against the FSA. The Great Depression threatened the social consensus known as the American dream—the ideology that in the United States anyone could prosper through hard work—so deeply that many people feared society would come unraveled. John Tagg denounces Roosevelt's New Deal as an attempt to shore up capitalism with the minimum expenditure of resources. He describes the New Deal as "a particular social strategy: a liberal, corporatist plan to negotiate economic, political, and cultural crisis through a limited programme of structural reforms, relief measures, and a cultural intervention aimed at restructuring the order of discourse, appropriating dissent, and resecuring the threatened bonds of social consent." Tagg writes that the New Deal used the FSA's documentary photography to "produce propaganda for its policies" but also to stake a claim to "truth in discourse, a status threatened by crisis but whose renegotiation was essential if social relations of meaning were to be sustained and national and social identities resecured, while demand for reform was contained within the limits of monopoly capitalist relations."[55] Tagg's critique might be extended to all uses of documentary photography to effect social change. To the Marxist, no change short of the replacement of capitalist economy ever suffices. Any improvement in people's circumstances only forestalls revolution.

Critics such as Sontag, Tagg, and others, who see only the big picture, fail to acknowledge that the New Deal fed, clothed, and sheltered people who would otherwise have gone hungry and been homeless, that Riis's efforts did help improve sanitation, housing, and education for New York tenement dwellers, and that without Hine, we might still have unregulated child labor. Theorists can and should think at the meta level, but individuals live their daily lives on the plane of reality where the basic needs for survival—food, clothing, and shelter—come before political theory. As for the charge of exploitation, the argument cuts in two directions. By impugning the motives of the photographers in the absence of any documentary evidence to support their charges, the theorists are advancing their own careers. Motivation is complex, and few people act from a single motive. It seems more appropriate to evaluate social documentary work based on its results instead of speculation about photographers' motives.

In the 1960s, a parallel initiative that grew out of European magazine photojournalism merged with the American social documentary tradition. In 1958, Cornell Capa, then a *Life* photographer, established a memorial fund to honor his brother Robert Capa, the legendary war photographer and cofounder of the Magnum Photos agency, and two friends: David Seymour, another co-founder, who went by the name "Chim," and Werner Bischof, a Magnum member. All three were killed on assignment. The fund gave cash awards to photographers to support their projects. Its purpose was "to promote the understanding and appreciation of photography as a medium for revealing the human condition."[56]

In 1966, it was absorbed into the International Fund for Concerned Photography in New York. A year later, Cornell mounted an exhibition featuring the work of Robert Capa, Seymour, Leonard Freed, and Dan Weiner at the Riverside Museum in New York City. *The Concerned Photographer,* a book based on the exhibition, was published in 1968, and the term *concerned photography* gained currency in discussing the work of photographers trying to combat global problems with their pictures. In describing the group and its impetus, Cornell articulated the social documentarian's faith in using photography to combat problems, but he expanded it to a global level. "The concerned photographer finds much in the present unacceptable which he tries to alter," Capa said. "Our goal is simply to let the world also know why it is unacceptable."[57] In 1974, Capa founded the International Center of Photography. Since his retirement, its exhibitions have broadened to include art photography, but it remains the foremost American museum dedicated to photojournalism and the documentary tradition.

The Capa brothers, whose family name was Friedman, were Hungarian Jews; Seymour was a Polish Jew. In the 1930s, as the Nazis dominated Germany and Eastern Europe, these photographers fled to France, finding work with the picture magazines. Their ideals of social justice merged with the tradition of French humanism and its concern for the human condition. Where the social documentary tradition in America was grounded in issues like poverty, child labor, and the Depression, the Europeans launched their careers exposing European fascism and covering the Spanish Civil War. Engaged partisan photographers, they did not worry about objectivity. Instead they supported the Spanish loyalists in their losing struggle against General Francisco Franco, who overthrew the democratically elected Spanish government. Instead of extended documentary projects, they produced concentrated news reports on the war. Much of their reportage was published in two Parisian magazines: *Regards* (*Glances*), a Communist weekly magazine, and *Vu* (*Seen*). Although *Vu* was mainstream with a larger circulation, it was no less concerned with the European political situation. It ran a weekly section called "Witness to Our Times," which highlighted major problems. This is one of the earliest instances of applying the term *witness* to the work of serious photojournalists.

Witness carries powerful resonances of standing for truth in the court of public opinion, of refusing to ignore the horrors that powerful men commit against their weaker fellow humans. James Nachtwey, widely regarded as the best war photographer working today, is one among many claiming this identification. "I have been a witness, and these pictures are my testimony," he declares. "The events I have recorded should not be forgotten and must not be repeated."[58] Susan Meiselas, another well-known war photographer and member of Magnum, writes:

> I see myself in that tradition of encounter and witness—a "witness" who sees the photograph as evidence. A lot of my work has been based on a concern about human rights violations. That's where that word is the most appropriate. But the other side of "witness" is that we do intervene, and we intervene by the fact

of our presence in a particular place. We change how people see themselves sometimes and how others may come to see them.[59]

Under the concept of witness, Meiselas, Nachtwey, and other magazine photojournalists have expanded the social documentary tradition from domestic issues of poverty and child labor to international problems of famine, ethnic cleansing, genocide, and, especially, war.

The Vietnam War marked a turning point in the way photographers covered war and the way they and the public thought about their work. For the first time, combat photography was perceived as being against American war policy. Earlier pictures might be read to oppose the horrors of war, but they did not challenge its justification. In the complex political and media environments of Vietnam, the antiwar movement appropriated still photos and television footage to expose the inhumanity of the war on soldiers and, especially, Vietnamese civilians. Photojournalists brought Vietnam into the nation's living rooms as no other previous war. Americans watched as their soldiers set fire to thatched huts with Zippo lighters. They saw photographs of wounded and dead GIs, as well as the bodies of Vietnamese civilians and opponents.

Technology played a big role in this increase of graphic imagery. The 35 mm camera let photographers capture the carnage of battles and bombing campaigns. Advances in film and logistics let television crews shoot, edit, ship, and broadcast stories while they were still timely. Minimal censorship was a second major factor. The South Vietnamese government was in charge of accreditation, and anybody with letters from two news organizations could get credentialed. Any westerner with credentials could travel freely on

U.S. military planes and helicopters. Many freelancers joined the professionals in trying to document the war.

In trying to explain how the United States lost the Vietnam War, many in the military and on the political right blame the media, characterizing its coverage as antiwar. With some exceptions, most of the press, including most photographers, supported the war effort until the Tet Offensive of 1968. During Tet, the Asian lunar new year, Vietcong and North Vietnamese army soldiers launched scores of coordinated attacks at key military and political targets across South Vietnam. Critics accuse the media of failing to report Tet as a major American victory, since the attackers were eventually driven back and failed to hold any of the sites they captured. This argument misses the larger point that all wars depend on public support. For months, President Lyndon B. Johnson, Secretary of Defense Robert McNamara, and General William Westmoreland, commander of U.S. forces in Vietnam, had been assuring the American public the war was almost won. McNamara quoted statistics, including body counts of the enemy, Johnson gave upbeat analyses, and at a November 1967 news conference, Westmoreland forecast a U.S. victory in the coming year by saying his military command could see "the light at the end of the tunnel."[60] As Americans watched televised accounts of Vietcong guerillas inside the U.S. embassy in Saigon, they realized their government had been lying to them.

Whether or not they opposed American war policy, photojournalists fueled antiwar sentiment simply by doing their jobs, showing the results of America's military prowess. Among the thousands of photographs taken during the Vietnam War, four have attained iconic status. Frequently published, they symbolize important aspects of the war. Malcolm Browne's 1963 image of the Buddhist monk Thich Quang Duc burning himself to death in protest against President Ngo Dinh Diem's persecution of Buddhists challenged U.S. support for this autocratic leader. Eddie Adams's 1968 picture of South Vietnamese general Nguyen Ngoc Loan summarily executing a suspected Vietcong captured the brutality of America's allies. Nguyen Cong Ut's photograph of nine-year-old Phan Thi Kim Phuc, severely burned by a "friendly" napalm attack, revealed the devastation that high-technology warfare inflicted on innocent victims. Sergeant Ronald Haeberle's photograph of victims of the My Lai massacre established that American soldiers committed atrocities against unarmed women and children. These and similar images seared Vietnam into the consciousness of the American public. By exposing the moral contradictions of U.S. involvement in southeast Asia, they helped mobilize antiwar sentiment. One photographer who openly opposed the war was Philip Jones Griffiths, a native of Wales and a member of Magnum. His 1971 book *Vietnam Inc.* is a scathing indictment of a high-tech war being waged by the world's most powerful country against an agrarian society.

Whatever other lessons the U.S. military learned, Vietnam reaffirmed its old beliefs about controlling the press during war. In Grenada, Panama, and the two Iraq wars, journalists had nothing close to the freedom of movement they enjoyed in Vietnam. In the complex exchange between photojournalists, government policy makers, military leaders, and the public over the issue of graphic war photographs, General Peter Dawkins offered the military's rationale for controlling photojournalists. "War is an ugly, dirty, obscene business, and if you take snippets of it and constantly expose the American public to its reality, then that is going to profoundly influence their attitude toward the enterprise. And I'm not sure that that reality, in itself, ought to be the controlling influence of what determines the public's attitude toward the policy."[61]

Others in government shared Dawkins's belief, including War-ren Christopher, U.S. secretary of state under President Clinton, who said, "Television cannot be the North Star of America's for-eign policy."[62] During the 1990s, a national debate emerged over the perception that horrific images were driving American foreign policy. Many believed, for example, that photographs of emaci-ated Somalis forced President George H. W. Bush to send Ameri-can troops in December 1992 to intervene in the civil war that was causing widespread starvation. "Every American has seen the shocking images from Somalia," Bush said.[63] "The people of So-malia, especially the children ... need our help," he stated later.[64] Opinion was just as certain that photographs of Somalis dragging a slain American pilot through the streets after an aborted raid in the fall of 1993 pressured President Clinton to withdraw the troops.

Broadcast journalist Cokie Roberts summarized this under-standing on ABC's *Nightline:* "It was pictures like these that pro-voked the U.S. to send over twenty-five thousand American troops to Somalia. . . . It may be pictures like these which finally make the U.S. leave. . . . We're seeing them again, pictures from another land so shocking that we're moved to call Congress, call the president, tell them what the United States should do."[65]

Drawing on numerous studies, media scholar David Perlmut-ter says the power of specific images and of the media in gen-eral to drive policy is limited. Based on a careful analysis of the photographs, events, and presidential statements about Somalia, he argues that instead of being forced by the photographs, both presi-dents used them to justify policies they had decided on for other reasons. "A striking, visually fascinating photograph or video ... has less political impact than we would assume or might attribute to it," he writes, insisting that independent evidence is required before accepting such claims.[66]

Other examples from the witness tradition include Gilles Caron's photographs of the famine and war in Biafra, Meiselas's pictures of the victims of the poison gassing of Iraqi Kurds under Saddam Hussein, David and Peter Turnley's coverage of the two Iraq wars, Gilles Peress's reporting on Kosovo, Nachtwey's story of American soldiers wounded in Iraq, and Ryan Spencer Reed's coverage of the rape and murder that the government-sponsored Janjaweed militias inflicted on the people of Darfur in Sudan. Such photographers earn their livings by selling timely photographs to newsmagazines, but like Jones Griffiths, many of them publish their collected images in books with greater impact and permanence—if smaller audiences—than ephemeral magazines. In taking a stand with the oppressed, they challenge the governments and individuals who perpetrated the oppression. They also force millions of Americans and Europeans to pay attention to these problems. In most cases, private citizens donate aid. Considering motivation and results, the tradition of being a witness can best be understood as extending the social documentary tradition to global problems.

In the United States, the struggle for racial justice and civil rights provided the opportunity to combine reformist photojournalism with spot news coverage. Charles Moore is the photographer most associated with the civil rights movement. He was a staff photographer on the *Montgomery Advertiser* in 1958 when he took an exclusive photograph of the Rev. Martin Luther King Jr. being roughed up as he was arrested and charged with loitering. Transmitted by the AP, Moore's photograph was published in *Life* and around the world. It helped transform a regional struggle into a national movement. Over the next seven years, Moore covered James Meredith integrating the University of Mississippi, the funeral of slain voting-rights activist Medgar Evers, King's "I have a dream" speech, the campaign to register African American voters, the Ku Klux Klan in North Carolina, the murder of three white Northern college students in Philadelphia, Mississippi, and numerous situations where state and local police attacked nonviolent freedom marchers.

His most frequently published image shows police officers setting their German shepherd attack dogs against African American protesters during the efforts to desegregate Birmingham, Alabama, in 1963. Part of a three-picture sequence published in *Life,* it shows one dog biting at the hip of a man as another lunges toward him with bared fangs. The man's trouser leg had been ripped from waist to ankle by a previous bite. "The police dogs were what really did it for me," Moore said. "The sight of snarling dogs, and the possibility of dogs ripping flesh, was revolting to me."[67] Many Americans shared his revulsion, and his photographs are credited with helping to spur passage of the Civil Rights Act of 1964. Referring to Birmingham police chief Theophilus Eugene "Bull" Connor, historian Arthur Schlesinger Jr. wrote, "The photographs of Bull Connor's police dogs lunging at the marchers in Birmingham did as much as anything to transform the national mood and make legislation not just necessary, which it had long been, but possible."[68]

During the civil rights era, most photographers remained detached from their subjects, most of whom quickly returned to anonymity. In one notable case, however, a photographer reconnected with his subjects and helped turn an instant of hate into a story of redemption. Three years after the Supreme Court overturned school segregation in its 1954 *Brown v. Board of Education* ruling, African American leaders in Little Rock, Arkansas, chose nine students to integrate Central High School. Playing to voters' racist instincts, Governor Orval Faubus ordered the National

Guard to prevent the black students from entering the school. Will Counts, a staff photographer for the *Arkansas Democrat,* recorded the opening-day events. He recorded a white mob viciously beating Alex Wilson, a black reporter for the Memphis *Tri-State Defender.*

In a second sequence, Counts followed fifteen-year-old Elizabeth Eckford from the point where the Guardsmen turned her away until she reached a bus stop and waited for a ride home. In a photograph memorable for its racist rage, Counts captured Eckford with her schoolbooks in her arms and a determined expression on her face (see figure 15). She is surrounded by a crowd of white students and adult men. At the center of the frame, high school student Hazel Bryan, her mouth open in an expression of hate, shouts a racial epithet at Miss Eckford, who absorbs it without reacting. Over the next forty years, the image took on iconic status, putting a human face on racism and its victim.

Counts's photographs, which were transmitted by the AP, played a leading role in changing the situation. Several made their way to the desk of President Eisenhower, who reportedly told an adviser, "I've got to do something." Eisenhower, who had been the Allied commander in World War II, ordered the 101st Airborne Division to Little Rock. The Arkansas National Guard stood down as the federal troops escorted the "Little Rock Nine" into school.[69]

The story might have remained there, except for the intervention of Counts and his wife, Vivian. In 1997, on the fortieth anniversary of the crisis, Little Rock planned a celebration of the racial harmony that had transformed Central High School. Counts returned to cover the events, which included President Bill Clinton presenting medals to the Little Rock Nine. With the help of Vivian, Counts got Elizabeth Eckford and Hazel Bryan Massery together for a new set of photographs in front of the school (see figure 16). It was a moment of reconciliation but also an opportunity for redemption for Massery. She had come to understand that her racist beliefs and actions that day were wrong. She felt haunted by the image and said she was tired of being the "poster child of the hate generation." She was grateful for the chance to apologize to Eckford. "My life has been more than that one moment," Massery said—a comment that gave Counts the title for his 1999 book, *A Life Is More Than a Moment,* which recounts the 1957 events and the women's reconciliation.[70]

Of the three traditions, the belief their pictures can make life better for their fellow humans remains the strongest motivation for photojournalists working today. Idealism runs high among students, and photojournalism instructors reinforce it by recounting the history of Riis, Hine, the FSA, the civil rights movement, and other crusading photographers. The tradition is also perpetuated in the W. Eugene Smith grant, the Robert Kennedy Award, and the World Understanding Award of the Pictures of the Year (POY) competition. The first two give financial support to photographers to pursue social documentary projects.

The social documentary tradition continues in the books of Donna Ferrato's images of spousal abuse, Eugene Richards's project on crack cocaine, Sebastião Salgado's photographs of third-world workers, and many hundreds of projects by newspaper and magazine photographers.

⬥

FIVE

THE PICTURE MAGAZINES

Photoreportage took its cues not from art or literature, but from the many and varied aspects of the condition humaine *itself. The emphasis was placed almost exclusively on the human element. The new photojournalism became a medium of human communication.*
—Tim Gidal

As press photography developed in American newspapers, a different tradition was born in Europe. In Berlin and Munich in the mid- to late 1920s, magazine photojournalism grew from three factors: a generation of innovative photographers and editors who pioneered a new form of visual reporting, a mass audience eager to see itself in illustrated magazines, and the 35 mm camera, which made the new picture-story format possible.

The Hungarian Stefan Lorant was especially instrumental in developing magazine photojournalism. Lorant, who edited both the *Berlin Illustrierte Zeitung* (*Berlin Illustrated Newspaper*) and the *Municher Illustriertre Presse* (*Munich Illustrated Press*), gave his photo reporters freedom to photograph their subjects as they saw best.

In his magazines, he presented picture stories "in as natural, simple, and un-manipulated a form as possible." His ideas about candid shooting and his focus on ordinary people in their everyday lives remain remarkably current. Lorant believed "the photograph should not be posed; that the camera should be like a notebook of the trained reporter, which records contemporary events as they happen without trying to stop them to make a picture; that people should be photographed as they really are and not as they would like to appear; that photo-reportage should concern itself with men and women of every kind and not simply with a small social clique; that everyday life should be portrayed in a realistic unself-conscious way."[1]

Instead of following the newspaper practice of publishing a single photograph that summarized an event, Lorant and his colleagues produced a sequence of pictures that told a story. These multipicture layouts typically clustered several small photographs around a dominant one on a two-page spread. They narrated events, explained complex situations, and expressed points of view. The picture-story format developed at the same time European directors were experimenting with cinema. In film, the term *montage* referred to cutting together sequences of wide, medium, and close-up shots. Magazine photojournalists adopted a similar approach to shooting and presentation.

Lorant's call to report on "men and women of every kind" acknowledged the magazines' practice of finding story subjects among their readers. This was part of a much larger trend as the period between the wars saw the rise of the common person. The centuries-long domination of the great man and great event was finally supplanted by the ordinary person's daily life. The shift was apparent across a wide spectrum. In architecture and product design, the Bauhaus attempted to reintegrate art with daily life. In cinema, Charlie Chaplin personified the "little man" in such films as *The Kid* and *Modern Times.* In sports, participation activities such as camping, skiing, hiking, and the physical culture movement attracted hundreds of thousands of enthusiasts. In literature, the hero was replaced by nonheroes, such as Leopold Bloom in James Joyce's *Ulysses* and Hans Castorp in Thomas Mann's *The Magic Mountain,* and by antiheroes such as Bardamu in Louis-Ferdinand Celine's *Journey to the End of the Night.* In politics, the shift manifested itself in the global rise of socialism and Communism. The title of a novel by André Malraux, *The Human Condition,* which celebrated a youth's political awakening, symbolized this sweeping social change among leftists during the 1930s.

Journalism contributed to the trend. During the 1920s, the German mass-circulation picture magazine was founded on the premise of portraying common people to themselves. "Photo reportage took its cues not from art or literature, but from the many and varied aspects of the *condition humaine* itself," wrote Tim Gidal, who photographed for the Berlin magazines. "The emphasis was placed almost exclusively on the human element. The new photojournalism became a medium of human communication directed primarily toward the individual in the mass."[2] The German approach spread to France, where Lucien Vogel launched *Vu* magazine in 1928. Vogel said *Vu* was determined to transmit "the vital rhythms of everyday life: political events, scientific discoveries, disasters, exploration, sports, theater, film, art, and fashion."[3] *Vu* and its competitors emphasized the *quotidian,* or everyday life, of ordinary people. "The press's creation of stars and heroes descends lower and lower into the social strata, even down to the murder of the week," explained Thomas Michael Gunther, a historian of French photography between the wars. "Instead of pieces on the actors and actresses, there are now pieces on the hair dressers, set designers, costume fitters."[4]

America came late to magazine photojournalism, translating European practices into its own flavor. After Hitler's National Socialist Party took power in Germany in March 1933, many Jewish editors and photojournalists fled to France, London, and New York. Among them, Kurt Korff, former editorial director of the Ullstein magazines in Berlin, was hired to help develop *Life* magazine. Also important to the new American magazines were the photo agencies that migrated from Germany and France to the United States. The best known is Black Star, founded in 1935 by Ernest Mayer and two partners. When Mayer escaped to New York, he slipped five thousand photographs out of Germany. In addition to selling from this stock to *Life* and other magazines, Black Star soon became an important broker between freelance photographers and magazine editors.

Chief among the technological developments in European magazine photojournalism was the Leica—its name was an acronym of *Leitz* and *camera*—which became the first practical 35 mm camera. Oskar Barnack built the first prototypes at the Leitz Optische Werke in 1913. He used standard cinema film but turned the image 90 degrees from its orientation in movie cameras, which enlarged its size. Barnack's motto, "Small negatives—large images," revolutionized photography. World War I interrupted development of the Leica, but it resumed in 1923. Introduced in 1925 in Leipzig, Germany, it became an immediate success.

The Leica was a radical departure from the view, press, and amateur cameras of the period. Small, candid cameras dated from the 1880s, but they were novelties. George Eastman introduced the handheld Kodak in 1888, but it was marketed to amateurs and was disdained by photographers with artistic aspirations. With a few exceptions, most art, studio, and press photographers in America rejected handheld cameras, because of the perceived inferior quality of their small negatives.

Several innovations made the Leica ideal for magazine photojournalism. Its small size, light weight, and quiet operation made it inconspicuous. This was a significant advantage for photographers who wanted to work surreptitiously. Its film cassette of thirty-six exposures permitted them to concentrate on moving subjects without having to reload after each picture. It also allowed for faster lenses with larger apertures, which let them photograph in low light without flash. The most important innovation was the Leica's viewfinder, which allowed the camera to be held to the eye instead of at waist level or on a tripod. With a Leica at their eye, photojournalists could easily track and capture moving subjects. People appeared natural because the shutter was clicked before they realized they were being photographed. Capturing spontaneity and naturalism was finally possible.

Magazine photojournalism began in America with the introduction of *Life* in November 1936, *Look* in 1937, and numerous imitators in the following months. *Life* was the dominant visual medium of the 1940s, and its coverage of World War II, the cold war, Korea, and Vietnam provides additional examples of the compulsion to witness history by individual photographers and by institutions such as *Life* itself. The magazines also advanced printing technology, bringing coated paper and color to photojournalism. Television eventually siphoned off advertising revenues, supplanting mass-circulation magazines as the dominant visual medium. In the early 1970s, both *Life* and *Look* ceased publication. While the traditional picture story continued to be practiced at *National Geographic,* long-form photojournalism has found little space in the niche magazines that proliferated from the 1970s to the present.

The idea of launching a picture magazine in the United States was in the air during the mid-1930s. Most people in the magazine industry knew the success of the German magazines and *Vu*. Several Americans entertained the idea, but Henry R. Luce was the first to implement it. In March 1923, he and Yale classmate Briton Hadden started *Time* magazine, the nation's first newsweekly. Its small staff did no original reporting but digested stories from major newspapers and the wire agencies, rewriting them in an idiosyncratic style of double epithets and reversed syntax. It enjoyed rapid success in circulation and profits with Hadden presiding over the editorial operation and Luce running the business. After Hadden's untimely death in 1929, both parts of the enterprise fell to Luce, who expanded the magazine into a media empire. He launched *Fortune* in 1930 and bought *Architectural Forum* in 1932. *Time* began presenting some of its stories on radio as a promotion for the magazine, and in 1931, Luce expanded these spots into a radio news program called *The March of Time*. Four years later, he added moving pictures, producing *March of Time* newsreels for movie theaters. Luce had the financial resources, business experience, and staff to develop a picture magazine. He also had a respect for photography's ability to communicate. When he interviewed Margaret Bourke-White for a job at *Fortune,* he told her, "The camera should explore every corner of industry . . . from the steam shovel to the board of directors."[5]

Still, *Life* might not have happened without the prodding of two people: Daniel Longwell, an editor at *Time,* and Luce's second wife, Clare Boothe Brokaw Luce. As the divorced wife of a wealthy New York clothing-store heir, Brokaw worked as an editor at *Vanity Fair* and wrote Broadway plays. In 1932, she sent a memo to *Vanity Fair's* owner, Condé Nast, proposing a picture magazine. "I should like to pattern an American magazine—and one bearing the title *Life* is admirably adapted to its contents— after the Parisian *Vu*," she wrote. The magazine would have "its own special angle, which would be reporting, not *all* the news nor, necessarily the most *important* news, but the most interesting and exciting news, in photographs." She envisioned a magazine with broad appeal, interesting to the author "Theodore Dreiser as much as the reader of the *Daily Mirror.*"[6] Luce divorced his first wife and, after a brief courtship, married Clare Boothe Brokaw in November 1935.

Longwell, who was generally seen as an idea man, had been pushing Luce to launch a picture magazine for some time. In one memo, he wrote, "Journalism itself has gone pictorial" since the birth of *Time* magazine. Intending to prod his boss, he said the *Time* staff could "stay as we are and have a comfortable old age ahead," taking afternoon tea and discussing "what our *confreres* on *Atlantic* and *Harper's* are doing, etc. etc." "But," he added, "the quick nervousness of pictures is a new language as sure as Rudyard Kipling or Ernest Hemingway were. Or *Time* itself."[7] Longwell accompanied his memo with a sixteen-page dummy of what such a picture magazine might look like. He sent it to the Luces while they were honeymooning in Cuba. "I don't really want more magazines," Luce reportedly told his bride, "but if it pleases you, we'll go ahead."[8]

Any reticence was gone by the time he returned to New York and announced, "I'm pregnant"—with ideas for the new venture.[9] He set up a planning team called the Experimental Department, which began to explore picture sources, contract with freelance photographers, gather sample picture stories, and produce dummy issues. To attract advertisers, a prospectus was written explaining the magazine's purpose, content, and advertising rates. It noted the magazine would average about two hundred photographs per week. Luce made a partial draft of the prospectus, then asked Archibald MacLeish, a writer for *Fortune* who later served as Librarian of Congress and won three Pulitzer Prizes for his poetry, to refine it. A portion of the prospectus appeared in the magazine's first issue and has become a credo for many photojournalists:

> To see life; to see the world; to eyewitness great events; to watch the faces of the poor and the gestures of the proud; to see strange things—machines, armies, multitudes, shadows in the jungle and on the moon; to see man's work—his paintings, towers, and discoveries; to see things thousands of miles away, things hidden behind walls and within rooms, things dangerous to come to; the women that men love and many children; to see and to take pleasure in seeing; to see and be amazed; to see and be instructed. Thus to see, and be shown, is now the will and new expectancy of half mankind. To see, and show, is the mission now undertaken by a new kind of publication.[10]

Several possible names were considered. The decision had been made to charge ten cents for the magazine at newsstands, and for a while memos referred to it as *Dime. Look* was also considered, as were *Album, Eye, Candid, Flash, Go, News Focus, Nuze-Vuze, Picture, Scan, Promenade, Quest, Snap, Vista, Witness, World, Spectator, See,* and *Wide Awake!*[11] In the end, Clare Luce's original proposal won. A humor magazine that originated in the 1880s already published under the name *Life.* Luce bought it for ninety-two thousand dollars, kept its name, and sold off its circulation. The title brilliantly symbolized the new magazine's contents and aspirations, but it also allowed Luce and his editors to equate their magazine with the pulse of its readers and their world.

Undeterred by the Great Depression, Luce and his team launched *Life* on November 23, 1936. Its masthead listed four photographers, Bourke-White, from *Fortune;* Alfred Eisenstaedt, who had built a strong reputation working for the German magazines; Thomas McAvoy, a *Time* photographer comfortable with the Leica; and Peter Stackpole, the youngest of the group, who had been freelancing for Luce publications for only a few years.

Bourke-White produced the first cover story, although nobody knew it would lead the issue when she drew the assignment to photograph the construction of a dam at Fort Peck, Montana. "We lack a good opening story—a smash!" managing editor John Billings wrote in his diary as the deadline approached. "And then Bourke-White's pictures on Whoopee at Fort Peck came in, as if in answer to our prayer."[12] Luce himself selected the photos and did a rough layout of the story. "If any Charter Subscriber is surprised by what turned out to be the first story in this first issue of *Life,* he is not nearly so surprised as the Editors were," an introductory note stated. "What the Editors expected—for use in some later issue—were construction pictures as only Bourke-White can take them. What the Editors got was a human document of American frontier life which, to them at least, was a revelation."[13] Bourke-White worked in two different approaches. Her cover shot showed the spillway of the dam as a pristine monolith, towering over two workers at its base (see figure 17). This photograph and a few inside reflected her specialization as *Fortune*'s foremost industrial photographer, who composed steel and concrete into patterns that symbolized America's economic might. Of the seventeen pictures, spread across nine pages, one shows huge cylinders of steel with workers clinging to their interior spokes. Another is an aerial view of Wheeler, Montana, one of six boomtowns that had sprung up around the dam project. The rest show people. Eight focus on the steamy side of life on this desolate frontier. They show workers drinking or dancing in the bars that had grown up to entertain them. Billings's "whoopee" comment referred to the story's headline, "10,000 Montana Relief Workers Make Whoopee on Saturday Night." The story examined the lives of people who had lost their jobs to the Depression and found a new start in this New Deal project. The text, written by MacLeish, pointed out that the $110 million dam project in northeastern Montana was providing jobs "to as many as 10,000 veterans, parched farmers, and plain unemployed parents." It emphasized the high incidence of bars and prostitution in the surrounding towns and concluded "Bourke-White's pictures enable you to observe at close range the labor and diversions of their inhabitants."[14]

Such attention to people was a shift for Bourke-White. Typically she included people in her *Fortune* photographs to show the scale of machines or buildings. Her large cameras precluded spontaneity. In most of her Fort Peck photographs, the people are clearly posing for the camera, and her control can be seen in the flash that illumines the indoor pictures. Even so, enough of the people strike candid poses that her story conveyed a sense of naturalism.

Loudon Wainwright, a senior editor who chronicled the magazine, believed this piece set the standard for *Life* picture stories for the next thirty-six years. Referring to the "rawboned" quality of its ordinary people, he wrote, "Whatever its preoccupations with royalty and politics and the high and low jinks of the famous, whatever its contributions in the understanding of art and science and the past, *Life*'s greatest resource for its picture stories would always be the lives of ordinary people, their work, their pleasure, their follies, their anguish. Such stories touched virtually every reader." They allowed *Life*'s readers to see themselves in its pages.

Echoing Gidal, Wainwright wrote, "This technique of holding up mirrors to its readers would quite transform the status of photojournalism" and become the essential factor in its success with readers.[15] While the Europeans invented magazine photojournalism, insiders claimed *Life* elevated the picture-story format to its classic level. Among other differences, the European magazines published a relatively small number of pictures typically confined to one spread. "Luce and the others did not realize it at the time," Maitland Edey, a *Life* editor, wrote of the Fort Peck story, "but they had just created the first true photographic essay ever made: a collection of pictures on a single theme, arranged to convey a mood, deliver information, tell a story, in a way that one picture alone cannot."[16]

Many photojournalists remember such classic picture stories, while forgetting *Life*'s other contents. The first issue forecasted a broad mix. A photograph of the birth of a baby boy filled the first full page of editorial content. Under the headline "Life Begins," a blurb stated, "The camera records the most vital moment in any life: It's beginning."[17] It was the kind of visual shock *Life* delivered repeatedly over the years. A metaphor for the magazine's own birth, it was also a declaration that *Life* would not shrink from publishing images that squeamish readers might find objectionable. The editors had taken Korff's advice that "it doesn't matter whether a certain group of readers is offended. To assail in an honest manner is always better than to bore."[18]

The ninety-six pages included many news photographs, an aerial view of the depository at Fort Knox, which would soon receive the nation's gold reserves, and a feature on how ordinary Russians relaxed. Three stories inaugurated what would be *Life*'s abiding promotion of culture: they profiled the Kansas painter John Stuart Curry, the Hollywood actor Robert Taylor, and Helen

Hayes, who was starring as Queen Victoria in a lavish Broadway production. The science department contributed stories on how the airlines were developing a pressurized plane that could fly above thirty-five thousand feet and a pictorial sequence of a black widow spider mating with and then devouring her unfortunate consort. The issue ended with "*Life* Goes to a Party," recording a hunting party for European royalty, hosted by a French noble. As the magazine matured, the editorial mix included heavy coverage of war, the space program, and modern living. There were also long text pieces by important writers such as Ernest Heming-way and political figures such as Winston Churchill and Harry S. Truman.

Luce's conservative political views permeated the first issue. Gushing with patriotism, the introductory note explained that so many of the stories were about Americans because they were at the top of their fields: "The Editors are particularly pleased that Art is represented not by some artfully promoted Frenchman but by an American [Curry] and that the Theatre is here in the person of an American lady who is being called the world's greatest actress [Hayes]."[19] Racism marred a story on Brazil. Calling the country "a colossal human failure," *Life* blamed its problems on miscegena-tion: "Brazilians are a charming people but are incurably lazy. The original Portuguese conquistadores ... married Indian aborigines, and their descendents added the blood of Negro slaves to the strain. The mixture did not work."[20] A story in the second issue applauded Argentine president Augustin Justo for seizing power in a coup, because he overthrew the democratically elected presi-dent who was a socialist. "Argentina's ruling class ... stand behind proud, big-fisted President Justo, head of the equivalent of the Republican Party," the story read. "He first got his job by an Army coup d'etat in 1930 that booted out the Argentine equivalent of

Franklin D. Roosevelt, the late New-Dealing President Irigoyen." The story also commended Argentine volunteers who were fighting in Spain "for the God-fearing Fascist Rebel side."[21]

In the concluding paragraph of their introductory note, the editors predicted a period of growing pains: "The first issue of a magazine is not the magazine," they pointed out. "It is the beginning. The Editors anticipate a strenuous and exciting year of growth and adventure."[22] There was a raw quality about volume 1, issue number 1, of *Life*. Notwithstanding the advice from Korff, the precedents of the European magazines, and the trial dummies, *Life* was an experiment in progress for the first several issues. On the content side, Billings lamented the lack of good pictures in his magazine: "Where are all the good pictures that are supposed to flow through this office?" he wrote. "We are always short on good pictures."[23] In March 1937, Luce took the occasion of the magazine's twelfth issue to assess *Life* against its stated purpose. In a long memo, he lamented the lack of truly informative science pieces and warned against gruesome photos and too many stories with an underlying sexual theme. He commented on the problems of finding a major news story every week that lent itself to pictorial treatment. In discussing the magazine's weekly feature piece, he reaffirmed his belief in photographic reporting. "The Feature," he wrote, is "a cinch—there's nothing to it—nothing except a crack photographer." Explaining that the managing editor didn't have to worry about it in advance, Luce continued, "Here's where you get that 'pure pictorial journalism' that the picture-fanatics love. . . . You can pick practically any damn human or sub-human institution or phenomenon under the sun, turn a crack photographer on it (after a little lecture by a journalist), and publish with pleasure in eight pages the resultant *photographic essay*. Fifty or twenty years ago, people used to write 'essays' for magazines. Essays for example on the bee. The essay is no longer a vital means of communication. But what is vital is *the photographic essay.*"[24]

Readers didn't notice the problems Luce enumerated or didn't care. From the beginning, *Life* was wildly successful on the newsstands. With no way to predict public interest, planners ordered an initial press run of two hundred thousand copies. It sold out a few hours after hitting the newsstands. Because of problems obtaining enough coated paper stock and assembling the stitched copies, the printers were able to add only another fifty thousand copies, but within three months they were printing a million copies, and by the end of the first year, a million and a half.[25] The newsstand success was offset by a greater advertising loss. Rates based on the two hundred thousand guaranteed circulation were locked in for a year. When *Life* could finally increase advertising rates, the cost for a full-page black-and-white advertisement quadrupled to $5,700. Adjusted for inflation, that would equal $85,341 in 2008 dollars.[26] *Life*'s circulation continued upward. During World War II, it grew to over 4 million. By 1956, it was 5.8 million, and in 1969, it peaked at 8.5 million.

Photographers were the celebrities at *Life*. In contrast to the press photographer, the new breed of magazine photographer was better dressed and better educated. Wainwright parodied the popular stereotype of the *Life* photographer:

> Miniature camera draped discreetly around his neck . . . a Gitane—its ash just at the breaking point—sending a plume of smoke past a cool, unblinking eye, trench coat slung carelessly over one shoulder, he looked in his Italian shoes and his calming suit from Cork Street like the kind of fellow who would be presentable—even desirable—in any situation. Definitely a romantic type, he starred in movies and plays (*Rear Window, The Philadelphia Story*), doubled

as a detective in mystery novels and was usually a wry, funny, sexy sort (brave, too, terribly brave, of course) who had been everywhere where he had done everything. . . . The *Life* photographer never pushed his subjects around, he just whipped out that little camera and took marvelous pictures before anyone knew what was happening. And when he left the scene, he usually took the best-looking woman in the place with him.[27]

Within photojournalism, a job at *Life* became highly coveted. *Life* paid better, gave credit lines, offered travel, used multiple images, and guaranteed a huge national audience. Its staffers were at the top of photojournalism's pecking order.

Notwithstanding this glamorous image, *Life* was produced by teams, and no matter how great their pictures, the photographers' role was narrowly circumscribed. The process could take as many as eight people to shepherd a story from conception to publication. To generate a large, steady flow of content, *Life* was organized into departments, such as science, religion, modern living, culture, and so on. Story ideas were generated by department heads based on their sense of what was important in their fields that would also make good pictures. Researchers fleshed out the idea with facts and found subjects willing to be photographed.

With the researcher's information, the department editor wrote a script that gave the photographer the story concept, a list of important people and situations to photograph, and a prediction of how much space the story might receive. Story scripts went to the picture editor, who managed both the staff and freelance photographers. He decided whether or not to assign a story and which photographer would get it. He also was the lifeline to photographers in the field, helping them deal with problems and keeping them aware of editorial thinking about their assignments.

Photographers were not expected to slavishly follow the script item by item but to bring their own talent and vision to the story. Everyone understood they would have to adapt to realities that often differed from the scripts.

With rare exceptions, *Life* photographers did not edit their contact sheets or print their negatives. Selection fell to the negative editor, who chose which frames would be enlarged from contact sheets, transparencies, or in a rush, from negatives. For most of *Life*'s thirty-six years, Peggy Sargent, formerly an assistant to Bourke-White, filled this role. She was a friend of the photographers, and many of them liked to hang out in her office. "For one and all," wrote Edey, "she performed the priceless service of making them look better than they were" by never allowing their bad frames to be printed or seen.[28]

Life operated on the strong-editor principle, with ultimate power residing in the managing editor, who was handpicked by Luce, answered directly to him, and except for his directives, had total control over the staff and the magazine's contents. They chose what stories would run, determined how much space to give each one, selected the images from the enlargements, and often laid out the stories. Instead of focus groups, marketing analysis, or committee decisions, *Life*'s six managing editors determined the magazine's contents and style based on their personal preferences as well as their professional experience.

This caused the magazine to shift emphasis and appearance over the years. The style of John Billings, the first managing editor, was described as rough, straightforward, but vital. Ed Thompson, whom many insiders considered *Life*'s greatest managing editor, loved breaking news and delighted in taking a crew to Chicago, where the magazine was printed, to tear up the opening section and replace it with a last-minute story. George Hunt increased color usage and emphasized long investigative-reporting articles.

Thompson also made the art director a key figure in the editorial process. Previously the art department staff was relegated to making the managing editor's ideas work, but Thompson gave design authority to Charlie Tudor during the 1950s and 1960s. Hunt replaced him with Bernie Quint. A perfectionist, Quint arranged photographs based on formal considerations as much as content. "Each picture has a design within itself. It has a pattern," he told an interviewer. "It has shapes and forms and gray values and color values, and if no attention were paid to the particular relationship of these values to the values of the type, as well as the relationship of one picture to another . . . you would end up with a hodgepodge."[29] Where word-oriented editors privileged point pictures, whose information advanced the story line, Quint gave prominence to the photographs' formal qualities and to the photographers' vision. For Edey, this "emergence of a true partnership among editor, photographer, and designer" marked the highest point in the evolution of the picture essay at *Life*.[30]

The final member of the team was the writer. Typically the writers were department heads, specialists in a topic, or reporters who accompanied photographers in the field. Their job was to captivate and amuse the reader, convey the story concept, and provide the verbal context necessary to understand the photographs, all in a short, brightly written blurb plus captions and headlines. Their work was almost always anonymous and always subject to being rewritten.

Although the public never saw it, there was resentment, even animosity, between the writers and photographers. "Many staff members didn't really like the photographers at all," Wainwright wrote, "and the photographers didn't like them, either."[31] Part of these feelings stemmed from the jealousy of editors and writers who resented all the glory going to photographers. Some reporters resented photographers who used "them like 'donkeys,' and 'caddies,' loading them up with heavy equipment, requiring them to make plane, hotel and restaurant reservations and treating them like lackeys."[32] Compounding such resentments were the old prejudices verbal journalists traditionally held against photographers. "Editors, writers and reporters often looked down on photographers, thinking of them as marginally talented, babyish, unreliable, opportunistic, self-important, boring and even stupid," Wainwright wrote. "For their part, photographers often considered the others … incapable of knowing the difference between a really good picture and some hokey setup shot banged off by the clowns at the wire services."[33] As a result of this tension, photographers had no voice in conceiving stories or in selecting and presenting their images.

Pettiness aside, *Life*'s staff was filled with exceptionally talented photographers. Some were generalists, but many excelled in specializations: Gjon Mili was a native of Albania whose engineering studies predisposed him toward the technical. He learned stroboscopic photography, a flash technology that made exposures in the range of 1/200,000 of a second. Its inventor, Dr. Harold Edgerton, of the Massachusetts Institute of Technology, used it to freeze bullets and drops of milk in midair. Mili applied it to dancers, athletes, and musicians so a succession of their movements overlapped to reveal motion through time and space.

As a U.S. Marine Corps combat photographer during World War II, David Douglas Duncan produced images that landed him a job with *Life* after the war. He covered the Korean and Vietnam wars and several smaller conflicts. His second specialty was the Spanish artist Pablo Picasso.

Philippe Halsman took portraits of the famous, with a twist. He asked them to jump and photographed them in midair. One such photograph of Marilyn Monroe appeared on *Life*'s November 9, 1959, cover, promoting "a jumping picture gallery" of Halsman's pictures inside.

Gordon Parks was an exceptional fashion photographer, but as *Life*'s only African American photographer, he is remembered for his stories on the Black Panthers and the Nation of Islam during the 1960s.

Among the generalists, Alfred Eisenstaedt gained fame for his single images. His most famous photograph, which shows a sailor kissing a nurse in New York City's Times Square on Victory over Japan Day, achieved iconic status as a symbol of the end of World War II.

As important as such specialists and generalists were to the magazine, the list of photographers who excelled at the picture story is relatively short. Some were freelancers, such as Berenice Abbott, Dorothea Lange, and Henri Cartier-Bresson. Among staffers, three stand out for their mastery of the form: W. Eugene Smith, Leonard McCombe, and Larry Burrows.

"Gene" Smith is probably the best known—a legend to many photojournalists because of his passionate dedication to truth in photography and his fierce refusal to compromise. He first gained attention for his dramatic World War II images showing the effects of the Pacific campaign on American soldiers and island natives. The war elicited his high standards and exposed his agonizing self-doubts. "In a few hours I shove off on something very tough—an effort to photograph 24 hours in the life of a soldier under fire," he wrote in a letter from Okinawa. "I am afraid that I cannot say what really must be said. . . . I cannot bear to fail. It would be much better to die tomorrow night than to live and fail these kids and in the battle for peace."[34]

Two days later, on May 22, 1945, Smith photographed an exploding mortar shell an instant before its shrapnel tore away much of his face and mangled his left hand. Before he passed out, he requested a pencil and paper and wrote out instructions about where to send his film.

Smith was one of five *Life* photographers wounded in action; another two were on ships hit by torpedoes, and one was taken prisoner of war. In January 1942, the Still Photographic War Pool was established with four members. The three major news organizations—the AP, Acme Newspictures, and International News Photos—could spread their costs, about four hundred thousand dollars per year, to members and clients. The fourth member was *Life*. AP photographer Joe Rosenthal's photograph of the raising of the American flag atop Mount Suribachi on Iwo Jima was the most memorable image of the war, and military photographers, including Steichen and his handpicked navy crew, made exceptional images. Overall, however, *Life* was the undisputed leader of American photojournalism's coverage of the war. With twenty-one photographers in the field, it exceeded the other pool members in numbers. But the extensive editorial space it devoted to the war, its picture-story approach, its national audience, and the caliber of its photographers, who included Robert Capa, Margaret Bourke-White, David Douglas Duncan, George Rodger, and Smith, all enhanced its dominance. All pool photographs were available to all American newspapers, but because *Life* was a weekly, photographs taken by its staffers that were not spot news were embargoed for release at the magazine's next publication.

Where World War I was concentrated along a single front in western Europe, World War II extended across "five continents, seven seas, and a dozen different fronts," making logistics a huge challenge.[35] Especially in the Pacific theater, finding a ride to the action and getting film back to the rear to be processed and then shipped to the States required great creativity. Many excellent pictures were never published because their events became outdated. For the first time, it was possible to transmit photographs by radio, but the quality was often poor, and the transmission points, controlled by the Army Signal Corps, were often filled with military traffic.

Censorship remained an issue. Film went from the front lines to theater headquarters, where it was processed and reviewed by military censors, who blocked anything that might give information to the enemy. Photographs that passed underwent a second round of scrutiny in Washington. The operating principle was President Roosevelt's dictum "the propaganda of truth," which expected the press to support America's war effort. As in World War I, military policy prohibited showing dead GIs. As the fighting ground on, Roosevelt and the War Department decided that showing the ultimate sacrifice soldiers were making would increase Americans' support for the war effort. In September 1943, censors reversed policy and released the first three photographs of wounded and dead GIs. One, taken by *Life* photographer George Strock, showed three dead soldiers sprawled in the sand on a beach in New Guinea. *Life* published it at full-page size. A text justified showing the dead Americans because "words are never enough." If the soldiers "had the guts to take it, then we ought to have the guts to look at it," it added.[36] Among the multitude of letters to *Life*'s editors were many from soldiers who praised running Strock's photograph, because they wanted civilians to understand what they were experiencing and they believed such images gave meaning to their sacrifices.

After extensive surgery and a long recuperation, Smith returned to *Life*. Over the next decade, he produced four classics in the history of the picture story: "Country Doctor," which told the story of Dr. Ernest Ceriani, the sole physician for the small Rocky Mountain town of Kremmling, Colorado, was published in 1948. "Spanish Village," shot in Deleitosa, Spain, in 1950, related the great themes of human existence in a remote village, set against the fascist regime of the dictator Franco. The following year, Smith photographed Maude Callen, an African American "Nurse Midwife," who assisted at the births of most of the black infants in the Pineville, South Carolina, area. His story noted how she wished for a modern clinic to better serve the residents in her county. *Life* readers contributed over twenty-eight thousand dollars, which was used to build and stock a cinder-block clinic in Pineville. Smith's last story for *Life* as a staff member portrayed Dr. Albert Schweitzer, who had recently received the Nobel Peace Prize for his writings and lectures on peace and for his treatment of leprosy patients at his Lambaréné hospital in Gabon, Africa. Titled "A Man of Mercy," it was published in 1954. Smith quit *Life* in a dispute about control of the story, including his printing and the amount of space it should be given.

Smith had several other major photographic campaigns, including a 1955 documentary project on Pittsburgh and patients in a schizophrenia ward in Haiti in 1958. His most famous project, photographed in 1971 and published in 1972, related the plight of Minamata, a Japanese fishing village. For years, Chisso, a chemical firm, had dumped mercury waste into Minamata Bay, which provided the villagers' major source of food. The mercury-contaminated fish caused neurological degeneration and horrific birth defects.[37]

Although some later stories were better printed and designed, "Country Doctor," published September 20, 1948, had the most influence on the development of the picture story. With a Shakespearean range, Smith portrays Ceriani, the only doctor serving some two thousand people in the town of Kremmling and its surrounding ranches. In Smith's somber photographs, Ceriani single-handedly combats accident, illness, and death. "For Smith life has always been tragic, full of injustice and hardship, but something which, if it is borne courageously and with dignity, brings out the nobility in man," Edey writes. "His Dr. Ceriani is such a man, dedicated, overworked, moving as best he can from one medical crisis to another—obscure, underpaid, aware of his own fallibility, but essentially noble. . . . All this shows in Ceriani's face, which is a marvelous reflector of his tensions, his relief, his fatigue."[38]

The story opens on a right-hand page with a single photo introducing the doctor (see figure 18). Preoccupied, weighted down by his heavy bag, he walks through a field of weeds past an unpainted fence. Ominous clouds in the background are balanced, however tentatively, by a few small flowers poking through the weeds. The first spread, titled "He must specialize in a dozen fields," shows the range of his daily challenges in nine pictures: he examines a four-year-old girl with tonsillitis, wraps the broken ribs of a rancher, stitches a boy's cut hand, and delivers a baby.

The second spread presents a story within the story. Three small photos show Ceriani taking a rare break from his duties to go trout fishing in the Colorado River. After half an hour, he is interrupted by the town marshal, who reports a child has been kicked in the head by a horse. The fourth photo shows the doctor treating the girl as her anxious parents watch. In the concluding picture, which fills the full right-hand page, he appears "worn out and tired" after stitching the child's forehead. His expression stems from concern about how to tell the girl's parents she will lose her left eye. In other short sequences, Ceriani sets a dislocated elbow, amputates a gangrenous leg, and attends the death of an eighty-two-year-old man.

The final spread lacks the coherence of the earlier ones. Its left page contains three photographs that normally would come near the beginning of a picture story to establish its setting. They show an aerial view of Kremmling, Ceriani's modest hospital, and the doctor with his wife and two children, watching a parade. The story ends with a full-page picture of Ceriani slumped on a counter, nursing a cup of coffee and the tail end of a cigarette. Dressed in a surgical gown after a crisis that ended at 2:00 A.M., he appears in deep introspection. Although *Life*'s caption did not disclose it, Ceriani had just conducted a cesarean section in which both the mother and baby died. While his expression may represent merely fatigue, it's possible to read in it the same frustration and self-doubt that Smith felt.

During the twenty-three days Smith spent shooting the story, he received repeated messages from *Life*'s picture editor Wilson Hicks, suggesting pictures to take and urging him to finish the story quickly. "They kept sending me messages, ordering me to return, or to go somewhere and do [another] story," Smith said later. "Finally, I kept sending back the same telegram, which was, 'Sorry, to leave now would jeopardize story.'"[39] Smith's insistence on adequate time stemmed from a previous story on a small-town doctor he photographed for *Parade* magazine in 1943. While some have seen this piece on Dr. Nathaniel P. Brooks of Croton-on-Hudson, New York, as a prototype for the Ceriani story, it seems more likely Smith considered it a failure he needed to rectify. A former newspaper reporter suggested the story to *Parade,* and most of the photographs were staged, with the reporter and his family acting roles.[40]

Rejecting such setups, Smith was determined to capture what really happened in the lives of Ceriani and his patients with a minimum of interference. In a new approach to magazine photojournalism, Smith wanted his pictures to emerge from carefully observing the subject while remaining unobtrusive. He rejected the old practice—implicit in the shooting script—of controlling the subjects in order to construct pictures based on editors' preconceived ideas.

"One of the first things Gene told me was, 'I want you to forget me,'" Ceriani recalled. "'Just don't pay any attention to me. I'll make the decisions whether something is worthwhile shooting.' . . . It didn't take very long for me to just totally ignore the guy, but the big problem was introducing him to the patients. . . . But finally Gene sort of became this community figure. He may not have known everybody, but everybody knew who he was. And you fell into this pattern: he was going to be around, and you just didn't let it bother you."[41] Some historians and *Life* insiders alike consider the "Country Doctor" to be the best picture story the magazine ever published.[42] Whatever its rank, it was a breakthrough in the genre. "'Country Doctor' was the harbinger of a new age in photojournalism," writes Smith's biographer Jim Hughes. "Gene had managed to produce, for a mass-circulation magazine, a true essay in a visual language that successfully combined the fictive power of the short story narrative with the verisimilitude of the camera as witness."[43] Edey cites it as an example of a great essay in which the photographer's personal involvement with the subject transcends both photographic technique and the magazine design process.[44]

A postmodern critique argues for a political reading of the "Country Doctor" by examining it against the political debate over medical policy in the late 1940s. Running for reelection in the fall of 1948, President Harry Truman campaigned on a promise of compulsory health-care insurance. Noting a shortage of doctors, he argued such a plan would encourage more young people to enter the field. The American Medical Association (AMA) labeled Truman's plan "socialized medicine." It insisted there was not a shortage of doctors but a problem in distributing them. It suggested small towns should raise money to buy modern equipment as incentives to attract doctors from large cities. When Barron Beshoar in *Life*'s Denver bureau looked for a subject for the story, he turned to Dr. Archer Sudan, former president of the Colorado State Medical Society. Sudan, who supported the AMA position, suggested Ceriani. Glenn Willumson, the photographic historian who pulled these threads together, said Smith probably did not realize how his story would figure in this debate. However, Willumson concluded, *Life* knowingly took an ideological position in selecting Ceriani and writing the text. "In essence, then, the *Life* magazine photo-essay became an extension of the medical association's public relations project," he wrote. "In recommending Kremmling and Dr. Ceriani, Dr. Sudan . . . was presenting a model of what the American Medical Association commission advocated: a community that had raised private monies to build a small hospital and hire nurses in an effort to attract a doctor." Instead of emphasizing training more physicians as *Collier's* and *Look* had done, "*Life* magazine endorsed the political position of the A.M.A.: that U.S. health care inadequacies were a matter of poor distribution rather than an inadequate supply of doctors."[45]

One point on which Smith would agree with postmodern theorists is the rejection of photography's objectivity. As a young photographer, he saw truth as requiring a purist approach. "My station in life is to capture the action of life.... A true picture, unposed and real," he wrote in 1936.[46] Like many of the FSA photographers, he stopped considering the photograph as an objective fact, embracing it instead as a vehicle for communicating his own subjective truth. His passion about the people he photographed and about photography's ability to make a difference in their lives led him to reject the straight photographers' dogma of never interfering with a subject or manipulating an image in the darkroom.

Although generally unobtrusive, he was not reluctant to control the situation when he felt it necessary. In the midwife story, for example, he moved the bed of a pregnant woman away from the wall so he could get a better angle of her giving birth. He inserted content into photographs, printing a handsaw from another negative into the foreground of a portrait of Schweitzer. And he effectively removed content by darkening the backgrounds of several of his prints. Discussing his picture of a Haitian schizophrenia patient, Smith justified lightening her eyes and burning out the background "as an effort to indicate the inner emotions that were going on at that time.... This is the way I feel it," he said, "and I think that this is perfectly legitimate in that photography has very little of reality in it.... I feel that everything that is honest to the situation is honest to the photograph."[47]

With many photojournalists, it is easy to separate the professional from the personal, but Smith's work intertwined with his turbulent life. Without applying the stereotype of the emotionally disturbed artist to Smith, it is important to note that he was addicted to alcohol and amphetamines. His family relationships were stormy, and his conflicts with magazine editors were legendary, causing him to lose work and often live in near poverty.

The dynamics of any personality are too complex to reduce to a few events and relationships, but his father's suicide when Smith was only seventeen had a major impact on his psychological development. Complicating the situation was his ambivalent relationship with his mother, Nettie Smith, a domineering woman who tried to live vicariously through her son. While Smith wrote long confessional letters to her, he also blamed her for his father's suicide. Explaining a portrait he made with her eyes in deep shadow, he told an associate, "I wanted to do a portrait of my mother to indicate that she doesn't see anything. She has no comprehension."[48]

Smith's altercations with editors stemmed in part from his high standards. "No man was ever more uncompromising on a creative point than Smith," said Hicks. "I have seen and heard him utterly crush editors with an almost demoniacal laugh."[49] Also crucial was his belief that his photographs could help their subjects. "I frequently have sought out those who were in the least position to speak for themselves," he said. "I can comment for them ... with a voice they do not possess."[50] When editors differed with Smith, he considered them obstacles to his mission to help the voiceless.

Seemingly, Smith was never satisfied with his work. Discussing the "Country Doctor" shortly after it was published, he told an interviewer, "I'm still searching desperately for the truth, for the answer to how to do a picture story.... I see deficiencies in ['Country Doctor'] myself, and the more compliments I receive, the more depressed I become."[51] More than two decades later in Minamata, he expressed the same self-doubts about his inability to capture the plight of Jitsuko-chan, a victim of fetal Minamata disease. Addressing a journal entry to her, he wrote, "To me, every photograph I have made of you is a failure."[52] On another occasion, he acknowledged, "For all my photographic life I have suffered these periods of extreme depression after not being able to reach the photographic heights I had tried for."[53]

Smith's subjectivity extended to personal involvement with his subjects and stories—often at inconvenience or danger to himself. In World War II, his desire to capture the intensity of combat caused him to stand up during battle, resulting in severe wounds. During the midwife story, he donated blood for a desperately ill infant. During the Minamata story, he and his wife, Aileen, who were nearly as impoverished as the villagers, lived among them and ate the same mercury-poisoned fish they did. In photographing a demonstration at a Chisso plant, he was attacked by company guards who smashed his head against a concrete wall. The resulting injuries caused intense headaches, the inability to bear the weight of his cameras around his neck, and loss of vision in his right eye. He could no longer photograph, but he continued making prints while Aileen took over photographing.[54]

Life published eleven of his Minamata photos on eight pages in its June 2, 1972, issue. In an editor's note, managing editor Ralph Graves commented on his commitment to his subjects: "The impact of Gene Smith's photography springs from his deep and usually agonized involvement with the life of human beings, their joys, and sufferings, their determination to prevail. This involvement runs like a thread through all his work."[55]

Minamata provided another occasion for Smith to defend subjectivity. He felt the Japanese press, which covered the victims' lawsuit with standard court reporting, was missing the true story by not focusing on the plight of the victims. He wrote in all capitals in one of his notebooks, "SUBJECTIVITY IS NOT A CRIME." In a letter to his daughter Juanita, he explained why he was making prints for an exhibition on Minamata so dark: "Facts just do not tell truth without poetry and drama."[56]

As published in magazines and books and shown in international exhibitions, Smith's Minamata story was a fitting culmination of a life spent using photography to help others. In a statement to accompany its publication in *Camera 35,* he expressed the hope of the social documentarian: "Daily, we are deluged with photography at its worst, until its drone of superficiality threatens to numb our sensitivity to all images," he wrote. "Then why photograph? Because sometimes ... photographs can lure our senses into greater awareness.... Someone—or perhaps many—among us may be influenced to heed reason and understanding until a way is found to right that which is wrong."[57]

No longer able to photograph, Smith began teaching at the Center for Creative Photography at the University of Arizona in Tucson. He died there in 1978, but his legacy continues in his images and in a fund created to support photographic projects. Since its inception in 1980, the W. Eugene Smith Grant in Humanistic Photography has annually awarded a stipend to support photographers working in the spirit of his "compassionate dedication." Recipients have included major figures in photojournalism—such as Sebastião Salgado, Gilles Peress, Donna Ferrato, Eli Reed, James Nachtwey, and Graciela Iturbide—often when they were near the beginning of their careers. In 2008, the stipend was thirty thousand dollars.

Though not as widely recognized as Smith, Leonard McCombe was another early master of the picture essay. An Englishman, he broke into *Life* in 1945 with a story on devastated German civilians and soldiers, who were struggling to return home and reunite with their families. Luce was reportedly so impressed with the pictures that he told his staff to hire the twenty-three-year-old McCombe immediately. His most important contribution to the picture-story genre was a concept that would become a common-place—an ordinary person who embodied an important trend. His best-known example conveys this idea in its title: "The Private Life of Gwyned Filling: The Hopes and Fears of Countless Young Career Girls Are Summed Up in Her Struggle to Succeed in New York."[58]

Like Smith, McCombe rejected shooting scripts and preconceived ideas in favor of candid photographs growing out of prolonged, close association with the subject. Departing from *Life*'s protocol, he located Gwyned Filling himself and worked without an assistant, compiling his own notes at the end of each day. His challenge was "to get her so used to his being around that she would ultimately begin acting naturally, so the real story could emerge." Complete investment of the photographer's time is crucial to such an approach. McCombe "arrived every morning at Gwyned's furnished room before she was up, then followed her through her day—in the street, in her office, with friends, on dates, at home with her roommate," Edey wrote. "He was on hand at three o'clock one morning when a lonely boyfriend called from San Francisco. . . . By that time Gwyned had become so accustomed to McCombe's presence that he was all but invisible."[59]

The intimacy McCombe achieved is remarkable. In twenty-four photographs over twelve pages, he shows her taking a morning bath, running for a bus, yawning during a meeting with her supervisor, working late at night on a project in her cramped bedroom, staunching a nosebleed, crying after an argument with a boyfriend, and being fitted for a dress. Where Smith recorded the life-and-death struggles of Dr. Ceriani, Maude Callen, and the residents of Minamata, McCombe captured small moments in the life of a young woman whose ordinariness was her reason for being photographed.

Furthermore, he did it with an anonymous style. Where dramatic composition and printing make Smith's photographs recognizable, McCombe effaced his own presence to enhance the realism of his images. His pictures are like windows into Filling's life, as if there were no camera or photographer mediating between the subject and the viewer. The effect is to allow the viewer to identify closely with the subject. As Edey wrote, "McCombe becomes one with his subject. The subject speaks directly to the reader. There is no one standing between."[60]

In contrast to the "Country Doctor" and Gwyned Filling stories, many of the stories produced by Larry Burrows show concentrated situations unfolding over a short time. Smith and McCombe produced mosaics, aggregations of images that *Life*'s designers synthesized into an overall impression. Burrows's story on a helicopter attack in Vietnam reads like a concise narrative.

As *Life*'s primary photographer of the Vietnam War from his arrival in 1962 until his death in February 1971, Burrows covered the daily impact of the war on American soldiers and South Vietnamese civilians alike. His single images of a bone-weary marine up to his chest in a swamp, a Vietcong suspect being beaten, a child being fitted for a prosthetic leg to replace the one she had lost to American bombs, and a Vietnamese woman consumed by grief as she slumps over a body bag all testify to the inhumanity of this conflict. He was equally adept at the picture story, producing eleven during his nine years in Vietnam. Working primarily in color, Burrows was an accomplished technician, but he also had the empathy that gave his photos emotional power.

He brought both dimensions together in his greatest story, "Yankee Papa 13," the designation of a Chinook helicopter. Photographed in 1965 as the buildup of American forces was accelerating, the story focuses on Lance Corporal James Farley, the marine helicopter's crew chief. Burrows had been photographing the unit for several days, establishing rapport with its men and officers. He got permission to ride on a mission ferrying South Vietnamese troops into battle. Working from inside the helicopter, Burrows would have been limited to photographing Farley from behind. For a better angle, he attached a remote-controlled camera to an external strut before the mission, aiming it back toward the door.

At the landing zone, a sister helicopter was disabled by enemy fire. As Farley ran to help rescue its crew, Burrows followed, photographing him. The pilot was already dead, but Farley helped the gunner and copilot back to his helicopter. Farley got the copilot, Lieutenant James Magel, onboard, but he was mortally wounded. "A glazed look came into his eyes, and he was dead," Burrows wrote. "Nobody spoke for a few seconds."[61] Burrows photographed Farley as he broke down crying on the helicopter and back at the base, his body racked in grief.

Like many photojournalists who witness death and emotional extremes, Burrows had doubts about the appropriateness of photographing them. "It's not easy to take a shot of a man crying, as though you have no thoughts, no feelings as to his sufferings," he wrote in *Life*. "It's not easy to photograph a pilot dying in a friend's arms and later to photograph the breakdown of a friend. I fought with my conscience. Was I simply capitalizing on someone else's grief? I concluded that what I was doing would penetrate the hearts of those at home who are simply too indifferent. I felt I was free to act on that condition."[62] Like many photographers on both sides, Burrows became a victim of the war. Covering the incursion into Laos in February 1971, he hitched a ride on a South Vietnamese helicopter that was shot down by antiaircraft fire, three months before his forty-fifth birthday.

• • •

Unknowingly, *Life*'s editors forecast its demise in its first issue. They devoted several pages to the National Broadcasting Company, which in 1936 was still a radio firm. Referring to one of NBC's affiliates, the Radio Corporation of America, the blurb writer stated, "At a special television demonstration on November 6, RCA President David Sarnoff, impressively televised, predicted that by 1946 the broadcasting of sight would be a commonplace."[63] World War II delayed Sarnoff's prediction, but by the end of the 1950s, most households in the United States owned one or more televisions. *Life* maintained its dominance through the 1950s. In 1956 its circulation was 5.8 million, with a readership estimated at 23 million. That year it earned $137 million in ad revenues; adjusted for inflation, that would equal about $1.07 billion in 2008 dollars.[64] During the 1960s, television became the dominant medium. As the public's habits changed, advertising dollars flowed from the picture magazines to television. Advertisers saw advantages in selling their products in a medium where images moved and had sound.

Niche magazines like *Fortune, Sports Illustrated, Playboy,* and women's and teen magazines retained their advertisers because they attracted readers who bought products related to their editorial contents. But *Life* was conceived and developed as a general interest magazine. "In addition to being a newsmagazine," one editor wrote, "*Life* is a combination of all general magazines, movie weeklies, the home publications, the scientific journals, *Harper's* and *The Atlantic,* fashion monthlies and the women's books."[65] By the 1960s, *Life* could no longer compete with television for ads across such a broad front.

Ad rates were based on circulation, and *Life* tried to remain competitive by increasing its guaranteed circulation numbers; this proved costly and, ultimately, ineffective. When the *Saturday Evening Post* died in 1969, *Life* bought its subscription list, increasing its guaranteed circulation to eight and a half million. With a pass-along factor of four, this meant as many as thirty-four million Americans saw the magazine every week.[66] As *Life* cut subscription rates and offered other inducements to keep its base, it became increasingly thinner because of a drop in ad pages. Near the end, it had only about eighty pages. Steep increases in the costs of paper and postage compounded its financial problems.[67] The situation became a downward spiral. *Life* published its last issue as a weekly at the end of 1972. The nation's premier picture magazine used only words on its last cover. A large sans serif title promoted "The Year in Pictures 1972." Its white letters stood in relief against a salad of red type of all faces and sizes, labeling the year's top stories: "Vietnam," "Olympics," "POW / MIA," "Godfather," "IRA," "Peace," "B-52," "Bugging," and so on. At the bottom right corner in capital letters was the word *goodbye.*

Wainwright and others see factors beyond advertising as the explanation for *the* demise. From its beginning, *Life* expressed a consensus of the American dream. Readers felt loyalty toward the magazine because "*Life* was playing back to these readers images of their country and of themselves that seemed authentic and reassuring," Wainwright maintained. "One could, figuratively speaking, find himself or herself in the magazine's pages, or recognize one's hopes or stoke one's indignation."[68] During the 1960s, the Vietnam War, the civil rights movement, political assassinations, student rebellions, and urban riots fractured any consensus of a shared American experience. While similar in scope and intensity, *Life*'s coverage of the Vietnam War did not bind its readers together as had its coverage of World War II and Korea. *Life*'s issue of June 27, 1969, which published headshots of most of the 242 GIs killed during one week's fighting, offers a good example. In addition to numerous cancellations of subscriptions, the piece prompted over thirteen hundred letters, revealing how polarized American opinion about the war was. Some called the article "ghoulish" or "cruel." Others thought it might have value in helping to end the war. "Somehow," Wainwright concluded, "the strong link that had formerly bound the magazine to its audience was gone.... Suddenly, it seemed, America had too many faces, and *Life* was having trouble keeping track of its own."[69]

Life went through several rebirths. Following its demise, it published numerous special reports and annual collections called *The Year in Pictures.* In 1978, the parent company Time, Inc., relaunched *Life* as a monthly magazine, with circulation of about 1.5 million. In 1991, it was back in its element, devoting four issues to the first Gulf War. It held on into the new century, closing for a second time in May 2000. In October 2004, it resurfaced as a weekly insert, distributed in about sixty newspapers. It could not compete with the established supplements *Parade* and *USA Weekend* and folded again in April 2007.

The postmodern critique begins with the charge that *Life* presented Luce's conservative politics as objective reality instead of a mediated point of view. Luce expected his writers and editors not just to report the news but to "make a judgment" on it.[70] In the prospectus for *Time,* Luce and Hadden compared their publication to the *Literary Digest,* which was as close as the United States had to a newsweekly at that time. "*The Digest,* in giving both sides of a question, gives little or no hint as to which side it considers to be right," they wrote. "*Time* gives both sides, but clearly indicates which side it believes to have the stronger position."[71] *Life*'s position was on the right. Critics document how Luce's conservative positions permeated his publications: from championing Republican politics and the Chinese leader Chiang Kai-shek to calling for U.S. entry into World War II. Many were especially critical of his call for American dominance after World War II. In his 1941 article "The American Century," Luce called for the United States to shoulder the burden of rebuilding Europe after the war but also to use its power to remold the world after American institutions.[72]

As the Soviet Union expanded its influence, Luce and his publications became staunch cold warriors in the battle against Communism. "I do not think there can be a peaceful co-existence between the Communist empire and the free world," he testified before a congressional committee.[73] Responding to critics from the political left and right, Luce said his perspective was no secret and implied readers should filter his publications' articles through that knowledge. He once commented that everyone should have "brains enough to know by now that I am a Presbyterian, a Republican and a capitalist, I am biased in favor of God, the Republican Party and free enterprise."[74]

For postmodernists, politics goes beyond partisanship to include the struggle for dominance among classes. From the Marxist perspective, Luce and his editors and business associates constituted an elite that attempted to maintain dominance by creating an ideology of a middle-class America that would disguise the disaffections and alienations of capitalism. *Life* "stood for certain things" as it joined in "the world-wide battle for men's minds," picture editor Hicks wrote.[75] American studies scholar Erika Doss responded, "The 'certain things' that *Life* 'stood for' were nationalism, capitalism, and classlessness, a sense of confidence, optimism, and exceptionalism, and the sure belief that the American way was the way of the world."[76]

In describing an exhibition of *Life* photographs, Robert R. Littman, director of the Grey Art Gallery at New York University, wrote, "*Life* had a decided editorial policy, perhaps unconscious, perhaps naive. It favored the inherent good in man; a positive future, apple pie . . . the forces of nature and the destiny of America."[77] While Littman intended his description to be positive, Doss reads *Life*'s editorial policy as an ideology intended to form the widest possible consensus through photography. "Pictures posited the seamless and integrated, independent and yet united American middle class that Luce and *Life*'s editors imagined," she writes, "solving the problems of inequity, poverty, racism, and alienation by simply imaging a better country and a better world." In doing this, *Life* failed to account for "the complex historical tensions of race, gender, and class in America" and "the nation's abiding patterns of systemic or institutional racism and class preference." The social cohesion that *Life*'s editors sought "was perhaps unattainable—because flux and uncertainty, rather than stability and resolution, were the key components in . . . modern America," she concluded.[78]

Postmodernists read *Life* from a meta perspective. Instead of focusing on individual photographers and the development of the picture story, they search between the lines and across the issues for institutional biases. In *Looking at "Life,"* a collection of essays edited by Doss, the authors examine the power politics at work in covering minorities, women, and homosexuals. Elite white editors shaped the representation of women and African Americans for predominantly white, middle-class readers. Although there was some gender and racial diversity on *Life*'s photographic staff, the editorial process neutralized differences in points of view. In a chapter analyzing *Life*'s five-part series on segregation, for example, Wendy Kozol points out how it framed the problem in moral, instead of political, terms. Published in 1956, two years after the Supreme Court overturned segregation in public education, the series made no mention of political activism within the African American community. Instead, it staged a debate between black ministers over whether the church was morally obligated to improve race relations. This transformed civil rights into a moral question, made blacks the problem, and shut off discussion of the social and political dimensions, Kozol wrote. The series illustrated "how the camera visualizes the problem" of race relations, "who the viewer gazes at," and the effects of those gazes on "the politics of representation," she added.[79]

In a variation on Wainwright's explanation of *Life*'s demise, Doss said it succumbed to "its own internal contradictions." "*Life* was always, of course, an elaborate fantasy: there never was an ideal American middle class, despite *Life*'s convincing visualization," she wrote. "But by staying committed to that imaginary vision, *Life* was stymied from committing to anything else or recognizing that the nation, as ever, had abandoned that particular picture and was now engaged in new images of national identity and purpose."[80]

At other magazines, editors commissioned photographers precisely because of their independence. In the spirit of New Journalism, which valued the personal voices of writers such as Tom Wolfe, Gay Talese, and Norman Mailer, they looked for photographers with idiosyncratic visions. Harold Hayes, the editor of *Esquire,* hired Diane Arbus to photograph a series of portraits of New Yorkers. "Her highly personal style matched the magazine's sophisticated sensibility—confident, critical, and offbeat," wrote curator Mary Panzer.[81] *Time* assigned Richard Avedon to apply his distinctive style of portraiture to the American diplomats and generals overseeing the Vietnam War, and *Rolling Stone* assigned him to cover the 1976 presidential election. The fashion photographer Irving Penn photographed for *Look.* Contributing to this move toward personalized photojournalism were books such as

William Klein's *Life Is Good and Good for You in New York* (1956) and Robert Frank's *The Americans* (1959). Under their influence, other photojournalists sought to publish their own books as a way to regain creative control of the presentation of their work. "The form began to outgrow its origins," Panzer writes. "A creation of the press, the photojournalist was beginning to claim a role beyond it."[82]

Two months after its birth, *Life* was followed by another large picture magazine. Although *Look's* first issue was dated February 1937, it appeared on newsstands in January. The two magazines are typically discussed as competitors, with *Look* always in second place. The reality is more complicated. Gardner "Mike" Cowles, the founder and force behind *Look's* success, had a strong commitment to photography. His brother John published the *Des Moines Register and Tribune* and the *Minneapolis Star.* Based on Gallup research that readers preferred photographs, the newspapers used pictures well. In 1933, the Cowles family launched a syndicate to sell their picture stories to other newspapers.[83]

The brothers were friends of Luce's, and at meetings during the fall of 1936, they told him about their plans to publish a picture magazine. In return, Luce showed them mock-ups of *Life.* Mike Cowles envisioned a different magazine from the one Luce was planning: *Life* would be a weekly with a news orientation, while *Look* would appear monthly, a time cycle that prevented spot news and mandated timeless features. As Cowles recalled the discussion, "*Life* would be a rather 'upscale' publication aimed at the relatively affluent, well-educated sort of people ... while *Look* would seek a more downscale audience."[84] Production values would match the audiences. *Life* planned to print on expensive glossy paper to appeal to advertisers as well as readers. *Look* planned to print on

cheaper paper and would run no ads until it established a circulation base. Based on these differences, Luce decided the magazines
would not be in direct competition and invested one hundred
thousand dollars for a 20 percent share in the Cowleses' magazine.

Some *Life* staff members were less accepting than Luce. When
the brothers visited the planning department of *Life*, there were
several mock-ups tacked on bulletin boards, including some with
the name *Look* on their covers. Wainwright implied they stole the
name. Longwell, who originally thought they were only interested
in syndicating *Life's* photographs, accused them of betraying his
trust. For his part, Cowles attributed his idea for a picture magazine to the Europeans. "Picture magazines such as *Vu* and *Pour
Vous* in France and *Illustrated London News* and *Weekly Illustrated* in
England, were already thriving in Europe and that had not gone
unnoticed by American publishing entrepreneurs," he wrote. "By
the time I began pasting up dummies for *Look* . . . in 1936, perhaps
half a dozen or more individuals and organizations were proceed-
ing with similar plans."[85]

Cowles's term *downscale audience* was a euphemism for his intention to emphasize sex and sensationalism. Time, Inc. executive Roy Larsen said his impression was that the *Look* proposal
was "too sensational." He predicted that its "appeal to the lower
instincts" of readers would succeed, but not at the level of a mass
circulation.[86]

Look's first issue certainly had plenty of sex and sensationalism.
The cover featured a large color photo of the Nazi war minister
Hermann Goering feeding a bottle of milk to a lion cub. Running
down the right side were small black-and-white pictures showing
President Roosevelt, the actress Joan Crawford, and a close-up of
a woman's legs. Inside were photographs from houses of prostitution in Japan and a sequence from a newsreel that showed a car

skidding into a pedestrian. A story entitled "When Is a Woman Actually a Woman?" discussed the subject of hermaphrodites. Two pieces were criticized for showing disrespect. Mrs. Harrison Williams, who had been selected as America's best-dressed woman of the year, was turned into the butt of a joke when her picture was composited with one of the burlesque queen Gypsy Rose Lee. In a fabricated conversation, a writer had the striptease dancer saying, "I never put off tomorrow what I can put off today."[87] Another photo sequence featured the many hats worn by Queen Mary of England. In one she was shown with her husband, King George V, who had been dead more than a year. A cartoonlike balloon with a comment attributed to the late king implied he was still alive.

Most salacious was the back cover, which featured a color photograph of the actress Greta Garbo. Rumor quickly spread that folding the cover in a certain way would reveal an image of a vagina. Many believed *Look*'s editors deliberately intended this. "Police in Montreal actually seized several hundred copies," Cowles wrote. "John and I decided we had no choice but to recall all of the unsold copies, which cost us over $100,000."[88] He recognized the problem created by the low editorial tone and changed the contents so *Look* would not seem "in bad taste" to "any substantial number of broadminded people."[89]

Taking advantage of *Life*'s mistakes, *Look*'s first issue had a press run of seven hundred thousand. Like *Life,* it enjoyed a rapid initial success and soon began publishing every two weeks, instead of monthly. Cowles elevated its tone, appealing to a more upscale audience. It soon became clear the two magazines were competitors, and in July 1937, the Cowleses bought back Luce's stock.

While the magazines were similar in format, *Look* was more liberal in its politics. As one example, it published stories and editorials that questioned the Vietnam War long before *Life* did. In

January 1969, *Look* published a cover story taken in Hanoi and North Vietnam by the French photojournalist Marc Riboud. It took the pragmatic position that the United States could not win the war because of the determination, ingenuity, and resilience of the North Vietnamese people.

Look fell victim to the same circulation and advertising pressures as *Life* and began losing money after 1967. By then, the Cowles family had diversified into other media areas and reincorporated itself as Cowles Communications. To keep *Look* afloat, it began selling off profitable properties, including the *San Juan Star* in Puerto Rico, *Family Circle* magazine, and a group of trade magazines, all to no avail.[90] The United States was in recession, advertising was down, and recent increases in postal rates added to the magazine's costs. In announcing the closing on September 16, 1971, Cowles said, "My heart said, 'Keep it going,' but my head said, 'Suspend it.'"[91] All that remained of Cowles Communications were the original newspapers and several radio and television stations.

National Geographic, America's remaining picture magazine, is qualitatively different from *Life* and *Look*. As the publication of a tax-exempt educational organization, it enjoys financial advantages, including lower mailing rates. Its format is much smaller, and although it attracts a large circulation, it is not a general-interest magazine offering a smorgasbord of contents. The house publication for members of the National Geographic Society, it is a quasiscientific publication that covers geography, world cultures, natural science, and conservation issues.

The society was founded in January 1888. In the first *National Geographic* magazine, published that October, it announced its mission to "increase and diffuse geographic knowledge."[92] The magazine was free to society members, who paid annual dues of five dollars. Early issues reflected the society's orientation toward professional geographers and federal employees involved in geographic studies of the American West. Articles were scientifically oriented. A decade later, Gardiner Greene Hubbard, the founding spirit and first president of the society, died. Leadership of the one thousand members passed to Hubbard's son-in-law Alexander Graham Bell, inventor of the telephone. He decided to appeal to a broader public by changing the magazine, which was heavily in debt, from a specialized journal to one with interesting articles, pictures, and maps. Several of the society's board members opposed this popularization.

Bell hired Gilbert Grosvenor, his future son-in-law, to be the magazine's first paid editor. Grosvenor resisted attempts by the purists to remove him as editor, but he genuinely thought they would succeed in firing him over the January 1905 issue. He was facing the December deadline with an eleven-page hole and no suitable article to fill it. He had recently received a packet of photographs of Lhasa, the remote capital of Tibet, and used them to fill the pages. Instead of being fired, he received praise from trustees and public alike. Emboldened, he published thirty-two pages of photographs on the Philippines a few months later. During 1905, membership in the society increased from thirty-four hundred to eleven thousand. Grosvenor's editorial judgment was confirmed, and the magazine increased its use of pictures. "Why not transform the Society's magazine from one of cold geographic fact, expressed in hieroglyphic terms which the layman could not understand, into a vehicle for carrying the living, breathing, human-interest truth about this great world of ours?" he wrote in a memoir. "Would not that be the greatest agency of all for the diffusion of geographic knowledge?"[93]

Grosvenor kept the job until 1954, putting his stamp on the magazine before passing it to his son and grandson. In a 1915 article addressed to readers, he articulated his seven principles for editing the magazine. Accuracy came first, but the second principle related directly to photographs: "Abundance of beautiful, instructive, and artistic illustrations." Two other principles have brought criticism to the magazine for what some consider its failure to take principled stands. Principle 5 held: "Nothing of a partisan or controversial nature is printed." Principle 6 extended this to nations as well: "Only what is of a kindly nature is printed about any country or people, everything unpleasant or unduly critical being avoided."[94] Grosvenor explained his rationale in his memoir: "I was brought up on the Golden Rule and was always taught not to criticize other people," he wrote. "That same rule pays off when you are dealing with countries.... Some people have to criticize—there is a need for it and someone has to do it. But I didn't want to; the world is so big and there is so much to say."[95] *National Geographic* remained above the fray during the world wars, the cold war, and other global conflicts, until the 1970s when Gilbert Melville Grosvenor, the third generation of the family to edit the magazine, stirred up controversy with articles on apartheid in South Africa, drug abuse in Harlem, and an admiring look at life in Communist Cuba. Soon, however, the magazine reverted to its speak-no-evil policy.[96]

Despite his conservatism, the elder Grosvenor made an editorial decision ahead of its time. In 1903, his cousin William Howard Taft, who would become the nation's twenty-seventh president, was governor-general of the Philippines. Taft sent him photographs that included one of two women, bare from the waist up, working in a rice paddy. Grosvenor was a scrupulously moral man. He did not smoke or drink and would not allow his staff to use profanity in his presence. Victorian mores, still in place, considered it highly improper for women to show any part of their bodies beyond hands and head. Nonetheless, Grosvenor felt the photograph was educationally important, because it accurately portrayed Filipino culture. He sought advice from Bell, who supported publishing it. Contrary to his fears, it drew almost no negative reaction. Perhaps readers concurred that the women's partial nudity was of justifiable anthropological interest. A postmodern explanation holds that this image and the many photographs of bare-breasted women that followed in *National Geographic* reduced women in colonial countries to objects. There was no shock, this argument maintains, because Western readers could not see half-naked colonial women as bearing any relationship to themselves. As one writer noted, "The only color of breasts that haven't been seen in the *National Geographic* are white ones."[97]

Devoting a substantial part of each month's issue to photographs put *National Geographic* ahead of newspapers and other magazines in the early twentieth century. Because of his limited budget, Grosvenor got many photographs from government agencies. Often he borrowed the engraving plates used in government publications and printed from them. Other ready sources were explorers and adventurers eager to offer photographic proof of their claims.

Beyond using photographs as illustrations, *National Geographic* pioneered many advances in photographic and printing technology. Some milestones include the first flash photographs of nocturnal animals (1906); an eight-foot-long panoramic photograph of a scene from the Canadian Rocky Mountains, which was the first of many foldouts (1911); and the first color photographs taken underwater (1926). The French oceanographer Jacques Cousteau took the first photographs of creatures in the ocean depths. In the

1920s, when few people had flown, the magazine showed its readers the world from above in black-and-white aerial photographs. Color aerial photographs posed a problem. With exposures fifty to sixty times longer than for black and white, color photographs were impossible because the airplane's motion would blur the images. Grosvenor had the idea of using slow-moving dirigibles. In the September 1930 issue, he published the first color aerial photograph. It was a view of the U.S. Capitol building taken by his son, Melville Bell Grosvenor, from the dirigible *Mayflower*.[98] In 1984, *National Geographic* also scored the first published hologram, a cover image of a bald eagle.

By today's standards, early color reproduction appears artificial. The magazine published its first color photographs in 1910, devoting twenty-four pages to "Scenes in Korea and China." The images were black-and-white photographs that had been hand-colored by a Japanese artist. Even so, they were a declaration of the magazine's intention to innovate in printing technologies. In 1959, color photographs appeared on the covers, replacing the practice of printing the table of contents there. In February 1962, *National Geographic* published its first all-color issue.

National Geographic's photography has been criticized on several grounds besides the charge of objectification. Some accuse it of aestheticizing problems. Instead of using photography to try to correct injustices, critics say, the magazine presents an impossibly perfect world. Writing in *Esquire* in 1963, Anne Chamberlin passed this judgment: "The *Geographic* has achieved such jewel-like tones in its reproduction of pictures on the rich glossy stock of its pages that even the suppurating sores of the filthiest betel-nut-chewing street urchin are somehow glamorized."[99] Her comment recalls a similar criticism—that *National Geographic* photographers control their photographs to make them more perfect than the reality they supposedly represent.

During the 1950s, for example, the so-called Red Shirt School of photography arose, in which *National Geographic* photographers encouraged their subjects to wear red or other bright clothing that would show up well on their color film. "Even though Kodachrome was already unnaturally bright," C. D. B. Bryan explained, "photographers . . . splashed the strongest possible colors in their pictures so that they would be more effective in print."[100] The impetus came from the top. "They'd go on these expeditions and everybody would be in khaki because that's the color of field uniforms," said Melville Bell Grosvenor. "And they'd come back with the dullest bunch of pictures you ever saw! You couldn't use them editorially because they had no color. So, we decided to have people wear colorful shirts."[101] In the 1950s and 1960s, such interventions were still commonplace in press photography and generally accepted as not transgressing ethical boundaries. The 35 mm ethic that every photograph should be pristinely unmanipulated had not yet pervaded American photojournalism.

That changed in the early 1970s under editor in chief Bill Garrett and picture editor Bob Gilka. They made a calculated decision to fill the vacuum created by *Life's* demise. They hired newspaper and wire service photographers committed to showing the world through spontaneous, unstaged photography. Gordon Gahan, who won a Silver Star for heroism at Dak To in Vietnam, earned a staff position based on his photographs of the mauling the 173rd Airborne Brigade took there. Bruce Dale came from the *Toledo Blade.* Gilka found Bill Allard driving a cab. Dave Harvey came from Richmond, J. Bruce Baumann from Evansville, Indiana, James Stanfield from Milwaukee, Jodi Cobb and Chris Johns from the *Denver Post,* Steve Raymer from Madison, Bob Madden from the University of Missouri's grad school. Freelance and contract photographers included Nathan Benn, later president of Magnum, Sam Abell, Steve McCurry, and Nachtwey. "Our mandate," said Raymer, "was to never set up—show it like it is. The moment is everything."[102] Over a period of fifteen years, Garrett increasingly brought substantive photography into the magazine. An early example was the July 1975 issue, which included two articles by Raymer on the global food crisis: "Can the World Feed Its People" and "Bangladesh: Nightmare of Famine." Garrett was fired in 1990, in a dispute with Gilbert Melville Grosvenor, then chair of the society.

Johns, a staff veteran who became editor in chief in 2005, continues to emphasize serious journalism in *National Geographic*'s editorial mix. In one example, Michael Finkel's December 2007 story on Bethlehem leads with the provocative statement: "The birthplace of Jesus is today one of the most contentious places on Earth. Israelis fear Bethlehem's radicalized residents, who seethe at the concrete wall that surrounds them."[103] A year earlier, Nachtwey reverted to black and white to photograph a story on medical treatment for American soldiers wounded in Iraq. In field hospitals, he showed burns, blood, shrapnel wounds, and soldiers who did not survive, despite the doctors' best efforts. Back in America, he photographed soldiers who had lost both legs or were suffering from traumatic brain injury, struggling to rebuild their lives. Few American newspapers would risk publishing photographs as emotionally powerful as Nachtwey's. During a war where Bush administration and Pentagon officials largely succeeded in minimizing negative pictures, Nachtwey and *National Geographic* continued the tradition of bearing witness.

Like *Life* and *Look, National Geographic* has seen a decline in membership and circulation. Its English-language edition dropped from a high of 10.9 million in 1989 to 6.05 million in early 2008.[104] Long before this occurred, however, it spun off several other magazines and diversified into book publishing, video, cable television, and more recently online multimedia. Because of its tax-exempt status, it has remained financially viable.

Near the end of the first decade of the twenty-first century, the state of magazine photojournalism, particularly the long-form picture story, is tenuous. The three major news magazines—*Time, Newsweek,* and *U.S. News and World Report*—publish thousands of single images a year and on important stories may devote three or four photographs, but they rarely practice the long-form photo-essay. During the 1980s and 1990s, the *New York Times Magazine* published serious essays by such photojournalists as Salgado, Nachtwey, and Meiselas. In the new century, it devotes most of its photographic space to fashion spreads. On a positive note, in 2004, *Harper's* editor Lewis Lapham made photojournalist Peter Turnley a contributing editor and began publishing his essays on a quarterly basis.

The market for magazine photojournalism thrives in Europe, but despite the few exceptions noted above, American magazine editors show little interest in photo stories. Two major photojournalists make this point. "When some of us began working in the early seventies, already the magazines of the sixties weren't hiring people to do what we dreamed we were going to do," Magnum photographer Meiselas says. "For my generation, those expectations weren't met. It is still tough for many of us with a lot of experience to get work today. Our production can no longer be sustained by editorial work alone."[105]

As an alternative to magazines, Mary Ellen Mark points to the importance of books and museum exhibitions. "When I began to take pictures, my inspirations were the many memorable documentary essays I saw in magazines," she says. "Now we all must work more independently to produce books and exhibitions."[106]

To books and exhibitions, technology has added the Internet. Newspapers and magazines have online editions. Some have exploited this transition as an opportunity to publish images that do not make the print edition, including documentary essays. Many freelance photographers use the Web to display their work and sell their stock. Internet technology is shifting the medium in yet another direction. To differentiate online from print editions, many publishers are pushing their photographic staff to produce audio slide shows and video stories.

SIX

FROM AN OCCUPATION TO
A PROFESSION

In 1945, as World War II was ending, a group of press photographers and newsreel camera operators launched an organization that would help transform their occupation into a profession. Their immediate goals were to improve working conditions and combat the negative stereotypes that tarnished press photographers. Their project coincided with a rapid growth in teaching photojournalism in higher education. During this era, several key newspapers emerged as centers of visual excellence, providing national leadership. All three factors combined to transform a second-class job into a profession.

Many causes contributed to press photographers' lowly status. They were latecomers to news operations that were organized to gather, process, and present verbal stories. Control was concentrated in the hands of "word" people. Although many publishers and senior editors valued the circulation increases that photographs produced, rank-and-file journalists did not automatically share their appreciation. Many reporters and editors held the common prejudice against photographs—that as a simplistic form of communication that appealed to the uneducated, they were inferior to the written word. Many reporters resented space going to pictures that could have been given to their stories. Moreover, most photographers came up through the ranks, learning their craft through an informal apprenticeship. At many newspapers, their on-the-job training was spotty, dependent on the willingness of senior photographers to share hard-won experience. At best, press photography was a craft with no sense of its own history, no power, and no voice.

Outside journalism, the public had its own negative perceptions. Press photography was highly competitive. Demanding editors pressured photographers to get the picture whatever the cost. The stereotype of a sharp-elbowed lout with a cigarette dangling from his lower lip, a press card jammed in the brim of his upturned hat, and a perpetually popping flash was common. One quip referred to a press photographer as "a reporter with his brains knocked out." Another said he "takes pictures or anything else he can carry away."[1] In 1946, a public relations journal described "the terrible picture-taker" with clear allusions to the Neanderthal:

> Whose finer sensibilities among us are not violated almost every time we attend a meeting of importance these days? The ubiquitous gentleman of the camera is always there. Carrying the accouterments of his trade, moving back and forth before the audience, peering into the face of first this person and that, he takes possession of the situation. And once the speaker mounts the rostrum, the fireworks begin. The cameraman stands up and studies his prey. Shall he take a front view? Or will it be better to catch the speaker in action from the side or rear? Maybe the thing to do is to take a shot of him from some high point. Perplexity wrinkles the brow of the cameraman. The weight of reaching a decision shows heavily upon his countenance. He walks about. He scowls. . . . He climbs

up on a chair and surveys his subject from aloft. Oblivious, or more possibly contemptuous, of the discomfort of the speaker and the audience, he plies the tools of his trade.[2]

Photographers and historians recognized this situation. Frank Scherschel, chief photographer of the *Milwaukee Journal,* wrote in 1940, "Not so long ago the news photographer was a dumb tough guy."[3] News photographers "earned a bad reputation almost immediately," wrote photographic historian Gisèle Freund. "For almost half a century the press photographer was considered inferior, a kind of servant who took orders, but who had no initiative."[4]

Like all stereotypes, this one exaggerated the behavior of some press photographers and generalized it to all members of the group. No matter how unfair the image, many photographers realized they needed to combat it with a positive version of their contributions. They also wanted to improve working conditions. Most press photographers performed physically grueling work, for low pay and little respect. A national organization promised solutions for such problems.

On March 29, 1945, a conference call among ten cities across the nation linked members of state and local associations. Burt Williams, chief photographer at the *Pittsburgh Sun-Telegraph,* was the driving force behind the meeting and launched it by urging the groups to unite into a national organization. "Let us get all of the press-photographer outfits in the country working for the same cause, cooperating for our common benefit." He emphasized the advantages of professionalization: "We can be a service for our newspapers and publishers, as well as for ourselves, if we raise up our own standards and set up a yardstick of ability." He also suggested the organization could work to curtail amateur photographers, called "Brownie Boys," who tried to crash news events. "The illegal and unorthodox behavior of hundreds of screwball photographers . . . has harmed the legitimate newspaper photographer for the last decade,"[5] Williams said. Other photographers from Los Angeles, Boston, and Washington, D.C., endorsed the idea.

Finally, the turn to speak passed to Joseph Costa, president of the New York Press Photographers Association and a respected photographer at the *Daily News*. While the others had been generally positive, Costa reviewed several negatives, especially the many photographers who were reluctant to work but quick to criticize those who did. "In listing the obstacles," he said, "No. 1 is the inherent lack of interest on the part of the press photographer in matters vital to his business when a little work or effort on his part is involved."[6]

On June 17, photographers met in Atlantic City to continue the momentum. They chose the National Press Photographers Association (NPPA) as the group's name and appointed an organizing committee, with Williams as chair, Costa as secretary, and Charles Mack of MGM News in Washington as treasurer. Costa was also named chair of a committee to draft a constitution. It listed ten principles ranging from fraternalism to opposing restrictions on photographers' rights to declaring the organization was not a labor union. The first and overriding purpose was the "advancement of press photography in all its branches."[7]

The country was organized into ten regions, and extensive efforts were made to invite all newspaper and newsreel photographers to join. By February 1946, almost three hundred had paid their six-dollar dues, and another sixty had applied but not sent their money. On February 23–24, regional leaders met in Manhattan and elected the organization's first officers. Costa nominated and supported Williams, but Williams demurred, arguing Costa would be a more effective leader. Costa was elected president, Williams, secretary, and Mack, treasurer.

In April, *National Press Photographer* magazine appeared, with a front-page headline proclaiming, "This is the voice of the press photographer" (see figure 19). The twelve-page publication evolved into a larger monthly magazine, which continues to publish under the title *News Photographer.*

In a front-page editorial, Costa developed the theme of having a voice:

> For more years than we should care to admit we've been taking a pushing around. And what have we done about it? Nothing, absolutely nothing! But all that is in the past. We're no longer going to permit ourselves to be relegated to the position of unwelcome but necessary stepchildren of the Fourth Estate. We've got a voice, finally, and we're going to make use of it.... We're going to yell so loud ... that those in this country who have been injuring us with scant courtesy will begin to realize that here is a new force to be reckoned with.[8]

After acknowledging that photographers needed to put their own house in order, he said it was time to stop being "mealy-mouthed" and demand "EQUAL RIGHTS FOR PHOTOG-RAPHERS!" "When we say 'equal rights,'" he explained, "we mean as compared with our best friends and severest critics—the reporters."[9]

Costa, who gained the nickname "Mr. Press Photographer," soon pressed his claim for equality in a speech to the American Society of Newspaper Editors. Tackling the stereotype head-on, he decried the myth "that to be good, a cameraman must be a screwball. Let me say, gentlemen, we'd prefer that any stories written about us play up our accomplishments in news photography, rather than our personal idiosyncrasies."[10]

In recruiting members, the NPPA posed a rhetorical question—"What do I get for my six dollars?"—and answered it by noting services for individuals and initiatives for the profession. Among those initiatives, leaders fought to extend freedom of information rights to photographers. The first battle was with federal marshals, many of whom prevented press photographers from photographing prisoners. In one notorious 1948 case, U.S. Marshal Fred Canfil ordered Betty Love of the *Springfield (Missouri) Leader* not to photograph two federal prisoners. When a reporter pointed out her First Amendment right to take the pictures, Canfil reportedly shouted, "The Constitution be damned! I have my orders not to let any pictures be made of federal prisoners, and you're not taking any."[11] The Justice Department under President Truman repeatedly assured the NPPA it was studying the problem, but no change occurred until the Eisenhower administration. On February 4, 1954, the department ratified the photographers' position in a directive: "United States marshals and their deputies shall, under no circumstances, interfere with a reporter, photographer, or other person seeking to take a photograph of a prisoner on the street or in other public places outside of the federal courthouse."[12]

The association fought similar battles against rules prohibiting television and radio coverage of committee meetings of the U.S. House of Representatives and a proposal for a similar ban in the Senate. Among the voices lending support was the CBS journalist Edward R. Murrow. The rules "represent both a threat of censorship and a denial of the right of television and radio to employ the tools of their trade to disseminate information," he charged.[13]

The NPPA campaigned for legislation to protect news photographers against the physical assaults that were common in the
1940s and 1950s. Scarcely an issue of *National Press Photographer*
passed without stories about photographers being attacked or
having their cameras damaged and negatives exposed by police,
military personnel, political-campaign operatives, and even crimi-
nal defendants. To many in press photography it seemed as if the
world had declared open season on their ranks and that law officers had joined the hunt. The assaults were especially vicious
because photographers with Speed Graphics to their faces were
vulnerable to being blindsided. The NPPA supported lawsuits
against the attackers and scored initial successes in getting antiassault laws passed in New York and New Jersey. In other states,
antiassault bills languished when opponents labeled them as class
legislation, designed to benefit a special group. Despite finding
sympathetic representatives to introduce a bill in Congress, the
campaign stalled at the national level also. Nonetheless, it raised
awareness of a problem that still continues.

In other initiatives, the NPPA established committees to improve working relationships with police and civil defense officials,
lobbied on Capitol Hill for repeal of a World War II excise tax on
cameras and photographic materials, pushed for better shooting
positions at professional sports events, launched a job bureau, negotiated group rates for life insurance for members, campaigned
to overturn the American Bar Association's Canon 35, which prohibited cameras in the courts, and battled for credit lines. In an era
when most newspapers gave bylines to reporters, credit lines for
photographers were nonexistent. During the Korean War, NPPA
president Ken McLaughlin contrasted photographers who had to
risk frontline action to word journalists in offices at the rear. "Reporters sitting at desks in the security of Tokyo and Washington,

men whose only danger is in tripping over a cuspidor on the way to the men's room, also receive credit lines." If any journalists "deserve credit and recognition," McLaughlin said, "it is certainly these boys who are sticking their necks out every day to bring the American public the activities of our men in the field."[14]

While these efforts were directed outward, the NPPA worked within its ranks to raise the skill and professionalism of members. Most press photographers had no formal training. Aspiring youths moved from being copy clerks to mixing chemicals in the photo lab to making prints and shooting studio setups. Finally, they graduated to outside assignments. If they were lucky, a veteran staffer might share advice and experience. If they were bookish, they might consult technical manuals. Otherwise, there were few ways to learn beyond the mistakes that came with experience. In the mid-1940s, few universities offered a course, let alone a major, in photojournalism. Even if they had, few photographers attended college.

The NPPA saw education as the primary means to fill this vacuum. Costa believed the "single most important committee in the NPPA" was the Education and Technical Committee. "Everything NPPA does is educational in nature," he said. "Whether it is education of our own men technically, whether it is education of editors with regard to understanding photographers and better use of pictures, whether it is education of public officials . . . or the public generally or the courts, it is all educational in nature."[15]

The Education and Technical Committee comprised photographers, university professors, and technical representatives from the photographic industry. Its first initiative centered on a decade-old idea, an intensive seminar called a short course. In 1937, Professor Clarence Smith offered the first news photography short course at the University of Oklahoma in Norman. With publicity from *Editor and Publisher* magazine, it drew 150 participants. When Smith moved to Kent State University in Ohio, he took the idea with him. Suspended during World War II, it resumed in 1946, attracting the support of the fledgling NPPA. Numerous officers and members lectured and made technical presentations. In May 1949, the NPPA sponsored its own short course for the first time. About thirty-five photographers attended the three-day event in Rochester, New York. The next year, the NPPA lent its support and expertise to the Carolinas Press Photographers Association to launch the Southern Short Course in Press Photography, which continues annually.

J. Winton Lemen, a Kodak representative and member of the committee, wrote a manual, explaining how to plan and organize a short course, printed two hundred copies, and circulated them to universities interested in hosting one. It recommended that all short courses include a mix of four kinds of sessions: lectures on fundamentals, inspirational talks, demonstrations of tools and techniques, and workshops. Members were hungry for such education. In the early 1950s, the committee polled the membership and identified the ten most popular topics. They ranged from the technical (improving flash pictures and using 35 mm cameras) to the aesthetic (composition, lighting, and shooting better sports photographs) to the conceptual (developing picture-story ideas and adding human interest to photographs). For some time, officers and members in the western region had complained of being neglected by the association. The Education and Technical Committee responded with a series of West Coast short courses. In November 1953, a program of speakers presented a two-day seminar at the University of Southern California in Los Angeles, flew to City College of San Francisco to give the same program, and gave it again at the University of Washington in Seattle. The experiment was so successful—about 650 photographers and editors attended the sessions—that it was repeated the following year. It became the basis for the Flying Short Course, which condensed the program to one day per stop. In 1958, the first Flying Short Course visited Los Angeles, Omaha, St. Louis, Tampa, and Schenectady, New York. The Flying Short Course has continued without a break, and organizers vary the locations to make it available to as many members as possible. A recent Flying Short Course included stops in Washington, D.C., Chicago, and San Jose, California. Speakers have included Pulitzer Prize and Emmy winners. Topics ranged from new media to covering the war in Iraq. The Flying Short Course and *News Photographer* magazine have been the two biggest tools for recruiting members for the organization, which numbered more than eight thousand at the end of 2008.[16]

Photographers returned from short courses inspired about their profession, ready to try new ideas and techniques, and eager to share their new knowledge. A typical reaction was, "I wish my editor would attend one of these courses so that he could get a firsthand picture of the photojournalism scene."[17] In response, the NPPA organized a management-level conference targeted to publishers, managing editors, photography department directors, picture editors, and printing department superintendents. Over 230 attended the Rochester Photo Conference in September 1953. Presentations ranged from the technical details of lithography to human perception of color to calls for greater imagination in assignments. Wilson Hicks of *Life* magazine advocated the use of 35 mm cameras "to picture life as it is—not as a photographer may revise it."[18] The NPPA repeated the conference in 1957, 1962, 1968, and 1975. In another educational venture, it published *The*

Complete Book of Press Photography, which was unveiled at its 1950 convention. As a public-relations gesture, Costa presented the ceremonial first copy to President Truman (see figure 20).

In 1976, the NPPA created the National Press Photographers Foundation, which encourages and funds a variety of educational activities, including the Stan Kalish Picture Editing Workshop, the Airborne TV Seminar, and the Awards for Research in Photojournalism. Under foundation president C. Thomas Hardin, it also administers funding for several college scholarships for students pursuing careers in both still and video photography.

Much of the criticism against press photographers from the 1920s through the 1940s implied they lacked personal and professional ethics. Costa had experienced firsthand the competitive era when photographers sabotaged each other's work, stealing film holders or exposing negatives left in unguarded bags. Those experiences resonated in the code of ethics he included in the constitution. It called on members to encourage and assist each other and to show "sympathy for our common humanity." Ethics are often associated with prohibitions, but Costa had the wisdom to frame the NPPA code as a positive statement about photojournalism as a public service. Rebutting the stereotypes and put-downs, he proclaimed that being a press photographer was not something to be ashamed of but a calling demanding its practitioners' very best. "The practice of press photography, both as a science and art, is worthy of the very best thought and endeavor of those who enter into it as a vocation," the code declared.[19]

The NPPA's code has evolved, responding in the early 1990s to digital photography. Although prohibitions were added, it retains a positive core. The latest version, adopted in 2004, declares photojournalists have a public trust to "report visually on the significant events and on the varied viewpoints in our common world" with a "faithful and comprehensive depiction of the subject at hand." It upholds the ideal that "photographic and video images can reveal great truths, expose wrongdoing and neglect, inspire hope and understanding and connect people around the globe through the language of visual understanding." It warns against the "great harm" photographs can cause "if they are callously intrusive or are manipulated." Echoing the NPPA's founding objectives, the code states the organization's purpose is "to promote the highest quality in all forms of photojournalism and to strengthen public confidence in the profession."[20]

The association's attitudes toward women were mixed. When a regional officer asked if he should accept the application of Effie Walton Giacomini, Costa wrote back, "Why not? She takes pictures and they are published."[21] But the sexism and paternalism of most city rooms extended into photojournalism as well. NPPA officers used the same gendered references, *cameraman* and *newsreel man,* as others in the industry. When the third issue of *National Press Photographer* published short biographies of six women who had joined, it referred to them as "ladies" and "girls."

As with Jessie Tarbox Beals, Frances Benjamin Johnston, and Consuelo Kanaga early in the twentieth century, the successes of Dorothea Lange in the Farm Security Administration and Margaret Bourke-White at *Life* were not typical for women in photojournalism and documentary photography in the middle decades. Patriarchal attitudes, good-old-boy networks, and men's desire to protect their dominance combined to keep the numbers of women in photojournalism small and to consign them to covering women's news and soft features, typically at lower salaries. At *Life,* for example, few women received assignments or had extended picture stories published during the magazine's first decade.[22] Of the 273 photographers included in the Family of Man exhibition, only forty were women. As late as the early 1970s, there were no women photographers or editors in the Associated Press's (AP's) picture operation in New York. Women employees were relegated to the level of photo librarians.

Such low numbers indicate a structural problem in the industry, but sexism manifested itself at the personal level as well. Constance Bannister recalled that in the 1940s, her male competitors put hypo in her developer and scratched her negatives.[23] Despite such obstacles, women excelled in photojournalism and documentary photography. In 1941, Lange became the first woman to receive a coveted Guggenheim grant, when she was photographing Japanese Americans confined at the Manzanar camp in northern California. Both Bourke-White and Lee Miller covered major campaigns and stories during World War II; their strongest photographs came from the liberation of the Nazi death camps. The war had the broader effect of increasing the number of women in all branches of photography. Rosie the Riveter symbolized women who stepped in to fill industrial jobs vacated by men drafted into the military, but the same process affected all sectors of the economy. The photography historian Naomi Rosenblum notes that the number of professional women photographers rose from eight thousand in 1937 to ten thousand in the mid-1940s.[24] The Army Signal Corps also opened its ranks to train members of the Women's Auxiliary Army Corps (WACs) as photographers. Elizabeth "Tex" Williams, who was the first African American woman admitted to the corps' photography school at Fort Monmouth, New Jersey, distinguished herself by graduating at the top of her class.[25]

After the war, in the early 1950s, Eve Arnold became the first woman to join Magnum Photos, the premier international photography agency, but again her accomplishment was not typical. As late as 1989, only five of the forty-nine Magnum members were women. They included Mary Ellen Mark, whose documentary subjects range from prostitutes in India to street kids in Seattle. Another prominent American woman in Magnum is Susan Meiselas, who followed her coverage of the civil war in Nicaragua by photographing the victims of Saddam Hussein's chemical attacks on the Kurds in northern Iraq in the 1980s. Meiselas is rare among photojournalists for the level of collaboration she achieves with her subjects. Her work was recognized with a MacArthur Fellowship, the so-called genius grant, in 1992.

Although parity for women in photojournalism still does not exist, the situation began to improve in the 1960s and 1970s. The feminist movement helped raise the nation's consciousness about gender issues, but the sexism embedded in the industry's structure would not have changed without the Civil Rights Act of 1964 and subsequent court rulings that mandated affirmative action for women and minority groups. Journalism along with other industries finally began to move toward greater gender diversity in hiring. Universities opened their programs to more women to help fill the jobs, and with time, women graduates returned to teach on photojournalism faculties. In the 1970s and 1980s, women moved from photographing to positions as picture editors at the *Atlanta Constitution, USA Weekend,* and the *New York Times Magazine.* Sandra Eisert left the picture desk at the *Louisville Times* to become photo editor for President Ford's White House. Women began appearing on Flying Short Course faculties and serving as regional and national officers in the NPPA. Still, it took until 1992 for *Washington Post* staffer Mary Lou Foy to become the first woman president of the NPPA. She was followed by Linda Asberry-Angelle in 1998 and Alicia Wagner Calzada in 2005.[26]

In 1989, women members formed their own group within the NPPA called Women in Photojournalism. It offers support, mentoring, and networking and promotes discussion of issues of special interest to women. It also sponsors an annual conference and contest through its Web site.[27]

Women also began taking top honors in national competitions. Notable examples include Carol Guzy, who has won three Pulitzer Prizes and, in 1990, became the first woman named Newspaper Photographer of the Year. She won that honor again in 1993 and 1997. Carolyn Cole became the first person to sweep photojournalism's top three awards, winning the Pulitzer, Photographer of the Year, and Best of Photojournalism in 2004. She also won Best of Photojournalism in 2002 and 2007 and has received the Robert Capa Award.

The story of African Americans is less positive. The association officially welcomed their membership. Asked by a regional officer in February 1954, "Do we accept Negroes?" Costa wired a one-word response: "Yes."[28] Later that year, President Art Whitman, in a letter to a Texas officer, wrote unequivocally, "Regarding the race questions—there is no Jim Crow in NPPA. Any photographer who applies for membership is evaluated in terms of his qualifications."[29] For many years, however, there were few minority press photographers. Most worked for African American newspapers and had few relationships with photographers at mainstream newspapers. It would be the 1970s before those newspapers would begin actively recruiting minority staffers. In the profession, Gordon Parks pioneered as a staff photographer for *Life*. Eli Reed became the first African American member of the Magnum Photos agency, and Michel duCille, a Jamaican American who won two

Pulitzer Prizes, was picture editor and later director of photography of the *Washington Post*. By 2008, there had still not been an African American president of the NPPA.

Concurrent with the NPPA's growth, higher education began working toward the shared goal of building a profession. It offered courses and, later, sequences and majors in photojournalism. In 1944, Congress passed the Servicemen's Readjustment Act, known as the GI Bill of Rights. One of its most popular services underwrote tuition up to five hundred dollars per year for college or vocational training. Over the ten-year life of the bill, 7.8 million veterans, or 48.8 percent of the 16 million eligible veterans, took advantage of the educational benefits.[30] Colleges and universities responded by increasing their enrollments.

Photojournalism courses rode this wave of academic growth. In 1943, Cliff Edom launched one of the earliest and most influential programs at the University of Missouri. Edom (who is credited with coining the word *photojournalism*) went beyond teaching classes to advance the profession nationally. Recognizing the advantages that reporters and editors gained from Sigma Delta Chi, their fraternal organization, he cofounded Kappa Alpha Mu for photojournalists. In 1949, he launched the Missouri Photo Workshop for working photographers who wanted to improve their skills, particularly their ability to create photo stories. Edom, who was not a photographer, said he started the workshop for his own benefit. "I wanted to learn from the greats in photojournalism but most of them were in the East and I couldn't afford the time or money to go there so I decided to bring them" to Columbia, he said.[31] Edom and his wife, Vi, ran the workshop for thirty-eight years, attracting top photographers and editors to tutor participants. Combining the documentary tradition with the picture-story format, the workshop took students to small Missouri towns to find subjects and tell their stories visually. At night, the students endured critiques—sometimes blistering—from the faculty. Modeled on the army boot camp, the workshop aimed to break students down at the beginning and rebuild them by the end of an intense week. Edom's other major contributions were launching the Pictures of the Year (POY) competition and the College Photographer of the Year contest.

Although the NPPA was intended for working photographers, it took an early interest in the education of students. In a chapter of *The Complete Book of Press Photography,* William Eckenberg, staff photographer for the *New York Times* and chair of the Education and Technical Committee, outlined an ideal curriculum for aspiring photojournalists. It started with technical aspects, such as cameras, lenses, filters, chemistry, and negatives, then moved to aesthetics, including lighting, camera angles, and cropping. After students mastered these, he advocated putting them on a rigid assignment schedule that would expose them to all kinds of situations. At the apex was indoctrination in ethics and people skills. Without the art of human relations, Eckenberg wrote, "their lot would be most difficult.... The press photographer comes in contact with people in every walk of life; ... he must often deal with difficult and sometimes unwilling subjects. Diplomacy and the art of getting along with people—in short, a knowledge of human relations—will be his biggest asset."[32]

Other photojournalism programs followed Missouri, including Syracuse University and the University of Minnesota, under Smith Schuneman. Somewhat later came the University of Kansas and Indiana University. Will Counts developed a strong photojournalism program at Indiana University, but his real accomplishment came at a broader level. Since the mid-1960s, the university's School of Journalism has required all majors to take a core course in visual communications, which features a hands-on photography component. This began under Dean John Stempel, who heeded the challenge of Basel Walters, executive editor of the Knight newspaper chain: "No man or woman should be permitted to have a journalism degree unless he or she has had at least an indoctrination course in news photography."[33]

After working as picture editor at the *Chicago Daily News* and the *Chicago Tribune,* Charles "Chuck" Scott moved to Athens, Ohio, in 1978, to launch the Institute of Visual Communications at Ohio University. It became the School of Visual Communications in 1986. Collaborating with him was Terry Eiler, who now runs the program. Western Kentucky University in Bowling Green has established a strong program, where majors take as many as seven courses. Students from Ohio University and Western Kentucky frequently take top honors in the Hearst competition and the College Picture of the Year. Other notable programs are at Syracuse University, San Francisco State, the University of North Carolina, the University of Texas at Austin, the University of Florida, Southern Illinois University, and the University of Nebraska.

In the mid-1940s, there was a plethora of contests for press photographers. Most were sponsored by trade agencies and associations—such as the Cigar Institute of America, the Coffee Institute, the Drinking Cup Institute, the National Fire Prevention Association, and the American Humane Association—to promote their products and causes. Within the profession, the Pulitzer board began awarding a prize for news photography in 1942. The first went to *Detroit News* photographer Milton Brooks for his picture of striking autoworkers attacking a dissenter. In higher education, the University of Missouri launched a contest in 1944 to pick the top fifty news and feature photographs of the year, and Kent State spotlighted the best news picture of the year.

NPPA leaders recognized the potential of contests to elevate the profession. "A photographer who covers his assignments with the thought in mind of winning prizes and honors in photo contests will inevitably be a better photographer, simply because he is trying to make better pictures," said Art Whitman, the NPPA's fifth president.[34] The leaders recognized that trade contests involved conflicts of interest, and they disliked competitions judged by nonphotographers. McLaughlin advocated "a contest for news photographers, judged by competent men in the trade," because "praise from fellow photographers" was "the highest accolade." He added, "the Pulitzer Prize has terrific prestige, but I think that in the years to come the NPPA prize ... can equal or even outrank it."[35]

Although most contests invite work from the previous calendar year, Costa felt the NPPA's first competition should recognize its members' entire careers. In 1948, "The Best Picture of My Life" contest drew more than nine hundred entries. First prize went to AP photographer Murray Becker for his 1937 picture of the explosion of the German dirigible *Hindenburg.* The one hundred top entries—comprising "sports and statesmanship, death and disaster, pathos and humor"—were exhibited across the country, including at the American Society of Newspaper Editors convention. The following year, the NPPA began an annual contest to select the Newspaper and Magazine Photographers of the Year.

During the next decade three competitions merged into one that dominated the profession. In 1944, Edom launched the Fifty Print Exhibition of Spot News and Feature Pictures at the University of Missouri, drawing 289 entries. By the end of the 1940s it combined with a contest sponsored by the *Encyclopaedia Britannica.*

The publisher provided funding, and Edom furnished the administration, the student workers, and the stature to attract large numbers of entries. In 1957, the NPPA joined Missouri and *Britannica* to sponsor the POY competition. Over time, corporate sponsorship passed to *World Book,* Nikon, Kodak, Canon, and MSNBC. From the beginning, winning entries were exhibited across the country and published in small-format collections. In 1974, Missouri and the NPPA began publishing large, glossy annuals titled *The Best of Photojournalism.*

In a disagreement over financing, the NPPA and Missouri ended their collaboration in 2001. The NPPA objected to Missouri's proposal to charge photographers entry fees to help cover costs. Missouri felt the NPPA had disrespected it by leaving logos of the university and the contest's corporate sponsors out of the 2000 edition of *The Best of Photojournalism.*[36] Despite urging from photojournalists, the two sides have not found a way to compromise and resume their cosponsorship of the contest. The NPPA conducts an annual competition called the Best of Photojournalism, while the University of Missouri continues to administer the more popular Pictures of the Year International (POYi). International was added in 2001, when Missouri globalized the call for entries and renamed the competition. In 2006, more than seventeen hundred newspaper and magazine photojournalists from four hundred publications in forty-five countries submitted over thirty-nine thousand entries. Awards were given in forty-six categories, including several for multimedia photojournalism.[37]

McLaughlin's prediction proved true. Although Pulitzer Prizes are better known to the public, within photojournalism the POY awards are the most coveted. Bill Garrett, former editor of *National Geographic,* called them the "Oscars of photojournalism."[38] George Smallsreed Jr. of the *Columbus (Ohio) Dispatch* summarized the attitude of many: "The only award I want . . . is the one called News Photographer of the Year. To me this is the big one. It is the one you have to earn."[39] Smallsreed got his wish in 1957.

In 1964, with the efforts of *Miami Herald* photographer Bob East, the NPPA launched a regional Photographer of the Year competition based on monthly judging of published clips. Top entries were published in *National Press Photographer,* and East devised a point system that designated regional winners. These contests helped advance the careers of winners. At most newspapers, the only promotion available to a staff photographer was to become chief photographer. Winning contests allowed many photojournalists to move from small newspapers to larger markets. Some have criticized the contests for creating a copycat syndrome. Picture-story topics or visual ideas that win are sure to be imitated the following year. Even so, as Whitman articulated, they have helped raise the technical, aesthetic, and conceptual levels of news pictures.

In the early years, there were intense debates over what kind of pictures the contest should honor. While many favored spot news pictures, others attributed them to luck and felt true skill showed when "the photographer has used his imagination and techniques to make something arresting out of the commonplace."[40] As a compromise, the University of Missouri and the NPPA based the top honor, Photographer of the Year, on portfolios of a year's work, but they also recognized single pictures in numerous categories, including spot news, features, sports, portraits, and picture stories.

The NPPA lobbied the Pulitzer board to broaden its awards as well. A 1954 editorial in *National Press Photographer* pointed out that there were as many or more kinds of photographs as written stories, which were recognized in many categories. "Year after year the Pulitzer Prize rules assign only one prize to news photography," it lamented. By lumping a wide variety of work into a single category, it concluded, "The Pulitzer Prize committee is bypassing the work of hundreds of competent press photographers. We believe they should get more consideration than this."[41] Change came slowly, but in 1968 the board added a Pulitzer for feature photography. The first award went to United Press International (UPI) photographer Toshio Sakai for his picture of an exhausted soldier in Vietnam, sleeping during a rainstorm after a firefight.

As television competed with and eventually replaced the newsreels, the NPPA welcomed television camera operators into the organization and offered them opportunities for professional development. In 1962, Costa and Ned Hockman of the University of Oklahoma began the TV NewsVideo Workshop with support from the U.S. Department of Defense. Dave Hamer, a veteran of television news in Omaha, Nebraska, was instrumental in two more of the NPPA's other major services for television members, the Quarterly TV News Contest in 1964 and the Airborne TV Seminar in 1993. All three continue today. The 2008 TV NewsVideo Workshop promised an immersion experience of twelve- to sixteen-hour days under a faculty with combined totals of eight Emmys, twenty-one Emmy nominations, and four Photographer of the Year Awards.[42]

In addition to the NPPA and higher education, the third factor in professionalization came as key newspapers, large and small, practiced a higher level of pictorial journalism and emerged as centers of photojournalistic excellence. An early leader was the *Milwaukee Journal*. Three dimensions made it distinctive. Its imaginative staff made photographs that went beyond the standard clichés, it pioneered several technical innovations and shared them with the industry, and it sent many leaders to the national level.

In the technical realm, *Journal* photographer Robert Dumke, who had studied electrical engineering, developed a device that synchronized a flashbulb with the Speed Graphic's focal-plane shutter, allowing exposures of 1/1,000 of a second. He also invented a camera that made three simultaneous exposures for color separations and an analyzer to check their color balance before engraving. In 1927, the *Journal* had begun publishing color photographs in its weekly rotogravure section, but they required a long lead time. In the mid-1940s, Dumke helped develop color printing in the daily newspaper. The *Journal* sold its color photographs to subscribing newspapers through the early 1970s. Another staff photographer, Edward Faber, helped develop an electronic strobe to replace flashbulbs. By October 1940, he and a partner had produced a strobe that could freeze action at 1/30,000 of a second. At twenty-five pounds, it was considered light enough to take on location.

Journal photographers were also early adopters of 35 mm cameras. Some bought them on their own, but by the late 1930s, the paper encouraged them to do so by providing interest-free loans. In 1954, it outfitted the entire staff with 35 mm cameras, becoming one of the first American newspapers to switch from Speed Graphics.

Although he was skeptical about the quality of 35 mm images, *Journal* picture editor Bob Gilka acknowledged the small camera had several advantages: People were less self-conscious about being photographed with a small camera. The cassette's thirty-six exposures made it easy to shoot sequences of pictures for a story. With faster lenses and film, the cameras let photographers shoot with less light, resulting in pictures that were more natural than those taken with flash. Also, the large Speed Graphic with its accompanying holders and flashbulbs signaled "press photographer," which caused some authorities to deny access. With a 35 mm camera, photographers could work inconspicuously.[43] Other newspapers began the transition after the 1956 political conventions when UPI photographers using 35 mm cameras beat the competition with naturalistic pictures from the convention floor.

Regarding national leadership, in the early 1930s, the *Journal*'s picture editor Ed Thompson launched a daily picture page. He then succeeded in taking control of the assignments from the city and news editors. Many photography staffs did not achieve this vital structural change until the 1960s and 1970s. Thompson went on to become managing editor of *Life* magazine from 1949 to 1961 and founding editor of *Smithsonian* magazine in 1970. The *Journal* also sent some of its photojournalists to the national level, including Joe Scherschel and Howard Sochurek (*Life*), James Stanfield and Thomas Abercrombie (*National Geographic*), Heinz Kluetmeier (*Sports Illustrated*), and Gilka (*National Geographic,* director of photography). In education, Angus McDougal became a professor at the University of Missouri, and John Ahlhauser taught at Indiana University. Robert Boyd and Ahlhauser became presidents of the NPPA. After retiring from Indiana University, Ahlhauser, with the help of his wife, Lois, founded the popular Stan Kalish Picture Editing Workshop, which helps photographers make the transition to the picture desk.

Other metropolitan newspapers that developed national reputations from the 1950s into the 1980s included the *Cincinnati Enquirer, (Louisville) Courier-Journal, Louisville Times, Dallas Times Herald, Denver Post, Norfolk (Virginia) Pilot / Ledger, Orange County (California) Register, Philadelphia Inquirer, Pittsburg Post-Gazette, St. Petersburg (Florida) Times,* and *Topeka (Kansas) Capital-Journal.* The national newspaper of record, the *New York Times,* began to improve its picture usage under picture editor John Morris in the 1970s. For many years during the 1990s, its Sunday magazine published picture stories on news events and global problems.

While the magazine has abandoned long-form photojournalism, the daily *Times* publishes graphic photographs of war, terror, and natural disasters that most newspapers avoid.

The most important institutional change at these newspapers occurred when photojournalists took control of the assignment and selection processes from word editors. In many newsrooms, assistant city editors, whose interest and expertise lay outside photography, had been responsible for generating assignments. They relied on cliché ideas and requests by people seeking publicity. The litany of bad assignments included check presentations, ribbon cuttings, posed handshakes (known as grip-n-grins), and pictures of groups (called firing squad shots, as in "line 'em up and shoot 'em"). These situations, often concocted by public relations firms, produced static results. As photojournalism moved from the Speed Graphic approach of posing subjects to the 35 mm aesthetic of capturing spontaneity, such assignments became untenable. At excellent newspapers, photojournalists and picture editors gained control of the assignment process. Photographers generated pictures on their own initiative. Chief photographers planned coverage of complex events. Picture editors coordinated with city, sports, features, and business editors to illustrate stories with visual potential. As photographers and picture editors demonstrated they could not merely take orders but initiate single pictures and photo stories, they earned the status of visual journalists.

One photojournalist who helped shape this transition was Rich Clarkson, who in 1957 became director of photography of a staff serving the *State Journal* and the *Daily Capital* in Topeka, Kansas. Clarkson was a born mentor and understood how to produce change. He convinced his publisher to adopt 35 mm cameras by arguing that it would save money on film. He broke the attitude that his staff was a service department by pushing them to develop "good editorial ideas" and build alliances with the best reporters in the newsroom. The staff was too small to have a picture editor, so Clarkson deputized all his photographers. "The first thing I want you to do as you go out and photograph every day is to think like a picture editor," he told them. "Think how the picture is going to be used.... Shoot both a vertical and a horizontal, do whatever you can to make it very usable. And then I want you to go to the state desk or modern living or whatever and act like a picture editor—sell the picture and work with them to get the size and the cropping and the play as close to" optimal as possible.[44]

When a photographer mastered that level, Clarkson moved her or him up a step. "Now I want you to think like a managing editor," he would say. Become aware of the total news situation "so you don't try to jam a picture down the new editor's throat for page 1 when, in fact, there is a big international or national story going that day." He taught his staff to think strategically, saving their best ideas for Sundays, which typically were the slowest days of the week.[45]

Clarkson sent many Topeka alumni to important photojournalism positions across the nation: After serving as UPI bureau chief in Saigon during the Vietnam War, Bill Snead became director of photography for the *Washington Post*. Pulitzer Prize–winner Brian Lanker rebuilt the *Eugene (Oregon) Register-Guard* into a top visual newspaper. After stints at the *Chicago Daily News* and the *New York Times,* Gary Settle became director of photography of the *Seattle Times.* Mark Godfrey became director of the New York office of Magnum Photos, and David Alan Harvey became president of Magnum U.S. After being publisher of *National Geographic Traveler,* Dave Johnson served as director of photography at the White House. Also at *National Geographic,* Sara Leen became senior photo editor, David Griffin, director of photography, and Chris Johns, editor in chief.

Clarkson's personal career provided a model for many ambitious photojournalists. In addition to twenty-three years at the *Capital-Journal,* he was director of photography and senior assistant editor at *National Geographic,* and assistant managing editor for graphics at the *Denver Post.* As a magazine contract photographer, he specialized in sports, covering eight Olympics and organizing coverage for *Time* and *Sports Illustrated* and other publications. In 1987, he incorporated Rich Clarkson Associates, which publishes books, creates exhibitions, and offers multimedia services for clients such as the National Collegiate Athletic Association and the Colorado Rockies. Clarkson gave back generously to the profession, serving as NPPA president in 1975, as head of the Flying Short Course for fourteen years, and as the creator of workshops in sports and wildlife photography.

Life magazine played a role in lifting the quality of newspaper photography. *Life* photographers led the transition to 35 mm cameras, and newspaper staffers attempted to emulate the technical achievements or innovative visual ideas they saw in the magazine. Many began producing the classic picture story as single pages or small sections. The influence extended to logistical practices as well. After *Life* chartered a plane to process, print, and lay out coverage of Winston Churchill's funeral as it flew from London to New York, Clarkson was inspired to process film in the trunk of his car. "Racing back to the office from the football stadium," he would stop "every ten minutes and go around to the back and pour out the developer and pour in the fixer" so he had negatives ready to print when he got to the office.[46]

Although most photojournalists lamented the demise of *Look* in 1970 and *Life* in 1972, one argued that it had a positive impact on

newspaper photojournalism. "The disappearance of strong magazine photojournalism may have been the best thing that ever happened to newspaper photographers," Professor Greg Lewis wrote.
"Without the mecca of magazines to monopolize their dreams
and without the magazine photojournalist to worship and imitate,
newspaper photographers at last were forced to focus on what was
essentially the only outlet left to them, the newspaper."[47]

Excellence never happens by accident; in each case there
were key photojournalists—chief photographers, department
managers, and picture editors—who did the tedious day-to-day,
person-to-person work to build a quality staff, gain control of
assignments and picture selection, and fight for space to publish
photographs at an effective size. Often these photojournalists
found allies among senior editors, such as Eugene L. Roberts Jr.
at the *Philadelphia Inquirer* and John Temple at the *Rocky Mountain
News* in Denver. On rare occasions, photojournalists rose to the
top ranks at newspapers—David Yarnold of the *San Jose Mercury
News* and J. Bruce Baumann of the Evansville, Indiana, *Courier and
Press* became managing editors, executive editors, and editors at
their newspapers. Excellence is also a fragile thing, and in many
cases when key leaders retired or moved on, the quality of photojournalism declined.

These three factors—NPPA programs, the increase in
college-educated photojournalists, and the leadership of excellent
newspapers—combined to produce a golden age of print photojournalism lasting roughly from the 1960s through the early 1980s.
A fourth factor also contributed. During the 1960s, television
displaced newspapers as the dominant medium. With declines
in newspaper circulation and advertising, publishers and senior
editors hoped photography would attract and hold readers. During the 1960s and 1970s, many newspapers increased their staffs,

devoted more space to photographs, added color, hired picture editors, and in many cases created the position of assistant managing editor for photography. Notwithstanding the character Animal on the *Lou Grant* sitcom, who resurrected all the old stereotypes, photojournalists were being accepted as professionals in the newsroom. Their increased skills in producing remarkable pictures in spot news, sports, features, and studio illustrations added to the respect.

The introduction of *USA Today* in 1983, with its emphasis on color graphics and small, often static photographs, halted this trend. Publishers shifted their hopes to color graphics, including charts, diagrams, timelines, and break-out boxes. Soon assistant managing editors for graphics replaced assistant managing editors for photography. This graphic revolution was advanced by the computerization of the newspaper industry, which changed the structure of newsrooms. As pagination replaced cold type in the late 1980s and 1990s and production moved from print shops to the newsroom, a new position arose. Page designers, working on computers, had control of the last step in the newsroom process before pages went to the platemakers. Their skills and thought processes inclined these designers toward graphics more than photography.

In the early twenty-first century, steep increases in the cost of newsprint and the migration of readers and advertisers to the Internet have compounded the squeeze on print photojournalism. Most newspapers are owned by public corporations that are traded on Wall Street. Analysts, who wield great power over stock prices, push these corporations to pursue profits, not serve the public trust. The recession of 2008, the financial problems of legendary newspapers such as the *Chicago Tribune,* and the bleak prospects for the newspaper industry have prompted deep cuts in staff and space. While photojournalism remains an important component, most photographs are confined to section fronts. Often page designers follow a formula that calls for a main photograph and one or two secondary ones. The lead photograph is not necessarily the best one available, but one chosen to illustrate the lead story.

Because of these and other stresses, many photojournalists have turned to book projects or found ways to display their work on the Internet, where space is less of an issue.

SEVEN

SEEING THE WORLD THROUGH
A HUMANIST VISION

Two great traditions have dominated Western culture. Christianity has emphasized the sinful nature of mankind and its need to seek forgiveness from a god of retribution. In contrast, the Greek tradition of humanism has, in the words of Protagoras, seen man "as the measure of all things."[1] Whatever their personal beliefs, most photojournalists work in the humanist tradition, inclined to see religion as one dimension of the human condition.

The term *humanism* can refer to a branch of ethics, a set of attitudes, or a modern movement. Italians coined the word *umanista* during the 1400s to refer to teachers and scholars of classical Greek and Latin literature. Their studies launched the Renaissance, which helped break the church's control over education and thought. The drive for knowledge and freedom to think led to the Reformation in the 1500s and the Enlightenment in the 1700s. Enlightenment philosophers in France and England rejected divine revelation in favor of scientific knowledge discovered by man. In politics, Enlightenment thought justified the American Revolution and inscribed freedom of the press and separation of church and state in the U.S. Constitution.

Humanism became institutionalized with the founding of the American Humanist Association in 1941 and the International Humanist and Ethical Union in 1952. The manifesto for the American Humanist Association defines humanism as "a progressive philosophy of life" that "affirms our ability and responsibility to lead ethical lives of personal fulfillment ... [for] the greater good of humanity."[2] The founding dates of the two groups bracket World War II and the birth of the United Nations. The United Nations embraced humanist principles in the prologue to its charter, declaring as its central purpose "to reaffirm faith in fundamental human rights, in the dignity and worth of the human person, in the equal rights of men and women and of nations large and small."[3] These ideals are part of the heritage of American photojournalists. The 1955 exhibition The Family of Man is a direct link between their ideals and the humanism of the United Nations.

For most photojournalists, humanism is a strongly held, if often unanalyzed, set of attitudes about themselves, their subjects, and the power of photography. These attitudes overlap with three core tenets of philosophical humanism: the belief that, at an essential level, every subject is on an equal plane with the photographer; the belief in the dignity and worth of each individual and in that person's right to self-fulfillment; and the belief that photography can help achieve a world in which every person is allowed to realize her or his dignity and self-worth.

Social documentary photographers from Hine to the FSA used humanism as a strategy to promote reform. This alignment of humanism with the political left was not just an American phenomenon. The oft-used phrase "the human condition" was the title of a novel about Communists in Shanghai, China, that the French leftist André Malraux published in 1933. During the 1930s, many European photojournalists—including Robert Capa,

David Seymour, and Henri Cartier-Bresson, who would influence American photojournalists—were engaged on the left. In Europe during this period, before Stalin's worst depredations were known, Communism was seen not as a totalitarian regime but as the only alternative to the fascism of Hitler, Mussolini, and Franco. During the Great Depression, many Americans, from intellectuals to union laborers, embraced the left as a corrective for the excesses of capitalism.

To the degree that *Life, Look,* and other picture magazines tried to show their readers to themselves, they advanced a humanism that coincided with their economic interests. Just as humanism was a successful strategy for the FSA photographers, so too it made sense for the picture magazines to include stories on people drawn from their readership. Leonard McCombe's essay on Gwyned Filling's attempts to launch a career in New York City was compelling because she typified so many *Life* readers.

Drawing on the FSA ethos and the picture magazines, a major exhibition marked the high point of twentieth-century photographic humanism. In 1955, Edward Steichen mounted The Family of Man exhibition at the Museum of Modern Art in New York. From there, it traveled the world and was seen by nine million people. Its enthusiastic reception by the public was matched by harsh criticism from the art world. While their comments offer important insights, these critics miss the exhibition's key point— Steichen conceived it as an argument against nuclear devastation. However much the art world rejects The Family of Man, photojournalists embrace its attitudes and themes and continue to work under its influence.

By 1955, Steichen had achieved a renowned career in photography. In the early 1900s, he figured prominently as a leader of pictorialism, the movement that succeeded in having photography recognized as one of the fine arts. After World War I, he became the premier photographer for *Vogue* and other Condé Nast magazines, as well as for the J. Walter Thompson public-relations firm. When the United States entered World War II, the navy put Steichen in charge of its photographic operations in the Pacific. He also was curator of several exhibitions at the Museum of Modern Art on the war effort. After the war, in a move to raise the profile of its photography department, the Museum of Modern Art hired Steichen as director of its photography department. After several smaller exhibitions, he began what he considered his greatest achievement, The Family of Man exhibition.

John G. Morris believes he influenced Steichen's thinking about the exhibition. As picture editor of the *Ladies Home Journal,* Morris commissioned Magnum photographers to record the everyday lives and problems of twelve families in twelve countries for a series entitled "People Are People the World Over." In his introduction to the first installment in the May 1948 issue, Morris noted the families represented "twelve countries, three races and five religious faiths. They speak eleven languages." He said the series would show "that people are pretty much people, no matter where you find them." Morris said Steichen was struck by the series so much that in 1949, he borrowed several of its pictures to make a window display to celebrate the anniversary of the United Nations. "Steichen began to dream, sharing his hopes with me, of an exhibition he would eventually call 'The Family of Man,'" Morris wrote.[4]

Despite their shared theme, Steichen did not mention Morris or his "People Are People" series in his acknowledgments in the exhibition book or in his autobiography. Instead he credited his brother-in-law Carl Sandburg, the poet and Lincoln biographer. Steichen recalled he was thumbing through Sandburg's biography of Lincoln when "I ran across a speech in which Lincoln used the term 'family of man.' Here was the all-embracing theme for the exhibition."[5]

Steichen said he wanted to show "the essential oneness of mankind throughout the world." In 1952, he sent out a general invitation to professional and notable amateur photographers around the world, calling for photographs that conveyed the exhibition's humanist theme. He requested "photographs, made in all parts of the world, of the gamut of life from birth to death with emphasis on the relationships of man to himself, to his family, to the community and to the world we live in—subject matter ranging from babies to philosophers, from the kindergarten to the university, from primitive peoples to the Councils of the United Nations."[6]

In addition to the thousands of submitted photographs, Steichen's assistant Wayne Miller examined two million photographs in the archives at *Life* magazine, the Farm Security Administration, Magnum Photos, and other collections. From an initial pool of about ten thousand, Steichen and his staff narrowed them to one thousand. "The final reduction from one thousand to five hundred . . . became a real struggle and was often heartbreaking," he wrote. "It involved the necessary elimination of many fine photographs."[7] The final selection comprised 503 images, taken by 273 photographers in sixty-eight countries. Steichen summarized their contents:

> Photographs of lovers and marriage and child-bearing, of the family unit with its joys, trials and tribulations, its deep-rooted devotions and its antagonisms. Photographs of the home in all its warmth and magnificence, its heartache and exaltations. Photographs of the individual and the family unit in its reactions to the beginnings of life and continuing on through death and burial. . . .

Photographs concerned with the religious rather than religions. With basic human consciousness rather than social consciousness. Photographs concerned with man's dreams and aspirations and photographs of the flaming creative forces of love and truth and the corrosive evil inherent in the lie.[8]

In what some have likened to Shakespeare's "seven ages of man," the photographs proceed from instances of love and courtship to marriage, pregnancy, and childbirth. Between birth and death are pictures of mothers nursing, cuddling, and instructing their children. Others show bonding between fathers and children. A father in Bechuanaland teaches his son to hunt with a spear, and a New York father and son share a couch as they read the newspaper. There are numerous photographs of children, including eighteen of groups playing ring-around-the-rosy.

In keeping with the exhibition's title, there are many images of the family, including four showing extended families in Sicily, Japan, Bechuanaland, and the United States. They are similar in size, square format, and photographic approach. In each, family members are frontally posed, gazing into the camera lens. There is a commonality in content as well. All make their livings directly from the land. Three are farm families; the African family, hunters. The Sicilian father wears patched pants and worn shoes. His wife has a safety pin on her dress where a wealthier woman might wear a brooch. The Japanese family, from toddler to stooped grandfather, stands in a rice paddy, the adults leaning on their cultivating tools. The American family encapsulates the midwestern farm ethos. Gathered around a potbelly stove, the men wear bib overalls and straw hats; the women, aprons. In the foreground, the matriarch sits in a rocking chair next to the youngest member, a chubby boy of about four years.

Central to all four images are expressions of love within and between generations. Mothers hold infants or toddlers, fathers extend a protective arm around children, husbands rest an affectionate hand on their wives' shoulder. The U.S. photograph extends beyond the three generations present. On the wall in the background are four large framed photographs from the 1800s that show the family's ancestors.

These images at the heart of the exhibition argue Steichen's thesis that, in essence, families are the same around the world. Differences in hairstyles, clothing, habitat, and dwelling—even polygamy in the African family—are inconsequential compared to the shared bonds that guarantee the species' continuity from one generation to the next.

Other photographs depict the theme of sharing: friends sharing drink and conversation and families around a table sharing food. There were numerous variations on the theme of work. Most celebrated the hand labor of sledgehammers, axes, and sickles, of harvesting, threshing, fishing, baking, and washing clothes. Some show the modernized work of tractors and assembly lines. Several demonstrate that laborers the world over suffer the same fatigue and thirst. As an antidote to the drudgery of work, The Family of Man documents many forms of play, from a game of checkers in a general store to swimming to card playing. In numerous pictures, people sing and play instruments. A few are professionals in jazz bands and symphony orchestras, but most are ordinary people: women singing at a quilting bee, a girl by a lake playing her recorder, an old man playing a mandolin in a dingy Italian street, and five Soviet friends playing chamber music. Repeated throughout the exhibition is a photograph of an Andean woman, her eyes twinkling and her mouth in a smile as she plays her wooden flute. Equally abundant are photographs of dance, ranging from ballet to the Scottish fling, from jitterbug to ballroom waltzes, from folk dances in Germany, Colombia, and Mauritania to sexual abandon in Brazil.

Education is represented by scenes from lecture halls and classrooms, children doing their sums on a blackboard, and a close-up of the hands of an old man learning to write the alphabet in a copybook. At the higher levels, a photograph showed Albert Einstein lost in thought; a second showed J. Robert Oppenheimer, head of the Manhattan Project, which developed the first atomic bomb, talking with physics students in a seminar at the Institute for Advanced Study at Princeton University. Several pictures captured religious piety, reverence, and longing. They include five women in Kasmir, praying toward Mecca; three boys reading the Torah in Czechoslovakia; and a street sweeper in Colombia kneeling in reverence as a priest walks by.

Balancing the overwhelming number of positive photographs are a small group that acknowledge global problems: scenes of Jews being marched through the Warsaw Ghetto on their way to the death camps, screaming Korean women demonstrating behind a barbed-wire barricade, a graffito on the side of an Indonesian streetcar demanding equality, and two men hurling rocks at a tank in eastern Europe. Images from the Great Depression show people in economic distress. Others show famine victims around the world, including a Chinese boy shivering in the cold and holding out his empty rice bowl to beg for food. Other images reflect law and government, including a trial in France, an American judge deep in contemplation, small political gatherings in America, South Africa, and Iran, and citizens voting in France, Japan, China, and Turkey.

From its opening to the present, critics have harshly criticized The Family of Man exhibition on political, aesthetic, and cultural grounds. Roland Barthes saw it as an example of using nature—the presumed universality of human experience—as a myth to conceal the injustices of history. Referencing Marxist thought, he argued that Steichen's show denied historical determinism by insisting that birth, death, work, religion, and other humanist themes are natural and thus beyond challenge. It is the economic specifics in which such universalities occur that are important. "True, children are *always* born," he wrote, but what is important is "whether or not the child is born with ease or difficulty, whether or not his birth causes suffering to his mother, whether or not he is threatened by a high mortality rate, whether or not such and such a type of future is open to him: this is what your exhibitions should be telling people, instead of an eternal lyricism of birth." Instead of the universality of work, investigate who profits from the laborer's toil, Barthes insisted. Emphasizing universals implies nothing can be done to correct specific injustices and inequalities. Barthes accused the exhibition of offering an alibi for inaction by positing "a 'wisdom' and a 'lyricism' which only make the gestures of man look eternal the better to defuse them."[9]

The postmodern photographer Allan Sekula offered a related Marxist critique. "The Family of Man universalizes the bourgeois nuclear family, suggesting a globalized, utopian family album, a family romance imposed on every corner of the earth," Sekula wrote. Calling the exhibition "the epitome of American cold war liberalism," he argued the United States saw itself as the powerful, controlling father in the global family of nations in which "the family serves as a metaphor also for a system of international discipline and harmony." Sekula pointed out the U.S. Information Service financed the circulation of the exhibition around the world as a vehicle to advance U.S. cultural dominance during the cold war.[10]

Christopher Phillips, in his postmodern account of the Museum of Modern Art's photography department, said the exhibition called up "very real social and political anxieties," which it tried to resolve facilely "with positive (imaginary) solutions." Phillips also criticized Steichen for imposing his own message on the 503 photographs instead of transmitting the vision and intentions of the individual photographers. According to Phillips, Steichen's method was to "prise photographs from their original contexts, to discard or alter their captions, to recrop their borders in the enforcement of a unitary meaning, to reprint them for dramatic impact, to redistribute them in new narrative chains consistent with a predetermined thesis." Thus the photographer slipped "from the status of autonomous artist to that of illustrator of" Steichen's ideas.[11]

Jacques Barzun, a professor of cultural history at Columbia University, criticized the exhibition for emphasizing mankind's "animal needs and sensual pleasures" above his intellectual achievements. He deplored its preference for primitivism over the accomplishments of Western intellect: "Whatever is formed and constituted (the work seems to say), whatever is adult, whatever exerts power, whatever is characteristically Western, whatever is unique or has a name, or embodies the complexity of thought, is of less interest and worth than what is native, common and sensual."[12]

The art critic Hilton Kramer criticized The Family of Man as superficial. He argued its theme of "the essential oneness of mankind" was based on a "vacancy of thought" that ignored "the nagging details of our actual lives."[13] Kramer was most disturbed by the exhibition's design, which he thought undermined photography's status as an art form. Unlike most museum exhibitions, which hang framed images of approximately the same size at the same height, The Family of Man was designed by an architect, who borrowed ideas from the picture magazines. The prints were not matted or framed. Many were wall size, but there were jolting shifts in scale. Several were suspended from the ceiling, and the photographs of children playing ring-around-the-rosy were mounted on a round wheel that visitors could spin. Literary quotations were substituted for the scholarly wall labels typical of museum exhibitions. Most significant, the photographs were not presented as the works of individual artists, but sequenced to advance Steichen's message. This was too much for Kramer, who insisted that a major museum should not subject art photography to such journalistic techniques. "What is disheartening," he wrote, "is to see the agency which claims to preside over the artistic values of photography tumble so easily into the vulgar ideological postures which, with less fanfare and less prestige, if also less taste, thousands of periodicals every day embrace as a matter of course."[14]

Postmodern critics have faulted Steichen for implying that photographers with Western biases could bridge the vast cultural gaps inherent in a collection of pictures from sixty-eight countries. Affirming an "unbridgeable distance between viewer and viewed," John Perivolaris castigated, "the presumptuous familiarity of humanist photography, which assumes that the most exotic subjects are readable because of their universal humanity."[15]

While these criticisms offer valid insights, none addresses Steichen's underlying objective for the exhibition or the historical context that shaped his thinking. The Family of Man did not champion humanism for its own sake, but as the world's best hope to avert a nuclear holocaust. In his autobiography, Steichen said he had intended three earlier exhibitions of war photography to be antiwar statements but had failed in his objective. "Although I had presented war in all its grimness in three exhibitions, I had failed to accomplish my mission," he wrote. "I had not incited people into taking open and united action against war itself. This failure made me take stock of my fundamental idea. What was wrong? I came to the conclusion that I had been working from a negative approach."[16]

In planning The Family of Man, he decided to try a positive approach, to present humankind as too valuable to be subjected to the ravages of another war. "What was needed," he wrote, "was a positive statement on what a wonderful thing life was, how marvelous people were, and above all, how alike people were in all parts of the world."[17]

Steichen's efforts must be seen against the widespread nuclear anxiety that followed World War II. Now, more than six decades after the United States dropped nuclear bombs on Hiroshima and Nagasaki, it is difficult to recapture the fear produced by the annihilation of those civilian targets. In 1952, when Steichen began assembling the exhibition, Europe and Japan were still recovering from the trauma of World War II, the Korean War was still being fought, and the cold war was threatening to ignite World War III. Everybody assumed it would be fought with nuclear weapons. By the time of the exhibition, the Soviet Union had developed its own nuclear arsenal, exploding an atomic bomb in 1949 and a hydrogen bomb in 1955. The American military regularly tested atomic bombs above ground. As the nuclear arms race accelerated, American school children practiced crouching under their desks.

In 1946, a group of physicists published an eighty-six-page booklet entitled *One World or None.* Several of its authors had been involved in the Manhattan Project, which had developed the atomic bombs dropped on Japan. Horrified by the devastation, they argued against any future military application, calling instead for the peaceful use of atomic energy under international control. Nobel laureate Albert Einstein wrote, "The construction of the atom bomb has brought about the effect that all the people living in cities are threatened, everywhere and constantly, with sudden destruction."[18] Oppenheimer, director of the Manhattan Project and widely known as the "father of the atomic bomb," wrote, "The conscious acquisition of these new powers of destruction calls for the equally conscious determination that they must not be used and that all necessary steps be taken to insure that they will not be used."[19]

While much of the development of America's nuclear arsenal was classified, the government did release selected details through the news media, including its nuclear tests in the Marshall Islands in the south Pacific Ocean. In 1952, the U.S. military tested its first nuclear fusion bomb in the Eniwetok Atoll. Ground zero, the island of Elugelab, was completely vaporized, leaving in its place a mile-wide crater. In 1954, less than a year before The Family of Man opened, Operation Castle on the Bikini Atoll unleashed over 20 percent more power than expected. This contaminated natives on islands several miles away and fishermen on the Japanese vessel *Lucky Dragon,* which was operating in the area. All twenty-three of them suffered radiation poisoning, and one soon died. American news media covered these stories prominently. *Life* magazine superimposed a map over an aerial view of the Eniwetok Atoll, with an outline where the island of Elugelab should have been. It published a close-up photograph of one of the Japanese fishermen, his face and ear showing radiation burns, his hair being tested by a Geiger counter. It also ran a story on plans to evacuate major U.S. cities in case of a nuclear attack, complete with maps showing circles radiating out from ground zero indicating the levels of destruction. These were only a few of the constant reminders that global devastation from a nuclear conflict was an imminent possibility.

That The Family of Man had a strong anti–nuclear war message has faded with time, primarily because most people know the project only through its book version, which omitted the most telling photograph. The front of the exhibition had an open design that allowed visitors to wander freely through large rooms, enjoying the positive pictures. As the exhibition built toward its climax, the space tightened. Baffles slowed visitors, encouraging them to spend more time contemplating pictures of contemporary problems. This section concluded with nine portraits of men, women, and children whose somber expressions seemed to interrogate the viewer. They were accompanied by a quote from the British philosopher Bertrand Russell: "The best authorities are unanimous in saying that a war with hydrogen bombs is quite likely to put an end to the human race. There will be universal death—sudden only for a fortunate minority, but for the majority a slow torture of disease and disintegration."[20]

Visitors then passed a photograph of a dead American soldier sprawled in a foxhole and entered a darkened room that contained "the single most arresting and important image of the exhibition."[21] The photograph was a mural-size enlargement of a hydrogen bomb explosion (see figure 21). The climax of Steichen's antinuclear message, it was the only picture that was not published in the book. It was also the only color image in the show, a transparency with rear lighting that made it glow. "After 450 black-and-white images," wrote photographic historian Eric J. Sandeen, "viewers were shocked back into poly-chromatic reality with this reminder of life in the modern world."[22]

Visitors entered the final room, where pictures of families and children were now seen in the context of the hydrogen bomb photograph. Portraits of seven couples, intended to represent all nations and ethnic groups, bore the same caption: "We two form a multitude." The label for a wall-sized photograph of the United Nations General Assembly quoted a portion of the U.N. Charter:

> We, the peoples of the United Nations, determined to save suc-ceeding generations from the scourge of war, which twice in our lifetime has brought untold sorrow to mankind, and to reaffirm faith in fundamental human rights, in the dignity and worth of the human person, in the equal rights of men and women and of nations large and small . . .[23]

Images of children filled the rest of the room. Just before exit-ing, visitors saw a photograph by W. Eugene Smith of his young children, walking past a dark foreground into a bright expanse of trees. A quote—"A world to be born under your footsteps . . ."—offered hope to the exhibition's visitors, but also implied the ne-cessity for them to choose.

The book conveys an antiwar message, but only the exhibition expressed the antinuclear message. None of the exhibition's critics have acknowledged Steichen's intentions or the historical context that produced them.

Whether or not photojournalists are aware of this antinuclear message, most have embraced its humanism either through study-ing the book or imbibing it indirectly through the humanist work of colleagues. As one example, the World Understanding category in the Pictures of the Year competition is a direct descendant of Steichen's exhibition.

Lest humanism seem inevitable, it should be noted that it is not the only option for documentary photographers and photo-journalists. Weegee, Lisette Model, Diane Arbus, Garry Win-ogrand, and Martin Paar, to name only a few, have expressed sar-donic views of humanity.

EIGHT

THE DIGITAL FUTURE

Of the many technological innovations that have advanced photography since 1839, the most profound is the transformation from film and chemistry to digital. This altering of the medium's fundamental base was not an evolutionary development, but a radical break. It unleashed a flood of innovations, improvements, and problems. At its beginning, photography relied on mechanical, optical, and chemical processes. Over time, the machine evolved from a simple wooden box with an opening and a few hinges to a computer-driven marvel of engineering. Optics evolved from a single lens to assemblies of several lenses working as a unit and ranging in focal length from fish-eye to extreme telephoto. Lenses also gained the abilities to admit more light, cover larger negatives, and zoom (change focal lengths).

Similar advances occurred in chemistry as emulsions became more light sensitive, letting photographers shoot in lower light and make faster exposures. The base of traditional photography was the film and print that held images in emulsions of silver or color dyes. Light reflected from the subject activates the silver or dyes, forming a latent image that is made visible by development in chemical baths. The resulting images are analog, or continuous. Even at high magnification, no breaks in their structure are visible.

While there is continuity in cameras and lenses, since the early 1990s digital technology has completely replaced the fundamental chemical-film-paper nature of photography. The digital process records light impulses as electronic charges stored on a memory card and then transferred to a computer. Instead of continuous fields of silver or dyes, a digital image is discontinuous—a matrix of rows and columns. They intersect to form tiny squares called picture elements, or pixels, which carry information about brightness and color. Each pixel exists separately from its neighbors. Typically the resolution, or number of pixels per inch, is so high that human vision synthesizes them into an image that appears unbroken. But when enlarged sufficiently, the boundaries between pixels are visible. As with all computerized technology, at the most basic level the information in each pixel comprises electronic pulses expressed as strings of zeros and ones. Digital photographs can undergo the same operations as all computer files, including being edited, stored, copied, transformed into a variety of formats, transmitted over the Internet, and deleted.

The development of digital photography occurred in two distinct phases: the digitized image preceded the digital camera. Digital photography had its origins in the 1960s as NASA scientists developed a method for Voyager space probes to send images back to Earth. The images were scanned, or reduced to ones and zeros, which could be transmitted as electronic signals. For several years, digital photography was limited to scanning analog prints or negatives into pixel files. In 1981, Sony introduced the first digital camera, the Mavica, making it possible to produce digital photographs directly with a camera. Improvements in speed and image quality increased rapidly, and the cost of digital cameras fell. Beginning in the early 1990s, photojournalists became the first group of photographers to use digital cameras extensively. Art photographers remain divided. Many use traditional film-based cameras and chemical processes, some work exclusively in digital processes, and many combine both approaches. Following the industry's lead, most amateurs have switched to digital cameras. As the industry persuaded millions of amateurs to scrap their film cameras as obsolete and buy digital ones, it reaped a financial windfall.

Digital technologies transformed the working methods of photojournalists on assignment. With traditional cameras, photographers are not sure what images they have until they process their film. Digital cameras feature liquid crystal display (LCD) screens that allow photojournalists to review what they have shot while still covering an event. They can decide whether they have the necessary story-telling photographs or need to pursue certain content. They can delete poor pictures, fill gaps in the visual narrative, and reshoot to correct problems in focus, exposure, and composition.

Early digital cameras produced images of low quality compared to analog prints. In 2000, photojournalists who wanted high-resolution images had to pay thirty-thousand dollars for Nikon and Canon single-lens reflex (SLR) cameras that Eastman Kodak retrofitted with digital sensors and processors. Quality, as measured in pixels per image, steadily rose and costs decreased. By late 2008, Canon's 14.7-megapixel PowerShot G10 was selling for five hundred dollars and Nikon's 24.5-megapixel D3X for eight thousand.

The capacity of memory cards also increased dramatically, leading to continuous recording. Motor-drive cameras that took up to four film exposures per second were available in the 1960s, but the photographer was still limited to thirty-six frames before having to change the roll of film. Digital cameras now offer the option of shooting still frames or switching to video mode for extended recording. These dual-mode cameras also make possible the production of videos for the Web editions of publications.

The digital camera has the potential for radically altering the practice of photojournalism. Since the advent of the 35 mm camera, news photographers developed their instincts and reflexes to get into position, anticipate the peak action, and press the shutter at the precise instant to capture it. Continuous recording threatens to devalue those skills by eliminating the need to concentrate on shutter timing. Anyone can press a button to start recording. The memory chip can be passed to an editor who will extract a frame showing the peak action or a revealing expression.

As a positive development, the digital environment has given photojournalists more input in the editing process. During the film-based era, at many newspapers and magazines, the picture editor would study contact sheets of a photographer's entire take and make the selection. There are no contact sheets with digital photography. While it is possible to download an entire take for a picture editor to review, in practice many photojournalists make an initial selection of a few images and forward them to the picture desk. This is particularly the case on assignments where the photographer does not come back to the office. As Dirck Halstead, former White House photographer for *Time* magazine, expressed, "The ability to edit our own takes has given back to us the creative process control we used to have." Referring to a three-picture spread in *Time* by photojournalist P. F. Bentley in 2001, Halstead, who is now editor and publisher of the *Digital Journalist,* said, "Although the editors had the final selection choice, P. F. was able to make the initial selection, Photoshopping them on his laptop. The ability to edit our own takes is like learning to take control of the creative process all over again."[1]

The digital process changed the time of the workflow to the advantage of both photojournalists and their publications. Eliminating the chemical phase saved considerable time formerly required to process film, make prints, and have them engraved. That time can now be spent covering the event. Significant time is also saved on getting images back to the publication. Instead of driving back to the office, photographers can plug a memory card into a laptop computer, select and caption the images, and transmit them by cell phone to their picture desk. This logistical advantage can happen from a football game across town or a war in a foreign country. It is particularly valuable when covering events on a tight deadline.

Conversion to digital brought economic benefits to news organizations. Substantial savings resulted from eliminating wet-chemistry darkrooms. Costly film, paper, and chemicals were no longer needed. A roll of film, for example, could be used only once, but a computer chip can be erased and reused continually. Darkroom space could be put to other uses, reducing overhead costs. Not having to dispose of dangerous chemicals reduced costs further and decreased photojournalism's impact on the environment. Despite the initial investment required for digital cameras, computer hardware and software, and storage capacity, conversion has brought a net savings for publishers.

Perhaps the greatest advantage to the publication is an operational one. Concurrent with the development of digital photography, newspapers and magazines transformed their printing process from the cold-type system, where printers pasted up pages in a back shop, to one where editors and designers produce them on computers in the newsroom. Thousands of printers' jobs were eliminated as pages went from the newsroom directly to the plate-making operation. Pagination requires computer-compatible images, and digital pictures merged seamlessly into this system. Since photographs no longer have to be engraved, many engravers' jobs were also lost. The printing operation has shrunk to making plates and running the presses.

Most newspaper and magazine publications now have online editions, and digital photographs meld just as smoothly into the production of these Web sites. They let photojournalists get more of their work published and have it available longer. Newsprint is expensive, making space for photographs in print publications limited. Compared to paper, the costs for computer servers and electricity for displaying images on the Web are minor, and the photographs can remain online as long as the publication chooses to archive them. Many newspapers have branches of their Web sites that showcase the work of their photojournalists. The *Washington Post* and the *San Jose Mercury News* have been leaders in this innovation.

In an attempt to distinguish themselves from print editions, many sites have moved beyond photography to multimedia. They include slide shows of still images accompanied by natural sound, interviews, and voice-over narration. A software application called Soundslides has made it relatively easy to produce such slide shows using Flash technology, which lets the pictures download rapidly. Propelled by the popularity of amateur video on such social networking sites as YouTube and MySpace, news organizations are also posting Web video. Organizations such as the NPPA and the Society of News Design offer workshops and sponsor competitions for Web videos.

Web video differs from television in several dimensions. Television has always been considered a close-up medium, but because Web videos are smaller than television screens, they are even more tightly focused. Television camera operators and editors followed their newsreel predecessors in adopting the principles of film continuity from cinema. Continuity requires constructing a montage of long, medium, and close-up shots with cut-ins, cutaways, and other transitional shots to avoid jump cuts. Many Web video journalists do not practice continuity, considering the ragged jump cuts as part of the aesthetic. Perhaps the most important distinction is the absence of the journalist. Most television reporters make themselves part of the story by cultivating a persona through stand-up appearances on camera and voice-over narrations. Most Web video journalists minimize their presence, telling their stories through the pictures and sound of their subjects alone. This replicates the still-photography tradition where photojournalists remained largely anonymous, except to their peers.

Although some photojournalists feel threatened and diminished by the prospect of an editor selecting frame grabs from a video, others see great potential working in a medium that offers sound and motion. Still others enjoy the challenge of working with still and motion at the same time. A similar situation existed during the 1930s and 1940s, before specialization set in, when some photojournalists shot both still photographs for magazines and film for newsreels. Henri Cartier-Bresson directed films on the Spanish Civil War and prisoners of war and displaced persons after World War II. One of the most famous portraits of the war photographer Robert Capa shows him with a movie camera—not a Leica—to his eye.

Other innovators are demonstrating how the Web can be used to revitalize classical long-form photojournalism. Foremost among them is Brian Storm, whose site MediaStorm.org has become a locus of compelling projects that draw on the traditions of witnessing history, exposing social and global problems, and humanism. "I want MediaStorm to be the *Life* magazine of this era," declares Storm. The stories he publishes, in video and in audio slide shows, range from a family struggling to rebuild after Hurricane Katrina to members of the "in-between generation" torn between an aging parent and young children, to a veteran of the Iraq War coping with suicidal tendencies. Storm has moved beyond presenting projects on the Web to publishing for multiple platforms, including DVDs, mobile phones, and other personal devices. To accomplish his goal of reaching as many viewers as possible, he is harnessing the viral boost that comes from a presence on social networking sites such as MySpace, YouTube, Flickr, and Facebook. While some photojournalists see the digital revolution as a threat, Storm embraces it: "I firmly believe that the Web is the savior of photojournalism."[2]

Fundamental to most ethical issues in photojournalism is the concept of photographic realism. It holds there is a causal relationship between what is in front of the camera when an exposure is made and the resulting image. Some commentators describe this as making a *trace* of the reality. Denying realism, postmodern theorists argue that since all knowledge is constructed by humans inside their brains, it is impossible to know external physical reality. Most postmodernists argue that all the decisions a photographer makes—camera angle, lens, exposure, instant of snapping the shutter, framing, and other compositional choices—infuse so much subjectivity into all photographs that it is meaningless to talk about them as conveying any objective record of reality. From their point of view, the photograph does not trace reality, it transforms it. For people who hold this view, the ethical debate is simplified: All photographs are faulty, inadequate, slippery, deceptive, mendacious. Anyone who claims otherwise is deluded or lying.

Instead of the old adage that the camera never lies, postmodernists insist, "The camera always lies." Instead of seeing the image as a representation of the external world, they see it as a construct of the image maker's consciousness and a revelation of how culture has determined his or her subjective vision. This is all the more insidious, they argue, because a realist style conceals the mediation of the photographer and camera between the subject and the viewer. The pretense that the photograph is a transparent window on the world is considered especially pernicious because so many unsophisticated viewers accept it. Complicating the debate is the confusion about the use of the term *objectivity*. Setting an impossibly high standard, the postmodernists define it as a one-to-one correlation between the image and the external world. Most photojournalists equate objectivity with a more modest nexus of values, including honesty, accuracy, fairness, and balance.

For those who continue to believe there is a causal relationship between reality and image, the primary ethical issue concerns the degree of the photographer's intervention between what was in front of the camera and the final image. Did the photographer direct the people and objects before making the exposure? Did he or she manipulate the negative or the print after exposure? Believers in photographic realism see such interventions as essentially different from subjective choices. Even if the photograph cannot capture external reality, most photojournalists believe nonintervention is an important ethical line that can be defined and must be respected. This position is not original to photojournalism. It arose about 1915 with Paul Strand and other straight, or purist, photographers. They practiced nonintervention and nonmanipulation on still lifes, landscapes, and nudes while making art photographs. Their ideas affected photojournalists and documentarians.

During the first half of the twentieth century, many photojournalists posed their subjects and manipulated images in the darkroom. The ethical line changed as technology evolved. It was several decades after the 35 mm camera made candid images possible before photojournalists finally rejected directing people and arranging objects in news pictures.

Darkroom manipulations were a separate issue. Many photojournalists embraced W. Eugene Smith's high standards of quality printing, altering their prints extensively from what appeared in front of their cameras. In what was laughingly called "hand of god" printing, they turned skies black and darkened backgrounds to the point of eliminating contents they considered distracting. At the other end of the tonal scale, they blocked light from the enlarger and used cyanide to bleach out details in highlights. The collective effect of such high-contrast printing was to devalue dramatic lighting when it appeared naturally. It was also blatantly obvious, because it left a halo of light between the principal subject and the darkened background. This printing style prevailed from the 1960s to the time when color replaced black and white, causing photojournalists to stop making prints.

Compared to darkroom manipulations, some critics believe digital manipulation constitutes a difference in kind. A trained eye could spot manipulations in an analog print. With digital manipulation, the argument goes, the changes are so subtle they are undetectable. An operator skilled in Photoshop software can add, delete, or move content, leaving a seamless image in which the changes are impossible to detect. Postmodernists use this as another argument for denying any truth-value to photography. Because manipulation is so easy to accomplish and so difficult to detect and because there is no negative against which to check a print, they argue that viewers should presume that all digital images have been manipulated.

The issue is complicated by photojournalists who argue that a certain level of digital manipulation is not only permitted but necessary. If a negative got scratched, the resulting line in the print was an artifact of the process, not part of the reality in front of the camera. Retouching such a line was never considered unethical. Further, there are differences between human vision and camera vision. The tonal scale, or range between lights and darks, that the human eye can see is much broader than what film can capture. Details visible to the human eye often block up in the shadows of a negative or get washed out in the highlights. Photojournalists always considered it appropriate to correct such problems in tonality when printing by controlling the exposure on their enlargers and by using paper with different degrees of contrast. They also compensated by lightening areas in the shadows (dodging) and darkening ones in the highlights (burning). When image-editing programs such as Adobe's Photoshop software replaced the wet-chemistry darkroom, photojournalists believed analogous corrections—intended to bridge the gap between human and camera vision and to compensate for limitations in the medium—were still acceptable. Most photojournalists drew the line, however, at adding, removing, or changing content in the print and at extending the frame by cloning.

Numerous cases of digital manipulation have occurred in both magazine and newspaper photojournalism. Most transgressions are discovered, reported to the public, and vigorously discussed in industry publications. In newspapers, they often result in the firing of the photographer and prompt apologies and pledges to prevent manipulations in the future from senior editors.

Several examples will characterize the types of manipulations and the discussions they provoke. One of the first cases to gain notoriety occurred on the February 1982 cover of *National Geographic*. Gordon W. Gahan photographed three men riding camels against the backdrop of the pyramids at Giza, Egypt. The photograph was horizontal, but the editors wanted to use it as a vertical image on the cover. Technicians digitally moved two pyramids closer together so the image could be cropped as a vertical. Wilbur E. Garrett, then editor of *National Geographic,* defended the alteration by arguing the photo could have been made if the photographer had changed his angle a few feet. The repositioning was not unethical, he argued, because the photograph was totally plausible. Notwithstanding Garrett's defense, many criticized, even lampooned, the magazine.

In June 1994, when the football star O. J. Simpson was charged with murdering his wife, *Time* magazine's editors directed staff artist Matt Mahurin to digitally darken Simpson's face in the police mug shot distributed by the AP. *Time* labeled the image as a photo illustration on its contents page but not on the cover. On newsstands across the nation, *Time* was displayed next to *Newsweek,* which published an unmanipulated, lighter image. *Time*'s change made Simpson look sinister, and many viewers saw blatant racism in its darkening of the skin of the African American athlete. The following week, *Time*'s editor James Gaines wrote an apology to readers, in which he said, "To the extent that this caused offense to anyone, I deeply regret it." In part explanation, part defense, he characterized the change as a photo-illustration that had been poorly labeled. "If there was anything wrong with the cover, in my view, it was that it was not immediately apparent that this was a photo-illustration rather than an unaltered photograph," Gaines wrote. "To know that, a reader had to turn to our contents page or see the original mug shot on the opening page of the story. . . . No single set of rules will ever cover all possible cases. It will remain, as it has always been, a matter of subjective judgment."[3]

Gaines failed to explain how simply altering a photograph's tonality changed it into an illustration or what point *Time* was trying to make in darkening Simpson's skin. Used in this sense, *illustration* seems to be a euphemism for manipulation. Gaines borrowed an argument from postmodernism as a defense. "Photojournalism has never been able to claim the transparent neutrality attributed to it. Photographers choose angles and editors choose pictures to make points . . . and every major news outlet routinely crops and retouches photos."[4]

Three years later, *Newsweek* was caught in a similar manipulation. In November 1997, when Bobbi McCaughey gave birth to septuplets, she and her husband Kenny were pictured on the covers of both *Time* and *Newsweek. Newsweek*'s cover showed her with perfectly straight, white teeth. In *Time*'s photo, they appear crooked and discolored. In an explanation that insulted his readers' intelligence as well as his staff's eyesight, Richard Smith, *Newsweek*'s editor in chief, said there was deep shadow over McCaughey's mouth. "The editors decided to lighten and improve the picture. In the process of doing that, the technical people went too far. The mistake was in guessing what was in the shadow and changing it."[5]

These examples illustrate the point that standards for magazine covers may be different than for photographs inside the same magazine. Editors see the cover as a marketing device intended to increase newsstand sales. This view sometimes tips decisions toward advertising practice, where any digital manipulation is acceptable. Also notable is that these examples were all done at the editorial level of the publication process. This is particularly troubling to photographic historian John Mraz, because the changes are made "not by those who were at the scene and experienced the event they photographed, but by computer technicians who have no sense of what really went on." They base changes on an idealized conception of what should have been, he says, "in line with a mentality increasingly governed by the conventions of advertising imagery."[6]

In contrast to magazines, most transgressions at newspapers have been committed by photographers, who often have been fired as punishment. Three cases illustrate the range of manipulation, the ensuing debate, and the consequences.

In covering the American invasion of Iraq, *Los Angeles Times* photographer Brian Walski transmitted a photograph that showed a British soldier brandishing a weapon in one hand and gesturing with the other to an Iraqi father holding his child to get down. The man appears to look at the soldier with a frightened and confused expression. The *Times* played the picture at the top of its front page and transmitted it to sister newspapers. When the *Hartford Courant* published it six columns wide on its front page, an employee noticed that some people in the background appeared twice in the photo. When a *Times* editor phoned Walski in Iraq, he admitted compositing two images—one with the gesturing soldier, the other with the father and child prominent—to make a more dramatic picture.

Walski, a twenty-year veteran in journalism, was summarily fired. The *Times* wrote an explanation to its readers, printing the two original photographs with the composite. Colin Crawford, the director of photography, framed the issue as one of honesty and trust between the paper and its readers: "What Brian did is totally unacceptable and he violated our trust with our readers." Although Crawford expressed regrets about having to fire Walski, he added, "The integrity of our organization is essential. If our readers can't count on honesty from us, I don't know what we have left."[7]

In a formal apology to the newspaper and his colleagues, Walski wrote, "I deeply regret that I have tarnished the reputation of the *Los Angeles Times,* a newspaper with the highest standards of journalism . . . and especially the very talented and extremely dedicated photographers and picture editors and friends that have made my four and a half years at the *Times* a true quality experience." He said he could not "truly explain my complete breakdown in judgment at this time. That will only come in the many sleepless nights that are ahead." Walski's tone was closer to desperation when he talked with a fellow *Times* staff photographer in Kuwait City a few hours after the incident. "I fucked up, and now no one will touch me," he said. "I went from the front line for the greatest newspaper in the world, and now I have nothing. No cameras, no car, nothing."[8]

Walski characterized his transgression as a single lapse done under the extreme stress of a combat situation. On the other hand, a 2007 case at the *Toledo (Ohio) Blade* involved scores of manipulations on routine assignments. Staff photographer Allan Detrich drew an assignment to cover the Bluffton University baseball team in its first game after five of its members were killed in a bus crash the previous month. Detrich and photographers from competing newspapers photographed the team kneeling in prayer in memory of their teammates. After the pictures appeared, some photographers alerted *Blade* editors to a major difference in Detrich's image. He had used Photoshop to eliminate the legs of a person standing behind a nearby banner. Detrich told his editors he had cloned out the legs in a version intended only for his own use and then mistakenly transmitted it for publication. When the director of photography began investigating his work, Detrich resigned. The investigation revealed that he had digitally altered seventy-nine images during the first fourteen weeks of 2007. In a letter to readers, executive editor Ron Royhab said the alterations "included erasing people, tree limbs, utility poles, electrical wires, electrical outlets, and other background elements from photographs" and inserting contents, "such as tree branches and shrubbery." In two sports photographs, Royhab wrote, Detrich "added a hockey puck and . . . a basketball, each hanging in mid-air."[9]

"When a *Blade* reporter or photographer covers a news event, the newspaper and its readers expect an accurate record of the event," Royhab wrote in an apology to readers. "Reporters and editors are not allowed to change quotes or alter events to make them more dramatic. Photographers and photo editors cannot digitally alter the content in the frame of a photograph to make the image more powerful or artistic."[10] He and other editors drew a hard line and promised to try to prevent such manipulations in the future. *Blade* assistant managing editor Luann Sharp said the newspaper has "zero tolerance" for digital manipulation. "To prevent this from happening again," she added, "we plan more spot checking of photojournalists' work in the future."[11]

In the case of *Charlotte (North Carolina) Observer* photographer Patrick Schneider, the ethical issue concerned aesthetics instead of content. Instead of adding or deleting contents or compositing images, Schneider's offense was intensifying the color in a July 2006 photograph he took of "a Charlotte firefighter on a ladder, silhouetted by the light of the early morning sun." In the unaltered photograph, the sky had a brownish gray color. With editing, "the sky became a deep red and the sun took on a more distinct halo." Editor Rick Thames quoted an *Observer* policy: "No colors will be altered from the original scene photographed."[12]

It was not the first infraction by Schneider. His supervisors had reprimanded him in 2003 for excessive burning and dodging of photographs that he submitted to a state press association contest. "Because of the most recent violation of our photo policy," Thames told readers, "Schneider no longer works at the *Observer.*" He apologized, adding, "Your trust is important to us. We will do all we can do to ensure the integrity of all our photos going forward."[13]

Thames insisted the color alteration was not merely a question of aesthetics and declared that accuracy must take precedence over art. "Journalism cannot be about original works of art unless it is labeled as such," he wrote. "That is why we label photo and art illustrations. It's why editorials go on pages labeled for opinion." He welcomed art, but only when photojournalists captured it as part of real life. And he allowed for tonal balancing to restore what the colors and values were in the original scene. "To the extent that we journalists are confident about what we saw or heard, we may rely on our memory to tone a photo to reflect the original scene photographed." But he concluded that "we should never alter the actual color of scenes photographed or invent quotes. . . . Our news stories and photos are not interpretive forms of art. When our tools and our human memory fail us, we must go out and try again to capture art in real life."[14]

In trying to enforce such high standards, editors and photography directors may soon have a new tool. Hany Farid and Alin Popescu, computer scientists at Dartmouth College, have developed a method for determining if a photograph has been manipulated by analyzing patterns in its structure of pixels. They have published scientific papers describing their discovery and plan to release it as a software application.[15]

Some commentators outside journalism say the blanket rejection of any manipulation misses the larger point of intention. Dan

Heller wrote, "To me, the matter of photo editing does not lie in the act itself, but in the end result: Why was the editing done? What did it accomplish? And what was the net effect?" He called for "judging these things on a case-by-case basis."[16] Comparing the three newspaper cases with another that surfaced in 2006 illuminates his point. Walski apparently edited to make a more dramatic picture that would secure prominent play and enhance his reputation as a photographer. Detrich removed the legs because he considered them a distraction from the main point of his photograph. Schneider intended to increase the aesthetic appeal of his color photograph. By contrast, editors at *El Nuevo Herald,* the Spanish language edition of the *Miami Herald,* composited a photograph of Cuban police officers with another showing a group of prostitutes on a Havana street. The fake photograph was intended to support an accompanying story that claimed the Castro government was ignoring prostitution. Its political motivation puts this manipulation in the same category as the composite photographs Senator Joseph McCarthy used during his anti-Communist crusade in the early 1950s.

Like most newspaper editors, leaders in photojournalism see digital manipulation as a threat to the credibility of the photographic image and thus to the profession itself. The National Press Photographers Association (NPPA) has responded by prominently publicizing cases of manipulation in *News Photographer* magazine and, in 1999, by adding a strong prohibition against digital manipulation to its code of ethics:

> As journalists, we believe that credibility is our greatest asset. In documentary photojournalism, it is wrong to alter the content of a photograph in any way (electronically or in the darkroom) that deceives the public. We believe the guidelines for fair and accurate

reporting should be the criteria for judging what may be done electronically to a photograph.[17]

In 2004, the code of ethics was updated to include nine standards that called for accuracy, avoiding "stereotyping individuals and groups," treating "all subjects with respect and dignity," and avoiding any attempt "to alter or influence events." In the clearest prohibition, Standard 6 states: "Editing should maintain the integrity of the photographic images' content and context. Do not manipulate images or add or alter sound in any way that can mislead viewers or misrepresent subjects." In addition to the standards, the code lists seven ideals, including a call for photojournalists to "respect the integrity of the photographic moment."[18]

Articles in *News Photographer* about cases of manipulation regularly include statements from NPPA officials strongly opposing manipulation. In response to the Detrich case, however, President Tony Overman framed the problem as one of education. "We will do all we can to meet the increasing needs for ethics outreach and training," he said. "We're not just going to condemn one series of incidents and then go away. We're going to promote ethics, ethical training, and ethical outreach again and again."[19]

Collectively, these statements by editors and industry leaders make the point that credibility lies with individual photojournalists, news organizations, and publications, not with the medium itself. Like words, photographic communication is capable "of subtlety, ambiguity, revelation, and distortion."[20] That words can be used to lie does not compromise the credibility readers give newspapers such as the *New York Times* and the *Washington Post*. Over time, specific newspapers and individual photojournalists establish a bond of trust with readers that they will not manipulate photographs. Acknowledging when transgressions slip past the gatekeeping function and following up with apologies and pledges of zero tolerance are part of maintaining that trust.

However sincere editors and industry leaders are about zero tolerance, in practice, many news organizations relax this stricture. Some newspapers have a high standard for their news and sports sections and a different one for feature sections. Digital photography has made it easy to produce illustrations that spring from the imagination, not the real world. Many newspapers publish them, and many journalists believe that if such images are clearly labeled as illustrations—typically in the credit line directly beneath the image—manipulation is acceptable. Others believe if an illustration shows a clearly impossible situation, there is no danger readers will take it literally. Putting an oversized head on a small body, for example, will clearly be understood as an illustration. According to this thinking, if there is no deception, intentional or actual, then there is no ethical transgression.

Manipulation is the standard practice in advertising, where products and the people who use them always appear perfect. In many magazines—particularly those in the beauty, fashion, preteen, and teen niches—the line between advertising and editorial content is extremely thin. These magazines routinely enhance composition, color, and the faces and bodies of models. Although the models are posed in studios under controlled lighting, the resulting images are not considered perfect enough. Every blemish is touched out, skin complexion and eye color are changed, highlights are added, and thin models are slenderized further. *Redbook* magazine's July 2007 cover photograph of country singer Faith Hill involved more than ten digital alterations to the original image. Her hair was augmented, shadows under her eyes were removed, her arm was extended to push her awkwardly positioned left hand out of the picture, and a bulge of flesh hanging over the edge of her dress was removed.[21]

If the only effects of such manipulations were to sell more magazines or more beauty products, that would be expected in a capitalist economy. But millions of women in the target audiences regularly see this impossible standard of beauty and internalize the message that their faces, their bodies, their selves are inadequate. This is especially pernicious for preteen and teenage girls still forming their self-image.

From practices in the advertising and magazine industries, digital deception has moved to the level of consumer products. In 2006, Hewlett-Packard added a slimming feature to its digital cameras that in the words of its ad "can instantly trim off pounds from the subjects in your photos!"[22] A virtual solution for a nation with an obesity problem.

Photojournalists do not live in a vacuum. They see such manipulations in the larger visual culture and are tempted to try them. Facing declining circulation, newspapers want to appear current to attract younger readers. So digital illustrations make their way into lifestyle and other feature sections. The end result of idealized perfection is to cheapen the value of good photographs that are captured under spontaneous situations. That the "decisive moment," when peak action and geometric composition coalesce, can now be constructed with Photoshop devalues honest images.

Two other aspects of the digital age have major implications for photojournalists and news publications. The ease and speed with which photographs can be accessed and transmitted has affected freelance photography in complex ways. Agencies that sell stock photos have existed for a long time, but in the analog era the process was cumbersome. Magazine picture editors had to telephone a request to the agency. A researcher would search the archives, pull together a selection, make prints or duplicates of slides, and send them to the editor. The editor would choose the desired image, and the agency would bill the publication. Now a picture editor can easily search an agency's entire stock online by subject, photographer, date, or other category; choose an image; pay for it electronically; and download it immediately.

Most professional photographers have contracts with large agencies, such as Corbis, Getty Images, and Black Star, as a way to gain residual sales of their work. But the burgeoning stock industry means many fewer assignments are being made to photographers. Magazine photographers may earn a day rate in the area of eight hundred dollars. If an editor can find and buy a stock photograph that adequately illustrates an article, there is little incentive to hire a photographer to make a fresh one.

The digital era has also opened up photojournalism to amateur photographers in dramatically new ways. During the analog era, amateurs who were lucky enough to be in the right place with their cameras could sell their newsworthy photographs for publication. Two of the most famous cases are Abraham Zapruder's film of the assassination of President John F. Kennedy and the picture of an Oklahoma City firefighter holding the lifeless body of one-year-old Baylee Almon, who was slain when Timothy McVeigh bombed the Murrah Federal Building. Taken by Charles Porter IV, it won the 1996 Pulitzer Prize for news photography.

Two factors make amateur news photography in the digital era qualitatively different. First is the proliferation of digital cameras to the point that many people carry them all the time in purses, backpacks, or briefcases; in addition, most cell phones also function as cameras. When terrorists bombed London subway trains in July 2005, passengers used cell-phone cameras to photograph their fellow riders being evacuated through the tunnels.

As newspapers adapt to the electronic era, they are exploiting the Web's potential for interactivity with readers. Many publishers and senior editors see readers as sources of free content and invite them to post both information and photos on their Web editions. More important, digital-photography technology has percolated down to the level that news organizations are no longer necessary for the mass distribution of photographs. Amateurs can create their own blogs and post photographs on Flickr and other sites. Millions upload videos to such social networking sites as YouTube and MySpace, and images can be widely distributed by e-mail or CDs. Such distribution of images outside normal journalistic channels means a loss of the gatekeeping function—checks on accuracy and decisions about significance, ethics, and taste—that editors have traditionally performed. Some deplore this loss; others celebrate it as a democratization of mass communication. For a generation that has grown up with the plethora of information on the Internet and the inclination to accept everything at equal value, the loss may not even be apparent. More significant, the rise of personal photography, much of which has banal content and poor aesthetic quality, may decrease the audience for serious news photographs.

The most important example of amateur photography in the early twenty-first century was the release of photographs of American soldiers abusing Iraqi detainees at the Abu Ghraib prison near Baghdad. First reported in April 2004 on CBS's *60 Minutes* and in the *New Yorker* magazine, the pictures reveal the physical abuse, psychological stress, sexual humiliation, and death that members of the U.S. 320th Military Police Battalion inflicted on Iraqi suspects (see figure 22). They show the Americans, grinning broadly and gesturing, as they humiliate the Iraqis. Taken primarily by Army Specialist Sabrina Harman, they record incidents a photojournalist would never have access to. Put on CDs, they were circulated to other soldiers for their amusement. Because digital photographs are so easy to copy and disseminate, they eventually found their way to news organizations, where their publication unleashed a firestorm of criticism against the U.S. military and President Bush's war strategy. They were quickly posted on the Web, bypassing journalism's gatekeeping function. They also circumvented control by the military, which would have suppressed the images if possible. While editors and industry leaders concentrate on the ethical issues created by the digital era, the effects of amateur access to the mass communication of images may be more profound.

While concerns about digital photography are justified, the most important aspects of photojournalism remain unchanged, including the ethics and values of the profession, the aesthetics of photography, how to think visually and journalistically, and how to approach a range of assignments, from news to sports, feature, portraits, and studio illustration. Nonetheless, the most significant aspect of technology in the digital era is how rapidly it continues to evolve. Driven by the profit motive, corporations develop new cameras, computers, and software at an increasingly rapid pace. Innovations are adopted first by organizations and professionals. Soon they become cheap enough for mass production and percolate down to the amateur level. Photojournalism will continue to undergo rapid technological transformation, and amateurs will follow close behind.

NINE

◇

A FINAL WORD

Every profession has its own methods of enculturating new members. In photojournalism, those methods are complex and work at many levels. As with most professions in the United States, a college education has replaced the on-the-job apprenticeships that sufficed to train press photographers a few generations ago. Professors transmit the three traditions of photojournalism—bearing witness to history, social documentary, and universal humanism—as they teach the history and ethics of photojournalism. Few photojournalism majors graduate without studying Lewis Hine's contribution to the regulation of child labor or Dorothea Lange's efforts to help victims of the Great Depression. Although they may not hear a thorough articulation of humanist theory, most student photojournalists have the term *the human condition* in their active vocabularies. They learn to take "people pictures," which treat their subjects with respect and capture empathetic moments.

If they do not become members of the NPPA as students, most photojournalists—encouraged by senior colleagues—join the association after they graduate and begin their first job. Its code of ethics, monthly magazine, and Web site reinforce the values they imbibed in college. Through such educational programs as the Flying Short Course, the Stan Kalish Picture Editing Workshop, and the TV News Video Workshop, photojournalists find opportunities for professional development to help them adapt to a rapidly changing media landscape. Many of these educational initiatives are tailored to help members cope with the technical revolution that is reshaping photojournalism from still photographs in newspapers, magazines, and books to multimedia presentations that feature video stories and audio slide shows.

Arguably the most powerful force for enculturation is the system of rewards that evolved during the second half of the twentieth century. At its apex stands the University of Missouri's Photographer of the Year International (POYi) competition. Ambitious photojournalists understand that winning a major POYi award is a stepping-stone to advancement at their own publication or to a job with a higher salary at a bigger organization. Not surprisingly, they carefully study and emulate the kinds of photographs and picture stories that win.

In the spring of 2008, as the 2007 competition was judged, the rewards went to photojournalists who excelled in the three traditions. Awards in the news categories went to photographers who had witnessed events and situations of historic magnitude, including the massacre at Virginia Tech, the assassination of former Pakistani prime minister Benazir Bhutto, and the unrest following the disputed election in Kenya. Numerous winning pictures were infused with humanism, including a mother cradling the body of her six-year-old son, slain by gunmen in Baqouba, Iraq; a grim-faced American boy waiting for his father to return from Iraq; marine veterans who lost legs in Iraq; a Boston family losing its home to the subprime mortgage crisis; and New Orleans residents trying to cope with homelessness two years after Hurricane Katrina.

In the reformist tradition, winners in other categories were trying to promote understanding of complex problems. The winning portfolio of Newspaper Photographer of the Year Stephen M. Katz included picture stories on the increase in leprosy in Nigeria and a platoon of American soldiers trying to help Iraqis. The World Understanding award went to Steve Liss for "Voices from Juvenile Detention," his documentary on how pretrial detention exacerbates the problems of more than six hundred thousand juvenile offenders each year—some of them only ten years old. Daniel Beltra won the Global Vision award for his project that linked clear-cutting of the Amazon forest in Brazil to the global warming that is causing the collapse of ice fields in the Antarctic. All fit within the social documentary tradition of exposing problems in the expectation that public awareness will cause them to be corrected.

Most Americans pick up their morning newspaper and see disconnected photographs of sports competitions and local, national, and world situations. Understandably, they assume photojournalism is about covering events. They may also believe the photojournalists producing those pictures are objective, detached, disinterested. From a meta perspective, both assumptions appear incorrect. The view from inside the profession and across several decades reveals that most photojournalists adopt a humanist point of view as they strive to make the world better with their pictures. Motivated by past victories over social problems, they work in the tradition of crusading journalism to expose problems and create understanding. They keep faith with President Franklin D. Roosevelt, who insisted during the Great Depression that problems created by humans can be corrected by humans. Their concerns have moved beyond child labor and poverty to include an array of issues from breast cancer to the stigmatizing of gay and lesbian teenagers, from autism to post-traumatic stress disorder, drug addiction, homelessness, spousal abuse, teenage suicide, juvenile crime, prostitution, polygamy, pollution, natural disasters, street violence, and a host of other national and global problems.

Although editors assign some of these stories, most are enterprise projects, generated by photographers personally committed to the issues. Their lack of objectivity is not a narrow partisanship. Rather, they believe they can prompt those who view their images in newspapers and on Web sites and television to create the political will to change things for the better. It is facile for postmodern theorists, who fail to offer their own solutions, to criticize such motivation as misguided idealism or self-serving opportunism.

In light of the cultural theorists' criticism, however, photojournalists should carefully examine their motives and the effects their practices have on the people they photograph. They should acknowledge that their photographs are only one part of a complex set of factors necessary to achieve positive change. Nonetheless, they should also take satisfaction—as individuals and members of a profession—that they are working for the good of humanity and that they have achieved a record of success.

NOTES

CHAPTER ONE

1. Wilson Hicks, *Words and Pictures: An Introduction to Photojournalism* (New York: Harper and Brothers, 1952), 100–101.

2. Susan D. Moeller, *Shooting War: Photography and the American Experience of Combat* (New York: Basic Books, 1989), 10.

3. Michael Carlebach, *The Origins of Photojournalism in America* (Washington, D.C.: The Smithsonian Institution, 1992), 1.

4. Caroline Brothers, *War and Photography: A Cultural History* (London: Routledge, 1997), 3.

5. Susan Sontag, *On Photography* (New York: Farrar, Straus and Giroux, 1977), 112.

6. Ibid., 178.

7. See Susan D. Moeller, *Compassion Fatigue: How the Media Sell Disease, Famine, War, and Death* (New York: Routledge, 1998).

8. Kevin G. Barnhurst, *Seeing the Newspaper* (New York: St. Martin's Press, 1994), 27.

9. Ibid., 35.

CHAPTER TWO

1. Census statistics are from the Inter-University Consortium for Political and Social Research, "Census Data for the Year 1840," http://fisher.lib.virginia.edu/cgi-local/censusbin/census/cen.pl?year=840 (accessed December 27, 2008).

2. Vicky Grocke, "Compulsory Education," History of American Education Web Project, Notre Dame, updated June 15, 2004, http://www.nd.edu/~rbarger/www7/compulso.html (accessed December 27, 2008).

3. E. L. Morse, ed., *Samuel F. B. Morse, His Letters and Journals* (New York: Houghton Mifflin Co., 1914), quoted in Robert Taft, *Photography and the American Scene: A Social History, 1839–1889* (New York: The MacMillan Company, 1938), 11–12.

4. Ibid., 12.

5. Ibid., 453.

6. Ibid., 16.

7. Ibid., 16.

8. Jack Wilgus and Beverly Wilgus, "What Is a Camera Obscura?" *The Magic Mirror of Life: An Appreciation of the Camera Obscura,* Bright Bytes Studio, http://brightbytes.com/cosite/what.html (accessed December 27, 2008).

9. Taft, *Photography and the American Scene,* 23.

10. Ibid., 44.

11. Ibid., 33–34.

12. Dr. John W. Draper, *Textbook of Chemistry* (New York: Harper and Brothers, 1846), 93, quoted in Taft, *Photography and the American Scene,* 33.

13. Charles Baudelaire, "Salon of 1859," *Révue Française* (Paris, June 10–July 20, 1859), reprinted in *Art in Paris, 1845–1862; salons and other exhibitions reviewed by Charles Baudelaire,* translated and edited by Jonathan Mayne (London: Phaidon Press, 1965), 152–53.

14. Taft, *Photography and the American Scene,* 33.

15. James F. Ryder, *Voightländer and I in Pursuit of Shadow Catching* (Cleveland: Cleveland Printing and Publishing Company, 1902), n.p., quoted in ibid., 48.

16. John Hannavy, ed., *Encyclopedia of Nineteenth-Century Photography,* vol. 1 (Abington, UK: Routledge, 2007), 366.

17. Taft, *Photography and the American Scene,* 84.

18. Undated article reprinted from the *Christian Watchmen* in *The Living Age* 9 (1846), quoted in *Photographic Art Journal* 9 (1855): 252, quoted in ibid., 68.

19. Nathaniel Hawthorne, *The House of the Seven Gables* (Columbus, Ohio: Merrill, 1969), 91.

20. William Henry Fox Talbot, *The Pencil of Nature,* facsimile of 1844–46 edition (Cambridge, Mass.: Da Capo Press, 1968), n.p.

21. Ibid.

22. Carlebach, *Origins of Photojournalism,* 39.

23. Taft, *Photography and the American Scene,* 39.

24. Undated "extract from the Congregationalist and Christian Times" quoted in *Amusing and Thrilling Adventures of a California Artist* (Boston: Published for the Author, 1854), 45, quoted in Martha A. Sandweiss, *Print the Legend: Photography and the American West* (New Haven, Conn.: Yale University Press, 2002), 51.

25. Sandweiss, *Print the Legend,* 51.

26. "Panoramic Excursions," *St. Louis Weekly Reveille,* April 22, 1850, quoted in ibid., 53.

27. Sandweiss, *Print the Legend,* 22.

28. The lithograph is reproduced in ibid., 37.

29. Ibid., 30.

30. Martha A. Sandweiss, Rick Steward, and Ben W. Husemann, *Eyewitness to War: Prints and Daguerreotypes of the Mexican War, 1846–1848* (Washington, D. C., and Fort Worth, Tex.: Smithsonian Institution Press and Amon Carter Museum, 1989), 37, quoted in ibid., 30.

31. Taft, *Photography and the American Scene,* 58.

32. Carlebach, *Origins of Photojournalism,* 25.

33. Quoted in Sarah McNair Vosmeier, "Photographing Lincoln, Part IV," *Lincoln Lore,* no. 1808 (October 1989): n.p., quoted in Harold Holzer, *Lincoln at Cooper Union: The Speech That Made Abraham Lincoln President* (New York: Simon and Schuster, 2004), 91.

34. Quoted in Roy Meredith, *The World of Mathew Brady: Portraits of the Civil War Period* (New York: Bonanza Books, 1988), 28.

35. Mathew Brady, "Address to the Public," reprinted in *Humphrey's Journal* 5 (1853): 16, quoted in Taft, *Photography and the American Scene,* 82.

36. *Official Description and Illustrated Catalog* (London: The Royal Commission, 1852), 3 vv.; v. 3, 1464, quoted in Taft, *Photography and the American Scene,* 70.

37. Quoted in Roy Meredith, *Mr. Lincoln's Camera Man, Mathew B. Brady* (New York: Charles Scribner's Sons, 1946), 59.

38. Ibid.

39. Silas Hawley to George W. Nichols, October 30, 1860, quoted in Harold Holzer, Gabor S. Boritt, and Mark E. Neely Jr., *The Lincoln Image:*

Abraham Lincoln and the Popular Print (New York: Charles Scribner's Sons, 1984), 67, quoted in Carlebach, *Origins of Photojournalism,* 59.

40. Holzer, *Lincoln at Cooper Union,* 100.

41. George Alfred Townsend, "Still Taking Pictures: Brady, the Grand Old Man of American Photography Hard at Work at Sixty-Seven," *The World* (April 12, 1891): 26, reprinted in "Reminiscences," The Daguerreian Society, http://www.daguerre.org/resource/texts/brady.html (accessed January 2, 2009).

42. *Frank Leslie's Illustrated Newspaper,* no. 14 (March 15, 1856): 214, quoted in Carlebach, *Origins of Photojournalism,* 25.

43. Ryder, *Voightländer and I,* 114, quoted in Carlebach, *Origins of Photojournalism,* 61.

44. Taft, *Photography and the American Scene,* 58–59.

45. Townsend, "Still Taking Pictures," 26.

46. Carlebach, *Origins of Photojournalism,* 70.

47. Ibid., 99.

48. The photograph and its caption are reproduced in Carlebach, *Origins of Photojournalism,* 78.

49. "Photographs of the War," *New York Times,* August 17, 1861, 4, quoted in ibid., 77.

50. Untitled note in *Humphrey's Journal* 13 (1861–62): 133, quoted in Taft, *Photography and the American Scene,* 228.

51. Carlebach, *Origins of Photojournalism,* 77.

52. George Hobart, *Masters of Photography: Mathew Brady* (London: Macdonald and Co.: 1984), 5.

53. "Brady's Photographs: Pictures of the Dead at Antietam," *New York Times,* October 20, 1862, 5. Quoted in Carlebach, *Origins of Photojournalism,* 93.

54. The younger Holmes recovered from his wounds. In 1902, President Theodore Roosevelt appointed him to the U.S. Supreme Court where he served for thirty years.

55. Oliver Wendell Holmes, *Atlantic Monthly* 12 (January 1863): 11, quoted in Taft, *Photography and the American Scene,* 236.

56. Townsend, "Still Taking Pictures."

57. Ibid.

58. Ibid.

59. William A. Frassanito, *Gettysburg: A Journey in Time* (New York: Scribner's, 1975), 24–28.

60. Ibid., 192.

61. Alexander Gardner, *Gardner's Photographic Sketch Book of the War,* vol. 1 (Washington: Philip and Solomons, 1864–65), plate 41.

CHAPTER THREE

1. Steven Schoenherr, "The New Journalism 1865–1919," University of San Diego, Department of History, http://history.sandiego.edu/gen/media/newjournalism.html (accessed December 27, 2008).

2. An advertisement with this slogan is reproduced in Henry Lieberman, Elizabeth Rosenzweig, and Push Singh, "An Agent for Integrated Annotation and Retrieval of Images," Media Laboratory, Massachusetts Institute of Technology, http://web.media.mit.edu/~lieber/Lieberary/Aria/Aria-CHI/Aria-CHI.html (accessed January 2, 2009).

3. Quoted in *Photojournalism* (New York: Time-Life Books, 1971), 12.

4. R. W. Amidon, Letter to the Editor, *New York Evening Post* (March 19, 1898): 7, quoted in Michael L. Carlebach, *American Photojournalism Comes of Age* (Washington: Smithsonian Institution Press, 1997), 11.

5. "Newspaper Pictures," *The Nation* 56, no. 1452 (April 27, 1893): 306, quoted in Carlebach, *American Photojournalism Comes of Age,* 12.

6. Stephen H. Horgan, "Photography for the Newspapers," *Philadelphia Photographer* 23, no. 269 (March 6, 1886): 141, quoted in Carlebach, *American Photojournalism Comes of Age,* 12.

7. Uncited quotation from an 1883 speech by Joseph Pulitzer, in Cyma Rubin and Eric Newton, eds., *Capture the Moment: The Pulitzer Prize Photographs* (New York: W. W. Norton, 2001), 6.

8. W. A. Swanberg, *Citizen Hearst: A Biography of William Randolph Hearst* (New York: Collier Books, 1986), 36, quoted in Carlebach, *American Photojournalism Comes of Age,* 14.

9. W. Joseph Campbell, *Yellow Journalism: Puncturing the Myths, Defining the Legacies* (Westport, Conn.: Praeger, 2001), 25.

10. Charlotte Perkins Gilman, "Newspapers and Democracy," *Forerunner*

(December 1916): 315, quoted in Carlebach, *American Photojournalism Comes of Age,* 13.

11. Campbell, *Yellow Journalism,* 63, 8.

12. Ibid., 26.

13. "A Step Too Far," *Journalist,* no. 12 (June 7, 1884): 3, quoted in Carlebach, *American Photojournalism Comes of Age,* 14.

14. "Photographs on the Wing," *Anthony's Photographic Bulletin* 16, no. 19 (October 10, 1885): 604, quoted in Carlebach, *American Photojournalism Comes of Age,* 18.

15. Raymond Fielding, *The American Newsreel, 1911–1967* (Norman: University of Oklahoma Press, 1972), 48.

16. John C. Hemment, *Cannon and Camera* (New York: D. Appleton and Company, 1898), 267, quoted in Moeller, *Shooting War,* 53.

17. Hemment, *Cannon and Camera,* 268, quoted in Moeller, *Shooting War,* 58.

18. James Burton, "Photographing Under Fire," *Harper's Weekly* (August 5, 1898): 774, quoted in Moeller, *Shooting War,* 57.

19. Quoted in Lewis Gould and Richard Greff, *Photojournalist: The Career of Jimmy Hare* (Austin: University of Texas Press, 1977), 11.

20. Ibid., 23.

21. Moeller, *Shooting War,* 56.

22. R. W. Stallman and E. R. Hagermann, eds., *The War Dispatches of Stephen Crane* (New York: Charles Scribner's Sons, 1926), 284, quoted in Gould and Greff, *Photojournalist,* 18.

23. Quoted in Moeller, *Shooting War,* 9.

24. Ibid., 82.

25. Ibid., 67.

26. Quoted in Marcus Wilkerson, *Public Opinion and the Spanish-American War* (Baton Rouge: Louisiana State University Press, 1932), 125–26, quoted in ibid., 67.

27. Moeller, *Shooting War,* 51, 68.

28. Carlebach, *American Photojournalism Comes of Age,* 34–35.

29. Ibid., 40.

30. "Taking Pictures for Fun," *New York Times,* November 11, 1883, 6, quoted in ibid., 50.

31. Edward Bok, "Is the Newspaper Office the Place for a Girl?"

Ladies' Home Journal 18, no. 3 (February 1901): 18, quoted in Carlebach, *American Photojournalism Comes of Age,* 49.

32. All biographical details about Beals are from the New York Historical Society, "Guide to the Jessie Tarbox Beals Photograph Collection [1900–1940]," http://dlib.nyu.edu/findingaids/html/nyhs/beals.html (accessed December 27, 2008).

33. Quoted in Alexander Alland Sr., *Jessie Tarbox Beals: First Woman News Photographer* (New York: Camera/Graphic Press, 1978), 53, quoted in Carlebach, *American Photojournalism Comes of Age,* 50–51.

34. Frances Benjamin Johnston, "What a Woman Can Do With a Camera," *Ladies' Home Journal* 15 (September 1897): 6, quoted in Carlebach, *American Photojournalism Comes of Age,* 50.

35. Judith Kalina, "From the Icehouse: A Visit with Consuelo Kanaga," *Camera 35,* December 1972, 54.

36. Mitchell Leslie, "The Man Who Stopped Time: Photographer Eadweard Muybridge Stunned the World When He Caught a Horse in the Act of Flying," *Stanford Magazine,* May/June 2001, http://www.stanford alumni.org/news/magazine/2001/mayjun/features/muybridge.html.

37. Carlebach, *American Photojournalism Comes of Age,* 78–79.

38. Ibid., 82.

39. "Army Heads Explain Press Censor Views," *New York Times,* July 7, 1916, 6, quoted in ibid., 84–85, 93.

40. Moeller, *Shooting War,* 114.

41. Wythe Williams, "The Sins of the Censor," *Colliers' Weekly* (January 12, 1918), 6, quoted in ibid., 115.

42. Moeller, *Shooting War,* 107.

43. Gould and Greff, *Photojournalist,* 119.

44. James H. Hare, "German Bombs Dropped on London," *Leslie's Weekly* (July 1, 1915), 8, quoted in Gould and Greff, *Photojournalist,* 123.

45. Carlebach, *American Photojournalism Comes of Age,* 91.

46. Schoenherr, "The New Journalism."

47. Moeller, *Shooting War,* 151.

48. Quoted in Louis Wiley, "Photographers as News-Reporters," *Photo-Era* 61, no. 4 (October 1928): 183, quoted in Carlebach, *American Photojournalism Comes of Age,* 152.

49. Silas Bent, "Journalistic Jazz," *The Nation* 122, no. 3169 (March 31,

1926): 341, quoted in Carlebach, *American Photojournalism Comes of Age,* 146.

50. Silas Bent, *Ballyhoo: The Voice of the Press* (New York: Horace and Liveright, 1927), 68, quoted in Carlebach, *American Photojournalism Comes of Age,* 169.

51. Simon Bessie, *Jazz Journalism: The Story of the Tabloid Newspapers* (New York: Russell and Russell, 1969), 224.

52. Claude Cookman, *A Voice Is Born* (Durham, N.C.: National Press Photographers Association, 1985), 30–31.

53. American Bar Association, Canons of Judicial Ethics, Judicial Canon 35, ABA Rep. 1134-1135 (1937), quoted in ibid., 153.

54. Arthur "Weegee" Fellig, *Naked City* (New York: Essential Books, 1945), 240.

55. Dickey Chapelle, *What's a Woman Doing Here? A Reporter's Report on Herself* (New York: William Morrow, 1962), 49, quoted in Carlebach, *American Photojournalism Comes of Age,* 159.

56. See Ray Boomhower, *"One Shot": The World War II Photography of John A. Bushemi* (Indianapolis: Indiana Historical Society Press, 2004).

57. Hal Buell, *Moments: The Pulitzer Prize Photographs; A Visual Chronicle of Our Time* (New York: Black Dog and Leventhan Publishers, 1999), 11.

58. Richard Lacayo and George Russell, *Eyewitness: 150 Years of Photojournalism,* 2nd ed. (New York: Time Books, 1995), 67.

59. Carlebach, *American Photojournalism Comes of Age,* 165.

60. Ibid., 40.

61. John Szarkowski, *From the Picture Press* (New York: Museum of Modern Art, 1973), 5–6.

62. Thomas F. Spidell, *The Milwaukee Journal: Six Decades; The News in Pictures* (Milwaukee, Wis.: Milwaukee Art Center, 1976), 11.

63. Larry Millett, *Strange Days, Dangerous Nights: Photos from the Speed Graphic Era* (St. Paul: Minnesota Historical Society, 2004), vii.

64. Oliver Gramling, *AP: The Story of News* (New York: Farrar and Rinehart, 1940), 334, quoted in Carlebach, *American Photojournalism Comes of Age,* 177.

65. Joseph Costa, ed., *The Complete Book of Press Photography* (New York: National Press Photographers Association, 1950), 48–52.

CHAPTER FOUR

1. U.S. Census Bureau, "Census of Population and Housing: 1890 Census," http://www.census.gov/prod/www/abs/decennial/1890.htm (accessed December 27, 2008).

2. Elizabeth V. Burt, ed., *The Progressive Era: Primary Documents on Events from 1890 to 1914* (Westport, Conn.: Greenwood Press, 2004), 5.

3. Alexander Alland Sr., *Jacob A. Riis: Photographer and Citizen* (New York: Aperture, 1974), 20.

4. Jacob Riis, *The Making of an American* (New York: Macmillan, 1901), 99.

5. Alland, *Jacob A. Riis,* 26–27.

6. Jacob Riis, *How the Other Half Lives: Studies Among the Tenements of New York* (New York: Scribner's, 1891), 123–24.

7. Alland, *Jacob A. Riis,* 33.

8. Stirred up by anti-Lincoln newspapers, rioters lynched several African Americans, burned an orphanage that housed over two hundred black children, and rampaged through the city. See Leslie M. Harris, *In the Shadow of Slavery: African Americans in New York City, 1626–1863* (Chicago: University of Chicago Press, 2003), 279–88.

9. Riis, *How the Other Half Lives,* 229.

10. Ibid., 54.

11. Ibid., 110.

12. Jacob A. Riis, *A Ten Years' War: An Account of the Battle with the Slum in New York* (Boston: Houghton, Mifflin, 1900), 263–64, 265.

13. Mary Panzer, *Lewis Hine* (London: Phaidon, 2002), 7.

14. Uncited quotation from *Child Labor Bulletin* (1914), in Walter Rosenblum, *America and Lewis Hine: Photographs 1904–1940* (New York: Aperture, 1984), reprinted at Lewis Hine: Articles, Masters of Photography, http://www.masters-of-photography.com/H/hine/hine_articles2.html (accessed January 2, 2009).

15. The History Place, "Child Labor in America 1908–1912: Photographs of Lewis W. Hine," http://www.historyplace.com/united states/childlabor (accessed December 27, 2008).

16. Panzer, *Lewis Hine,* 8.

17. History Place, "Child Labor in America."

18. Robert Leggat, "A History of Photography from Its Beginnings Till the 1920s," s.v. "Hine, Lewis Wickes," http://www.rleggat.com/photo history/history/hine.htm (accessed December 27, 2008).

19. Quoted in Panzer, *Lewis Hine,* 10.

20. Robert W. Marks, "Portrait of Lewis Hine," *Coronet* (February 1939): 147–57, quoted in "Lewis W. Hine," Luminous-Lint—For Collectors and Connoisseurs of Fine Photography, http://www.luminous-lint.com/app/photographer/Lewis__Hine/A/ (accessed January 2, 2009).

21. Wayne Andrews, ed., *The Autobiography of Theodore Roosevelt, Condensed from the Original Edition, Supplemented by Letters, Speeches, and Other Writings* (New York: Charles Scribner's Sons, 1913, reprinted 1958), 246–47.

22. Franklin D. Roosevelt, "Second Inaugural Address," January 20, 1937. Text of speech located at http://www.bartleby.com/124/pres50.html.

23. Herbert Hoover Presidential Library and Museum, "Gallery Six: The Great Depression," http://www.hoover.nara.gov/exhibits/Hoover story/gallery06/gallery06.html (accessed December 27, 2008).

24. Franklin D. Roosevelt, "Presidential Nomination Address," Democratic National Convention, July 2, 1932. Text of speech located at http://newdeal.feri.org/speeches/1932b.htm.

25. Roy E. Stryker and Nancy Wood, *In This Proud Land: America 1935–1943 as Seen in the FSA Photographs* (Boston: New York Graphic Society, 1973), 7.

26. Thomas H. Garver, ed., *Just Before the War: Urban America from 1935–1941 As Seen by Photographers of the Farm Security Administration* (Balboa, Calif.: Newport Harbor Art Museum, 1968), n.p., quoted in F. Jack Hurley, *Russell Lee: Photographer* (Dobbs Ferry, N.Y.: Morgan and Morgan, 1978), 18.

27. Stryker and Wood, *In This Proud Land,* 7.

28. John Vachon, "Standards of the Documentary File," Roy Stryker Papers, University of Louisville Photographic Archives, Louisville, Ky., reprinted in Miles Orvell, ed., *John Vachon's America: Photographs and Letters from the Depression to World War II* (Berkeley: University of California Press, 2003), 285.

29. Library of Congress, "Photographers of the FSA: Selected Portraits," http://memory.loc.gov/ammem/fsahtml/fsap.html (accessed December 27, 2008).

30. Quoted in James R. Mellow, *Walker Evans* (New York: Basic Books, 1999), 265.

31. Walker Evans, unpublished note written in 1961, quoted in Landon Nordeman, "Walker Evans Revolutionizes Documentary Photography," introduction, created May 31, 1997 (updated February 28, 2007), http://xroads.virginia.edu/~ug97/fsa/intro.html (accessed January 2, 2009).

32. F. Jack Hurley, *Portrait of a Decade: Roy Stryker and the Development of Documentary Photography in the Thirties* (Baton Rouge: Louisiana State University Press, 1972), 46.

33. Ibid., 64.

34. James Agee and Walker Evans, *Let Us Now Praise Famous Men* (Boston: Houghton Mifflin, 1960), 116–17.

35. Dorothea Lange, *The Making of a Documentary Photographer* (Berkeley: Regional Oral History Office, Bancroft Library, University of California, 1968); Dorothea Lange, interview by Richard K. Dowd, May 22, 1964, transcript, archives of American Art, Smithsonian Institution, p. 13, quoted in Karin Becker, *Dorothea Lange and the Documentary Tradition* (Baton Rouge: Louisiana State University Press, 1980), 2.

36. Lange, *Making of a Documentary Photographer,* 17–18, 19, quoted in Becker, *Dorothea Lange,* 56.

37. Lange, interview by Dowd, 3, quoted in Becker, *Dorothea Lange,* 22.

38. Daniel Dixon, "Dorothea Lange," *Modern Photography* 16 (December 1952): 73, 75, quoted in Becker, *Dorothea Lange,* 23.

39. Nat Herz, "Dorothea Lange in Perspective," *Infinity* 12 (April 1963): 9, quoted in Becker, *Dorothea Lange,* 24.

40. Ben Clarke, "Introduction to Image and Imagination: Encounters with the Photography of Dorothea Lange," Oakland Museum of California, http://www.freedomvoices.org/stories/langclar.htm (accessed December 31, 2008).

41. Becker, *Dorothea Lange,* 102.

42. Ibid., 111.

43. Rondal Partridge, interview by Karen Becker Ohrn, May 29, 1974, quoted in ibid., 56.

44. Paul Taylor, *Paul Shuster Taylor: California Social Scientist,* vol. 1, *An Interview by Suzanne Rice* (Berkeley: Regional Oral History Office,

Bancroft Library, University of California, 1973), 133, quoted in Becker, *Dorothea Lange,* 56–57.

45. Becker, *Dorothea Lange,* 61.

46. Lange, *Making of a Documentary Photographer,* 206, quoted in ibid., 103.

47. Dorothea Lange and Paul Taylor, *An American Exodus: A Record of Human Erosion* (Paris: Jean-Michel Place, 1999), 129.

48. Robert Coles, *Doing Documentary Work* (New York: Oxford University Press, 1998), 150.

49. Stryker and Wood, *In This Proud Land,* 9.

50. Dorothea Lange, "The Assignment I'll Never Forget: Migrant Mother," *Popular Photography* (February 1960): n.p., quoted in "Migrant Mother, 1936," EyeWitness to History (2005), http://www.eyewitnessto history.com/migrantmother.htm (accessed December 31, 2008).

51. Quoted in Geoffrey Dunn, "Photographic License," *New Times,* http://web.archive.org/web/20020602103656/http://www.newtimes-slo .com/archives/cov_stories_2002/cov_01172002.html#top (accessed December 31, 2008).

52. Ibid.

53. Ibid.

54. Quoted in Michael E. Staub, *Voices of Persuasion: Politics of Representation in 1930s America* (Cambridge: Cambridge University Press, 1994), 14.

55. John Tagg, *The Burden of Representation: Essays on Photographies and Histories* (Amherst: University of Massachusetts Press, 1988), 8–9.

56. "Memorial," on Alice Han and Ben Shneiderman, "Chim: A Web Biography of David Seymour," based on hypertext database, 1986 (University of Maryland at College Park: 1998), http://museum.icp.org/ museum/collections/special/chim/bio/memorial.html.

57. Quoted in Katherine A. Bussard, Gregory J. Harris, and Newell G. Smith, "The Concerned Photographer," The Art Institute of Chicago, http://www.artic.edu/aic/exhibitions/concerned.html (accessed December 31, 2008).

58. James Nachtwey, "Witness: Photography by James Nachtwey," http://www.jamesnachtwey.com/ (accessed December 27, 2008).

59. Ken Light, *Witness in Our Time: Working Lives of Documentary Photographers* (Washington, D.C.: Smithsonian Books, 2000), 106–7.

60. Quoted in eHistory Archive, "America in Vietnam," Ohio State

University Department of History, http://ehistory.osu.edu/vietnam/books/aiv/0028.cfm (accessed December 27, 2008).

61. Columbia University Graduate School of Journalism, *The Military and the News Media: The Correspondent Under Fire,* Media and Society Seminars, produced in association with WQED, Pittsburgh; WNET, New York; and the Bonneville Broadcast Group, New York (1985), program transcript, p. 14, quoted in Moeller, *Shooting War,* 364.

62. J. Urschel, "Caution: Don't Base Policy on Emotions," *USA Today,* February 10, 1994, 10A, quoted in David R. Perlmutter, *Photojournalism and Foreign Policy: Icons of Outrage in International Crises* (Westport, Conn.: Praeger, 1998), 3.

63. "Address to the Nation on the Situation in Somalia," weekly compilation of presidential documents: administration of George Bush, December 1992, 2329, quoted in Perlmutter, *Photojournalism and Foreign Policy,* 94.

64. C. P. Freund, "Images from Somalia," *Washington Post,* December 6, 1992, C3, quoted in Perlmutter, *Photojournalism and Foreign Policy,* 94.

65. Cokie Roberts, *ABC Nightline,* October 5, 1993, quoted in Perlmutter, *Photojournalism and Foreign Policy,* 145.

66. Perlmutter, *Photojournalism and Foreign Policy,* 19.

67. Michael S. Durham, *Powerful Days: The Civil Rights Photography of Charles Moore* (New York: Steward, Tabori and Chang, 1991), 28, quoted in Davi Johnson, "Martin Luther King Jr.'s 1963 Birmingham Campaign as Image Event," *Rhetoric and Public Affairs,* Spring 2007, http://muse.jhu.edu/journals/rhetoric_and_public_affairs/v010/10.1johnson.html (accessed December 31, 2008).

68. Quoted in Durham, *Powerful Days,* 32.

69. Will Counts, *A Life Is More Than a Moment: The Desegregation of Little Rock's Central High* (Bloomington: Indiana University Press, 1999), xv.

70. Ibid., xvii.

CHAPTER FIVE

The epigraph is from Tim Gidal, *Modern Photojournalism: Origin and Evolution, 1910–1933* (New York: Collier Books, 1973), 5.

1. From an uncited article in *Modern Photography* as quoted in John R. Whiting, *Photography Is a Language* (New York: Ziff-Davis Publishing, 1946), 22.

2. Gidal, *Modern Photojournalism,* 5.

3. Lucien Vogel, *Vu* 1, no. 1 (March 21, 1928): 3. (Translated from the French by the author.)

4. Thomas Michael Gunther, interview with author, April 4, 1990.

5. Quoted in Loudon Wainwright, *The Great American Magazine: An Inside History of "Life"* (New York: Alfred A. Knopf, 1986), 7.

6. Uncited memorandum from Clare Boothe Brokaw to Condé Nast, May 1931, quoted in Wainwright, *Great American Magazine,* 4.

7. Uncited memorandum from Daniel Longwell to Henry Luce, 1936, quoted in Wainwright, *Great American Magazine,* 21.

8. Quoted in Alden Whitman, "Henry R. Luce, Creator of Time-Life Magazine Empire, Dies in Phoenix at 68," obituary, *New York Times,* March 1, 1967, available at http://www.nytimes.com/learning/general/onthisday/bday/0403.html.

9. Josh Billings, diary entry for February 1936, quoted in Wainwright, *Great American Magazine,* 21.

10. "Introduction to the First Issue of *Life,*" *Life,* November 23, 1936, 3.

11. Wainwright, *Great American Magazine,* 47.

12. Josh Billings, diary entry for November 1936, quoted in Wainwright, *Great American Magazine,* 70.

13. "Introduction," *Life,* 3.

14. "10,000 Montana Relief Workers Make Whoopee on Saturday Night," *Life,* November 23, 1936, reproduced in Maitland Edey, *Great Photographic Essays from "Life"* (Boston: New York Graphic Society, 1978), 24.

15. Wainwright, *Great American Magazine,* 71, 26.

16. Edey, *Great Photographic Essays,* 1.

17. "Introduction," *Life,* 2.

18. Kurt Korff, "Essential Outline for a New Illustrated Magazine," undated memorandum, quoted in Wainwright, *Great American Magazine,* 27–28.

19. "Introduction," *Life,* 3.

20. "Brazil," *Life,* November 23, 1936, 40.

21. "The Argentine," *Life,* November 30, 1936, 57.

22. "Introduction," *Life,* 3.

23. Josh Billings, diary entry for January 26, 1937, quoted in Wainwright, *Great American Magazine,* 88.

24. Henry Luce, "Redefinition," memorandum to *Life* editors, March 1937, quoted in Wainwright, *Great American Magazine,* 89 (emphasis and ellipsis in the original).

25. Wainwright, *Great American Magazine,* 81.

26. Federal Reserve Bank of Minneapolis, "What is a dollar worth?" rate calculator, http://www.minneapolisfed.org/research/data/us/calc (accessed January 2, 2008).

27. Wainwright, *Great American Magazine,* 150–51.

28. Edey, *Great Photographic Essays,* 7.

29. Quoted in Wainwright, *Great American Magazine,* 306.

30. Edey, *Great Photographic Essays,* 20.

31. Wainwright, *Great American Magazine,* 149.

32. Ibid., 150.

33. Ibid., 149.

34. Letter from W. Eugene Smith to Shelly Mydans published in P. I. Prentice, "A Letter from the Publisher," *Time,* July 2, 1945, n.p., quoted in Jim Hughes, *W. Eugene Smith: Shadow and Substance* (New York: McGraw Hill, 1989), 168.

35. Moeller, *Shooting War,* 181.

36. "Three dead Americans on the beach at Buna," photograph, *Life,* September 20, 1943, 35. In Moeller, *Shooting War,* 206.

37. Hughes, *W. Eugene Smith,* 480.

38. Edey, *Great Photographic Essays,* 64.

39. Taped conversations between W. Eugene Smith and Robert Combs, 1968, quoted in Hughes, *W. Eugene Smith,* 220.

40. Hughes, *W. Eugene Smith,* 79.

41. Dr. Ernest Ceriani, interview by Jim Hughes, June 28, 1981, quoted in ibid., 216.

42. Erika Doss, *Looking at "Life" Magazine* (Washington, D.C.: Smithsonian Institution Press, 2001), 7.

43. Hughes, *W. Eugene Smith,* 222.

44. Edey, *Great Photographic Essays,* 20–21.

45. Glenn Willumson, *W. Eugene Smith and the Photographic Essay* (Cambridge: Cambridge University Press, 1992), 55.

46. W. Eugene Smith in a letter to Nettie L. Smith, December 8, 1936, quoted in Hughes, *W. Eugene Smith,* 36.

47. Taped conversation among W. Eugene Smith, Aileen Mioko Sprague, and Mr. Hori, August 1970, (courtesy of Leslie Teicholz), quoted in Hughes, *W. Eugene Smith,* 388.

48. Ted Castle, interviews by Jim Hughes, October 19, 1981–February 24, 1982, quoted in Hughes, *W. Eugene Smith,* 224.

49. Wilson Hicks, "Classics of Photography 8: W. Eugene Smith— Passionate Involvement with Life," *Modern Photography* (January 1970): 93, quoted in Hughes, *W. Eugene Smith,* 219–20.

50. Quoted in Hughes, *W. Eugene Smith,* viii.

51. James L. Collings, "Smith Carries Torch with His Camera," *Editor and Publisher* (October 2, 1948): 46, quoted in Hughes, *W. Eugene Smith,* 223.

52. W. Eugene Smith, "Minamata, Japan: Life—Sacred and Profane, A Photographic Essay on the Tragedy of Pollution, and the Burden of Courage," *Camera 35,* April 1974, 34, quoted in Hughes, *W. Eugene Smith,* 484.

53. Quoted in Wainwright, *Great American Magazine,* 158.

54. Hughes, *W. Eugene Smith,* 489.

55. Ralph Graves, "The Picture Signature of Gene Smith," *Life,* June 2, 1972, 3, quoted in ibid., 493.

56. Letter from W. Eugene Smith to Juanita Smith, September 2, 1974, Center for Creative Photography, University of Arizona, Tucson, quoted in Hughes, *W. Eugene Smith,* 494.

57. *Camera 35,* April 1974, 34, quoted in Hughes, *W. Eugene Smith,* 498.

58. Leonard McCombe, "The Private Life of Gwyned Filling," *Life,* May 3, 1948, 103.

59. Edey, *Great Photographic Essays,* 50.

60. Ibid., 40.

61. Larry Burrows, *Vietnam* (New York: Alfred A. Knopf, 2002), 100.

62. Quoted in Wainwright, *Great American Magazine,* 380.

63. "N.B.C.," *Life,* November 23, 1936, 37.

64. Federal Reserve Bank of Minneapolis, rate calculator.

65. Undated memorandum from Daniel Longwell to Henry Luce, quoted in Wainwright, *Great American Magazine,* 141.

66. A. J. van Zuilen, *The Life Cycle of Magazines* (Uithoorn, the Netherlands: Graduate Press, 1977), 248.

67. John Tebbel and Mary Zuckerman, *The Magazine in America 1741–1990* (New York: Oxford University Press, 1991), 247.

68. Wainwright, *Great American Magazine,* 179.

69. Ibid., 339.

70. John Kobler, *Luce: His Time, Life, and Fortune* (Garden City, N.Y.: Doubleday, 1968), 149.

71. Quoted in Whitman, "Henry R. Luce."

72. See Henry R. Luce, "The American Century," *Life,* February 17, 1941, 61.

73. U.S. Congress, Senate, Government Operations Committee, Subcommittee on National Policy Machinery, *Organizing for National Security, Hearings,* 86th Cong., 2d sess., 1960, 923.

74. Quoted in Kobler, *Luce,* 152.

75. Hicks, *Words and Pictures,* 85.

76. Doss, *Looking at "Life,"* 11.

77. Robert R. Littman, *Life 1936–1945: The First Decade* (Boston: New York Graphic Society, 1979), n.p.

78. Doss, *Looking at "Life,"* 12.

79. Wendy Kozol, "Gazing at Race in the Pages of *Life,*" in ibid., 173.

80. Doss, *Looking at "Life,"* 7, 18.

81. Mary Panzer, *Things As They Are* (New York: Aperture Foundation, 2005), 21–22.

82. Ibid.

83. Tebbel and Zuckerman, *Magazine in America,* 230–31.

84. Gardner Cowles, *Mike Looks Back: The Memoirs of Gardner Cowles, Founder of "Look" Magazine* (New York: Gardner Cowles, 1985), 59.

85. Ibid.

86. Quoted in Wainwright, *Great American Magazine,* 61.

87. Quoted in Wainwright, *Great American Magazine,* 61.

88. Cowles, *Mike Looks Back,* 221.

89. Wainwright, *Great American Magazine,* 62.

90. Zuilen, *Life Cycle of Magazines,* 240–41.

91. Cowles, *Mike Looks Back,* 221.

92. C. D. B. Bryan, *National Geographic Society: 100 Years of Adventure and Discovery* (New York: Harry N. Abrams, 1987, 1997), 28.

93. Gilbert H. Grosvenor, *The National Geographic Society and Its Magazine* (Washington: National Geographic Society, 1936), 23.

94. Gilbert H. Grosvenor, "Report of the Director and Editor of the National Geographic Society for the Year 1914," *National Geographic,* March 1915, n.p., quoted in Bryan, *National Geographic Society,* 115–16.

95. Anne Chamberlin, "Two Cheers for the *National Geographic*," *Esquire,* December 1963, 300.

96. Robert M. Poole, *Explorers House: National Geographic and the World It Made* (New York: Penguin Press, 2004), 267.

97. Howard S. Abramson, *National Geographic: Behind America's Lens on the World* (New York: Crown Publishers, 1987), 143.

98. Ibid., 137.

99. Chamberlin, "Two Cheers for the *National Geographic,*" 300.

100. Bryan, *National Geographic Society,* 294–95.

101. Quoted in ibid., 295.

102. Steve Raymer, e-mail message to author, December 31, 2007.

103. Michael Finkel, "Bethlehem 2007," *National Geographic* 212, no. 6 (December 2007), unpaginated table of contents.

104. Julie Crain, National Geographic Society, Communications Department, e-mail message to author, March 21, 2008.

105. Meiselas, interview by Light, no date, quoted in Light, *Witness in Our Time,* 107.

106. Mary Ellen Mark, interview by Ken Light, no date, quoted in Light, *Witness in Our Time,* 83.

CHAPTER SIX

1. Quoted in Cookman, *A Voice Is Born,* 3.

2. Quoted in ibid., 3.

3. Willard D. Morgan and Henry M. Lester, *Graphic Graflex Photography: The Master Book for the Larger Camera* (New York: Morgan and Lester Publishers, 1940), 258, quoted in George J. Lockwood, *Six Decades: The News in Pictures* (Milwaukee: Milwaukee Art Center, 1976), 11.

4. Gisèle Freund, *Photography and Society* (Boston: David R. Godine, 1980), 113.

5. Quoted in Cookman, *A Voice Is Born,* 9.

6. Quoted in ibid., 10.

7. Quoted in ibid., 14.

8. Quoted in ibid., 18.

9. Ibid.

10. Quoted in ibid., 20.

11. Quoted in ibid., 104.

12. Quoted in ibid., 104.

13. Quoted in ibid., 107.

14. Quoted in ibid., 114.

15. Quoted in ibid., 92.

16. E-mail from James Straight, executive director of NPPA, to the author, December 29, 2008.

17. Cookman, *A Voice Is Born,* 99.

18. Quoted in ibid., 99.

19. Quoted in ibid., 15.

20. National Press Photographers Association, "NPPA Code of Ethics," http://www.nppa.org/professional_development/business_practices/ethics.html (accessed December 27, 2008).

21. Quoted in Cookman, *A Voice Is Born,* 64.

22. Naomi Rosenblum, *A History of Women Photographers* (New York: Abbeville Press, 1994), 187.

23. Ibid., 188.

24. Ibid., 181.

25. Ibid., 181–82.

26. National Press Photographers Association, "NPPA Past National Officers," http://www.nppa.org/about_us/history/officers (accessed December 27, 2008).

27. "Women in Photojournalism Conference," Women in Photojour-

nalism, http://www.womeninphotojournalism.org/ (accessed December 31, 2008).

28. Quoted in Cookman, *A Voice Is Born,* 65.

29. Quoted in ibid., 65.

30. U.S. Department of Veterans Affairs, "GI-Bill History," http://www.gibill.va.gov/GI_Bill_Info/history.htm (accessed December 27, 2008).

31. Quoted in Bill Garrett, "Cliff Edom," *Editor and Publisher,* October 30, 1999, 51.

32. Costa, *Complete Book,* 102.

33. Quoted in ibid., 100.

34. Quoted in Cookman, *A Voice Is Born,* 141.

35. Quoted in ibid., 142.

36. Donald R. Winslow, "*National Geographic* Backs POYi, Withdraws Offer to Host Talks," National Press Photographers Association, http://www.nppa.org/news_and_events/news/2007/12/contest01.html (accessed December 27, 2008).

37. Pictures of the Year International, "Missouri School of Journalism Names 63rd Annual POYi Contest Winners," http://www.poyi.org/63 (accessed December 27, 2008).

38. Garrett, "Cliff Edom," 51.

39. Quoted in Cookman, *A Voice Is Born,* 145.

40. Ibid.

41. Quoted in ibid., 147.

42. National Press Photographers Association, "NewsVideo Workshop," http://www.nppa.org/professional_development/workshops_and_seminars/NewsVideo_workshop/2008 (accessed December 27, 2008).

43. Lockwood, *Six Decades,* 17.

44. Rich Clarkson (founder and CEO, Rich Clarkson Associates), telephone interview with author, August 16, 2007.

45. Ibid.

46. Ibid.

47. Greg Lewis, *Photojournalism: Content and Technique* (Dubuque, Ia.: William C. Brown, 1991), 309.

CHAPTER SEVEN

1. Carol Poster, "Protagoras (c. 490–c. 420 BCE)," *The Internet Encyclopedia of Philosophy,* 2006, http://www.iep.utm.edu/p/protagor.htm (accessed January 5, 2009).

2. American Humanist Association, "Humanism and Its Aspirations," Humanist Manifesto III, a successor to the Humanist Manifesto of 1933, http://www.americanhumanist.org/3/HumandItsAspirations.php (accessed December 27, 2008).

3. United Nations, "Charter of the United Nations—Preamble," http://www.un.org/aboutun/charter/preamble.shtml (accessed December 27, 2008).

4. John G. Morris, *Get the Picture: A Personal History of Photojournalism* (New York: Random House, 1998), 120–21.

5. Edward Steichen, *The Family of Man* (New York: Museum of Modern Art, 1955), n.p.

6. Ibid.

7. Edward Steichen, *A Life in Photography* (Garden City, N.Y.: Doubleday and Co., 1963), n.p.

8. Steichen, *Family of Man,* n.p.

9. Roland Barthes, *Mythologies* (New York: Hill and Wang, 1957), 101–2.

10. Allan Sekula, "The Traffic in Photographs," *Art Journal,* Spring 1991, 19.

11. Christopher Phillips, "The Judgment Seat of Photography," *October,* Fall 1982, 46.

12. Jacques Barzun, *The House of Intellect* (New York: Harper and Brothers, Publishers, 1959), 29.

13. Hilton Kramer, "Exhibiting the Family of Man," *Commentary,* October 1955, 366.

14. Ibid.

15. John Perivolaris, "Mirrors and Windows: Photography after Postmodernism," *Bigger Picture Redeye Newsletter,* Autumn 2004, 20.

16. Steichen, *Life in Photography,* n.p.

17. Ibid.

18. Albert Einstein, "The Way Out," in Dexter Masters and Katherine

Way, eds., *One World or None: A Report to the Public on the Full Meaning of the Atomic Bomb,* rev. ed. (New York: New Press, 2007), 76.

19. J. R. Oppenheimer, "The New Weapon: The Turn of the Screw," in Masters and Way, *One World,* 25.

20. Steichen, *Family of Man,* n.p.

21. Eric J. Sandeen, *Picturing an Exhibition: The Family of Man and 1950s America* (Albuquerque, N.M.: University of New Mexico Press, 1995), 48.

22. Ibid., 93.

23. United Nations, "Charter."

CHAPTER EIGHT

1. Dirck Halstead, "Digital Photojournalism Turns a Corner," editorial, *The Digital Journalist,* January 2001, http://digitaljournalist.org/issue0101/editorial.htm.

2. Brian Storm, MediaStorm.org, e-mail message to author, November 30, 2007.

3. Quoted in Sophie Hayard and Dan Jung, "Enhancing the Moment?" NYC24.com, issue 4, http://www.nyc24.org/2001/issue04/story02/page2.html (accessed December 27, 2008).

4. Ibid.

5. Quoted in Kenneth N. Gilpin, "Second 'Miracle' for Iowan: A Touch-up," *New York Times,* November 26, 1997. Also available online at http://query.nytimes.com/gst/fullpage.html?res=9E06E6D7173AF935A15752C1A961958260.

6. John Mraz, "What's Documentary About Photography? From Directed to Digital Photojournalism," ZoneZero, *Magazine,* January 2003, http://www.zonezero.com/magazine/articles/mraz/mraz01.html.

7. Quoted in Kenny Irby, "L.A. Times Photographer Fired over Altered Image," *Poynter Online,* April 2, 2003, http://www.poynter.org/content/content_view.asp?id=28082.

8. Quoted in Irby, "L.A. Times Photographer."

9. Ron Royhab, "A Basic Rule: Newspaper Photos Must Tell the Truth," *Toledo (Ohio) Blade,* April 17, 2007. Quoted in Donald R. Winslow, "Toledo Blade Discovers Dozens of Doctored Detrich Photos,"

News Photographer Magazine, April 15, 2007, http://www.nppa.org/news_and_events/news/2007/04/toledo05.html.

10. Ibid.

11. Quoted in Winslow, "Toledo Blade Discovers Dozens."

12. Ibid.

13. Quoted in ibid.

14. Ibid.

15. Hany Farid, "Digital Doctoring: How to Tell the Real from the Fake," publication of Institute for Security, Technology, and Society, Dartmouth College, http://www.ists.dartmouth.edu/library/315.pdf (accessed December 27, 2008).

16. Dan Heller, "Digital Manipulation: Responsibilities of Photojournalism," http://www.danheller.com/biz-manipulation.html (accessed December 27, 2008).

17. National Press Photographers Association, "NPPA Code of Ethics," http://www.nppa.org/professional_development/business_practices/ethics.html (accessed January 5, 2008).

18. Ibid.

19. Tony Overman, "NPPA President's Statement on Toledo's Detrich and Ethics," April 19, 2007, http://www.nppa.org/news_and_events/news/2007/04/nppa_statement.html.

20. Fred Ritchin, *In Our Own Image: The Coming Revolution in Photography; How Computer Technology Is Changing Our View of the World* (New York: Aperture, 1990), 1.

21. "Photoshop of Horrors: Here's Our Winner! *Redbook* Shatters Our 'Faith' in Well, Not Publishing, but Maybe God," *Jezebel,* July 16, 2007, http://jezebel.com/gossip/photoshop-of-horrors/heres-our-winner-redbook-shatters-our-faith-in-well-not-publishing-but-maybe-god-278919.php.

22. Hewlett-Packard, "Slimming Photos with HP Digital Cameras," http://www.hp.com/canada/portal/hho/digital_photography/tours/slimming/index.html (accessed December 27, 2008).

SELECTED BIBLIOGRAPHY

Agee, James, and Walker Evans. *Let Us Now Praise Famous Men.* Boston: Houghton Mifflin, 1960.

Alland Sr., Alexander. *Jacob A. Riis: Photographer and Citizen.* New York: Aperture, 1974.

Anderson, Duncan. *Glass Warriors: The Camera at War.* London: Harper Collins, 2005.

Angle, Paul M. *A Pictorial History of the Civil War Years.* Garden City, N.Y.: Doubleday, 1967.

Arnold, Eve. *The Unretouched Woman.* New York: Alfred A. Knopf, 1976.

Barnhurst, Kevin G. *Seeing the Newspaper.* New York: St. Martin's Press, 1994.

Barthes, Roland. *Mythologies.* New York: Hill and Wang, 1957.

———. *Camera Lucida: Reflections on Photography.* New York: Hill and Wang, 1981.

Baughman, James L. *Henry R. Luce and the Rise of the American News Media.* Boston: Twane, 1987.

Becker, Karin. *Dorothea Lange and the Documentary Tradition.* Baton Rouge: Louisiana State University Press, 1980.

Benjamin, Walter. *Illuminations.* New York: Schocken Books, 1968.

Berch, Bettina. *The Woman Behind the Lens: The Life and Work of Frances Benjamin Johnston, 1864–1952.* Charlottesville: University Press of Virginia, 2000.

Berger, John. *Ways of Seeing.* New York: Penguin Books, 1972.

———. *About Looking.* New York: Vintage Books, 1980, 1991.

Best of Life, The. New York: Time-Life Books, 1973.

Bolton, Richard, ed. *The Contest of Meaning: Critical Histories of Photography.* Cambridge, Mass.: The MIT Press, 1996.

Brennen, Bonnie, and Hanno Hardt, eds. *Picturing the Past: Media History and Photography.* Urbana, Chicago: University of Illinois Press, 1999.

Brothers, Caroline. *War and Photography: A Cultural History.* London: Routledge, 1997.

Bryan, C. D. B. *The National Geographic Society: 100 Years of Adventure and Discovery.* New York: Harry N. Abrams, 1997.

Buell, Hal. *Moments. The Pulitzer Prize Photographs: A Visual Chronicle of Our Time.* New York: Black Dog and Leventhal Publishers, 1999.

Bunnell, Peter C. *Inside the Photograph: Writings on Twentieth-Century Photography.* New York: Aperture, 2006.

Burt, Elizabeth V., ed. *The Progressive Era: Primary Documents on Events from 1890 to 1914.* Westport, Conn.: Greenwood Press, 2004.

Callahan, Sean, ed. *The Photographs of Margaret Bourke-White.* New York: Bonanza Books, 1972.

Campbell, W. Joseph. *Yellow Journalism: Puncturing the Myths, Defining the Legacies.* Westport, Conn.: Praeger, 2001.

Capa, Robert. *Slightly Out of Focus.* New York: Henry Holt and Co., 1947.

Carlebach, Michael. *The Origins of Photojournalism in America.* Washington, D.C.: The Smithsonian Institution, 1992.

———. *American Photojournalism Comes of Age.* Washington, D.C.: The Smithsonian Institution, 1997.

Carnes, Cecil. *Jimmy Hare, Photographer: Half a Century with a Camera.* New York: MacMillan, 1940.

Cashman, Sean D. *America in the Gilded Age.* New York: New York University Press, 1988.

Chapnick, Howard. *Truth Needs No Ally: Inside Photojournalism.* Columbia, Mo.: University of Missouri Press, 1994.

Cohen, Lester. *The New York Graphic: The World's Zaniest Newspaper.* Philadelphia: Chilton Books, 1964.

Coles, Robert. *Doing Documentary Work.* New York: Oxford University Press, 1998.

Collier's Photographic History of World War II. New York: P. F. Collier and Son, 1946.

Cookman, Claude. *A Voice Is Born.* Durham, N.C.: National Press Photographers Association, 1985.

———. *The People's America: Farm Security Administration Photographs 1935–1943.* Bloomington: Indiana University Art Museum, 1997.

Corbett, B. *A Simple Guide to Digital Photography.* New York: Amphoto Books, 2002.

Costa, Joseph, ed. *The Complete Book of Press Photography.* New York: National Press Photographers Association, 1950.

Counts, Will. *A Life Is More Than a Moment: The Desegregation of Little Rock's Central High.* Bloomington: Indiana University Press, 1999.

Cowles, Gardner. *Mike Looks Back: The Memoirs of Gardner Cowles Founder of* Look *Magazine.* New York: Gardner Cowles, 1985.

Daniel, Pete, and Raymond Smock. *A Talent for Detail: The Photographs of Miss Frances Benjamin Johnston 1889–1910.* New York: Harmony Books, 1974.

Diner, Steven J. *A Very Different Age: Americans of the Progressive Era.* New York: Hill and Wang, 1998.

Documentary Photography. New York: Time-Life Books, 1972.

Doss, Erika, ed. *Looking at* Life *Magazine.* Washington: Smithsonian Institution Press, 2001.

Duncan, David Douglas. *War Without Heroes.* New York: Harper and Row, Publishers, 1991.

Edey, Maitland. *Great Photographic Essays from* Life. Boston: New York Graphic Society, 1978.

Eisenstaedt, Alfred. *Eisenstaedt's Album: Fifty Years of Friends and Acquaintances.* New York: Viking Press, 1976.

Eisinger, Joel. *Trace and Transformation: American Criticism of Photography in the Modernist Period.* Albuquerque, N.M.: University of New Mexico Press, 1999.

Evans, Jessica. *The Camerawork Essays: Context and Meaning in Photography.* London: Rivers Oram Press, 1997.

Faber, John. *Great News Photos and the Stories Behind Them.* 2nd ed. New York: Dover Publications, 1978.

Ferrato, Donna. *Living with the Enemy.* 4th ed. New York: Aperture, 2000.

Fielding, Raymond. *The American Newsreel, 1911–1967.* Norman: University of Oklahoma Press, 1972.

Frassanito, William A. *Gettysburg: A Journey in Time.* New York: Scribner's, 1975.

Freund, Gisèle. *Photography and Society.* Boston: David R. Godine, Publisher, 1980.

Fulton, Maryanne. *Eyes of Time: Photojournalism in America.* Boston: Little, Brown, 1988.

Galassi, Peter, and Susan Kismaric. *Pictures of the Times: A Century of Photography from the New York Times.* New York: Abrams, 1996.

Gandal, Keith. *The Virtues of the Vicious: Jacob Riis, Stephen Crane, and the Spectacle of the Slum.* Oxford: Oxford University Press, 1997.

Gauvreau, Emile. *My Last Million Readers.* New York: E. P. Dutton, 1941.

Gidal, Tim. *Modern Photojournalism: Origin and Evolution, 1910–1933.* New York: Collier Books, 1973.

Goldberg, Vicki. *Margaret Bourke-White: A Biography.* New York: Harper and Row, Publishers, 1986.

———. *The Power of Photography: How Photographs Changed Our Lives.* New York: Abbeville Press, 1991.

Gould, Lewis, and Richard Greff. *Photojournalist: The Career of Jimmy Hare.* Austin and London: University of Texas Press, 1977.

Great Themes, The. New York: Time-Life Books, 1970.

Guimand, James. *American Photography and the American Dream.* Chapel Hill, N.C.: University of North Carolina Press, 1991.

Halsman, Philippe. *Philippe Halsman's Jump Book.* New York: Simon and Schuster, 1959.

Hariman, Robert, and John L. Lucaites. *No Caption Needed: Iconic Photographs, Public Culture, and Liberal Democracy.* Chicago: University of Chicago Press, 2007.

Harrison, S. L. *Twentieth-Century Journalists: America's Opinionmakers.* New York: University Press of America, 2002.

Hawthorne, Nathaniel. *The House of the Seven Gables.* Columbus, Ohio: Charles E. Merrill Publishing Co., 1969.

Hendrickson, Paul. *Bound for Glory: America in Color 1939–43.* New York: Harry N. Abrams, 2004.

Hicks, Wilson. *Words and Pictures: An Introduction to Photojournalism.* New York: Harper and Brothers, 1952.

Horton, Brian. *The Associated Press Photojournalism Stylebook.* New York: Addison-Wesley Publishing Co., 1990.

———. *The Associated Press Guide to Photojournalism,* 2nd ed. New York: McGraw-Hill, 2001.

Hoy, Frank. *Photojournalism: The Visual Approach.* 2nd ed. Englewood Cliffs, N.J.: Prentice Hall, 1993.

Hughes, Jim. *W. Eugene Smith: Shadow and Substance.* New York: McGraw Hill Publishing, 1989.

Hunter, Jefferson. *Image and Word. The Interaction of 20th Century Photographs and Texts.* Cambridge: Harvard University Press, 1987.

Hurley, F. Jack. *Portrait of a Decade: Roy Stryker and the Development of Documentary Photography in the Thirties.* Baton Rouge: Louisiana State University Press, 1972.

Kaplan, Daile, ed. *Photo Story: Selected Letters and Photographs of Lewis W. Hine.* Washington: Smithsonian Institution Press, 1992.

Kemp, John R. *Lewis Hine: Photographs of Child Labor in the New South.* Jackson, Miss.: University Press of Mississippi, 1986.

Kobler, John. *Luce: His Time, Life, and Fortune.* Garden City, N.Y.: Doubleday, 1968.

Kobre, Ken. *Photojournalism: The Professionals' Approach.* 6th ed. Boston: Focal Press, 2008.

Kozol, Wendy. *Life's America: Family and Nation in Postwar Photojournalism.* Philadelphia: Temple University Press, 1994.

Kramer, Hilton. "Exhibiting the Family of Man." *Commentary.* October 1955.

Lacayo, Richard, and George Russell. *Eyewitness: 150 Years of Photojournalism.* New York: Time Books, 1990, 1995.

La Grange, Ashley. *Basic Critical Theory for Photographers.* Boston: Focal Press, 2006.

Lange, Dorothea, and Paul Taylor. *An American Exodus: A Record of Human Erosion.* Paris: Jean-Michel Place, 1999.

Legends: The Century's Most Unforgettable Faces. New York: Time-Life Books, 1997.

Lester, Paul Martin. *The Ethics of Photojournalism.* Durham, N.C.: National Press Photographers Association, 1990.

Lewis, Gret. *Photojournalism: Content and Technique.* Dubuque, Ia.: Wm. C. Brown, 1991.

Life: The First Decade, 1936–1945. Boston: New York Graphic Society, 1979.

Light, Ken. *Witness in Our Time: Working Lives of Documentary Photographers.* Washington: Smithsonian Books, 2000.

Lockwood, George J. *Six Decades: The News in Pictures.* Milwaukee: Milwaukee Art Center, 1976.

Lutz, Catherine A., and Jane L. Collins. *Reading National Geographic.* Chicago: University of Chicago Press, 1993.

Maddow, Ben. *Let Truth Be the Prejudice: W. Eugene Smith His Life and Photographs.* New York: Aperture, 1985.

Malcolm, Janet. *Diana and Nikon: Essays on the Aesthetic of Photography.* Boston: David R. Godine, 1980.

Masters, Dexter, and Katherine Way, eds. *One World or None: A Report to the Public on the Full Meaning of the Atomic Bomb.* Rev. ed. New York: New Press, 2007.

Maynard, Patrick. *The Engine of Visualization: Thinking Through Photography.* Ithaca and London: Cornell University Press, 1997.

McDougall, Angus. *A Photo Journal from the Glory Days of the* Milwaukee Journal. Columbia: Missouri School of Journalism, 2001.

Mellow, James R. *Walker Evans.* New York: Basic Books, 1999.

Meredith, Roy. *The World of Mathew Brady: Portraits of the Civil War Period.* New York: Bonanza Books, 1988.

Mich, Daniel D., and Edwin Eberman. *The Technique of the Picture Story.* New York: McGraw-Hill, 1945.

Millett, Larry. *Strange Days, Dangerous Nights: Photos from the Speed Graphic Era.* St. Paul: Minnesota Historical Society, 2004.

Millstein, Barbara, ed. *Committed to the Image: Contemporary Black Photographers.* New York: Brooklyn Museum of Art, 2001.

Moeller, Susan. *Shooting War: Photography and the American Experience of Combat.* New York: Basic Books, 1989.

————. *Compassion Fatigue: How the Media Sell Disease, Famine, War, and Death.* New York: Routledge, 1998.

Moore, Charles, and Michael S. Durham. *Powerful Days: The Civil Rights Photography of Charles Moore.* New York: Steward, Tabori and Chang, 1991.

Morris, John G. *Get the Picture: A Personal History of Photojournalism.* New York: Random House, 1998.

Newhall, Beaumont. *The History of Photography.* New York: The Museum of Modern Art, 1982.

Newton, Julianne H. *The Burden of Visual Truth: The Role of Photojournalism in Mediating Reality.* Mahwah, N.J.: Lawrence Erlbaum, 2001.

Norback, Craig T., and Melvin Gray. *The World's Great News Photos 1840–1980.* New York: Crown Publishers, 1980.

Orvell, Miles. *American Photography.* Oxford: Oxford University Press, 2003.

———, ed. *John Vachon's America: Photographs and Letters from the Depression to World War II,* Berkeley: University of California Press, 2003.

Panzer, Mary. *Lewis Hine.* London: Phaidon, 2002.

———. *Things As They Are.* New York: Aperture Foundation, 2005.

Parks, Gordon. *A Choice of Weapons.* New York: Harper and Row Publishers, 1966.

Peden, Charles. *Newsreel Man.* Garden City, N.Y.: Doubleday, Doran and Co., 1932.

Perivolaris, John. "Mirrors and Windows: Photography after Postmodernism." *Bigger Picture Redeye Newsletter.* Autumn 2004.

Perlmutter, David D. *Photojournalism and Foreign Policy: Icons of Outrage in International Crises.* Westport, Conn.: Praeger, 1998.

Phillips, Christopher. "The Judgment Seat of Photography." *October* (Fall 1982).

Photojournalism. New York: Time-Life Books, 1971.

Poole, Robert M. *Explorers House: National Geographic and the World It Made.* New York: Penguin Press, 2004.

Price, Jack. *News Pictures.* New York: Round Table Press, 1937.

Rabaté, Jean-Michel. *Writing the Image after Roland Barthes.* Philadelphia: University of Pennsylvania Press, 1997.

Richards, Eugene. *Cocaine True, Cocaine Blue.* Millertown, NY: Aperture, 1994.

Riis, Jacob. *How the Other Half Lives: Studies Among the Tenements of New York.* New York: Scribner's, 1891.

———. *A Ten Years' War: An Account of the Battle with the Slum in New York.* Boston: Houghton, Mifflin and Co., 1900.

———. *The Making of an American.* New York: MacMillan, 1901.

Ritchin, Fred. *In Our Own Image: The Coming Revolution in Photography:*

How Computer Technology Is Changing Our View of the World. New York: Aperture, 1990.

Rosenblum, Naomi. *A World History of Photography.* New York: Abbeville Press, 1997.

———. *A History of Women Photographers.* New York: Abbeville Press, 2000.

Rosenblum, Walter. *America and Lewis Hine: Photographs 1904–1940.* New York: Aperture, 1984.

Rothstein, Arthur. *Photojournalism: Pictures for Magazines and Newspaper.* New York: American Photographic Book Publishing Co., 1956.

Rubin, Cyma, and Eric Newton, eds. *Capture the Moment: The Pulitzer Prize Photographs.* New York: W.W. Norton, 2001.

Sandeen, Eric J. *Picturing an Exhibition: The Family of Man and 1950s America.* Albuquerque, N.M.: University of New Mexico Press, 1995.

Sandweiss, Martha A. *Print the Legend: Photography and the American West.* New Haven, Conn.: Yale University Press, 2002.

Sekula, Allan. *Photography Against the Grain. Essays and Photo Works 1973–1983.* Halifax: The Press of the Nova Scotia College of Art and Design, 1984.

———. "The Traffic in Photographs." *Art Journal.* Spring, 1991.

Shawcross, Nancy M. *Roland Barthes on Photography: The Critical Tradition in Perspective.* Gainesville, Fla.: University Press of Florida, 1997.

Sontag, Susan. *On Photography.* New York: Farrar, Straus and Giroux, 1977.

———. *Regarding the Pain of Others.* New York: Farrar, Straus and Giroux, 2003.

Spidell, Thomas F. *The Milwaukee Journal: Six Decades: The News in Pictures.* Milwaukee, Wis.: Milwaukee Art Center, 1976.

Squiers, Carol. *The Critical Image: Essays on Contemporary Photography.* Seattle: Bay Press, 1990.

Staub, Michael E. *Voices of Persuasion: Politics of Representation in 1930s America.* Cambridge: Cambridge University Press, 1994.

Steel, Andy. *Photojournalism: The World's Top Photographers and the Stories Behind Their Greatest Images.* Mies, Switzerland: RotoVision, 2006.

Steichen, Edward. *The Family of Man.* New York: Museum of Modern Art, 1955.

————. *A Life in Photography.* Garden City, N.Y.: Doubleday, 1963.

Stryker, Roy E., and Nancy Wood. *In This Proud Land: America 1935–1943 As Seen in the FSA Photographs.* Boston: New York Graphic Society, 1973.

Szarkowski, John. *Walker Evans.* New York: Museum of Modern Art, 1971.

————. *From the Picture Press.* New York: Museum of Modern Art, 1973.

Taft, Robert. *Photography and the American Scene: A Social History, 1839–1889.* New York: Dover Publications, 1938.

Tagg, John. *The Burden of Representation: Essays on Photographies and Histories.* Amherst, Mass.: The University of Massachusetts Press, 1988.

Talbot, William Henry Fox. *The Pencil of Nature.* Facsimile of 1844–1846 edition. Cambridge, Mass.: Da Capo Press, 1968.

Tausk, Petr. *An Introduction to Press Photography.* Prague: International Organization of Journalists, 1976.

Tebbel, John, and Mary Zuckerman. *The Magazine in America 1741–1990.* New York: Oxford University Press, 1991.

Thomas, William F., ed. *Images of Our Times: Sixty Years of Photography from the* Los Angeles Times. New York: Abrams, 1987.

Trachtenberg, Alan. *Reading American Photographs: Images As History, Mathew Brady to Walker Evans.* New York: Hill and Wang, 1989.

van Zuilen, A. J. *The Life Cycle of Magazines.* Uithoorn, the Netherlands: Graduate Press, 1977.

Wainwright, Loudon. *The Great American Magazine: An Inside History of* Life. New York: Alfred A. Knopf, 1986.

Weinberg, Adam D. *On the Line: The New Color Photojournalism.* Minneapolis: Walker Art Center, 1986.

Wheeler, Thomas H. *Phototruth or Photofiction? Ethics and Media Imagery in the Digital Age.* Mahwah, N.J.: Lawrence Erlbaum, Publishers, 2002.

Willis-Thomas, Deborah. *An Illustrated Bio-Bibliography of Black Photographers, 1940–1988.* New York: Garland Publishing, 1989.

Willumson, Glenn G. *W. Eugene Smith and the Photographic Essay.* Cambridge: Cambridge University Press, 1992.

INDEX

Claude Cookman has taught visual communications and the history of photography at Indiana University's School of Journalism since 1990. He is the author of *A Voice Is Born,* about the founding of the National Press Photographers Association, and has written numerous journal articles on French magazine photojournalists. His professional career includes more than twelve years as a picture editor at the Associated Press in New York City, the *Louisville Times,* and the *Miami Herald.* He shared in the 1976 Pulitzer Prize for Feature Photography, awarded to the combined photography staff of the *Louisville Times* and the *(Louisville) Courier-Journal.* He earned his PhD in the history of photography from Princeton University, where he wrote his dissertation on Henri Cartier-Bresson.

Richard B. Stolley is senior editorial adviser of Time, Inc., the former editor of both *People Weekly* and the monthly *Life* magazines, the former editorial director of Time, Inc., and the editor of the best-selling *Life: Our Century in Pictures.*